A PARTIAL
ENLIGHTENMENT

A PARTIAL ENLIGHTENMENT

WHAT MODERN LITERATURE AND BUDDHISM CAN TEACH US ABOUT LIVING WELL WITHOUT PERFECTION

AVRAM ALPERT

Columbia University Press   *New York*

Columbia University Press
Publishers Since 1893
New York   Chichester, West Sussex
cup.columbia.edu
Copyright © 2021 Columbia University Press

Library of Congress Cataloging-in-Publication Data
Names: Alpert, Avram, 1984– author.
Title: A partial enlightenment : what modern literature and Buddhism can teach us about living well without perfection / Avram Alpert.
Description: New York : Columbia University Press, 2021. | Includes bibliographical references and index.
Identifiers: LCCN 2020035621 (print) | LCCN 2020035622 (ebook) |
ISBN 9780231200028 (hardback) | ISBN 9780231200035 (trade paperback) |
ISBN 9780231553391 (ebook)
Subjects: LCSH: Buddhism—History—20th century. | Literature, Modern—20th century. | Enlightenment (Buddhism) | Reincarnation—Buddhism. | Salvation—Buddhism. | Buddhist modernism.
Classification: LCC BQ 316 .A47 2021 (print) | LCC BQ 316 (ebook) | DDC 294.3/442—dc23
LC record available at https://lccn.loc.gov/2020035621
LC ebook record available at https://lccn.loc.gov/2020035622

Columbia University Press books are printed on permanent and durable acid-free paper.
Printed in the United States of America

Cover design: Noah Arlow
Cover image: Anthea Behm, *A/B Extract; Ed Ruscha, City, 1968, Custom Blur*, 2011

CONTENTS

Acknowledgments   *vii*

Introduction   1

1 Enlightenment   27

2 Reincarnation   63

3 Liberation   103

4 Authenticity   139

Coda   173

Notes   *177*
Bibliography   *221*
Index   *243*

ACKNOWLEDGMENTS

This book formed through much of the same research as my previous one, *Global Origins of the Modern Self*, and so many of the acknowledgments made there also apply here. I would never have learned what I needed to learn to write this book without a semester spent at the Institute of Buddhist Dialectics in spring 2005, organized by Tara Doyle of Emory University. It was in those months that I first began to understand how little I knew about Buddhism in the modern world, and how much more I had to learn. The relentlessly patient Geshe Dorje Damdul also answered every conceivable philosophy question that I put to him in those months. I realized that I could actually write a book about modern Buddhism and literature when I taught a seminar on the topic at Rutgers University in 2014. It was my first opportunity to teach a course of my own design, and I could not have been luckier than to have had the group of students we did. We formed a remarkable community that showed me just how much these texts could matter for all of us as we try to make sense of our place in the world. I received generous feedback on parts of this book from Michael Allan, Ben Baer, Wendy Belcher, Billy Galperin, Colin Jager, Priya Joshi, David Kurnick, Justin Neuman, Yi-Ping Ong,

Jean-Michel Rabaté, Eileen Reeves, Adam Spanos, Mimi Winick, several anonymous readers who read earlier versions of some of the chapters, and a few others, I'm sure, to whom I must apologize for forgetfulness. Jean-Michel deserves special notice for the sheer volume of pages I've sent him over the years, and his always speedy and generous replies. The Princeton Writing Program hosted a workshop of the chapter on reincarnation, in which my interdisciplinary colleagues helped me see new angles on my argument and how to improve it. The most important moment in the written life of this book was when the Princeton University Center for Human Values sponsored a book workshop with Justin McDaniel, Gauri Viswanathan, and Rebecca Walkowitz. Over one long afternoon they not only broke down the first draft of this book but also helped me see how to rebuild it. I can't thank them enough for the generosity of their time and engagement. It saved this book. And I cannot think of a better editor for this project than Wendy Lochner, who completely understood the argument and what I was trying to do. She offered excellent advice on completing the manuscript and found two wonderful readers to offer feedback and guidance. Her enthusiasm for scholarship and the life of the mind is infectious. The rest of the team at Columbia University Press has made completing this book a very easy and enjoyable process, and I thank them for their diligence.

My old friend Zach Luck took time out from parenting and lawyering to give me feedback on how to make the book more interesting for people outside the academy. And my mother, Rebecca Alpert, as always, is my swiftest and most generous reader. She made incisive comments on several drafts of this book. The rest of my immediate family—Lynn, Christie, Jodi, and Joel—gave me the support throughout my life and the years of writing that made this work possible. I won't even begin to list all the wonderful support from my friends and colleagues. But I will say that my wife, Anthea Behm, has made my life such a joy that it almost brings me to doubt my own claim in this book that there are irremovable dissatisfactions in human experience.

Still, as I write these words in May 2020, in the midst of the social upheavals of Covid-19 and the protests against state violence, inaction, and inequality, it would be inappropriate not to acknowledge that all the good fortune I have had to be able to read and write is less because of any particular merit or hard work on my own part, and more because I have benefited from a world that unequally rewards some of us. Modern Buddhism, as I will argue in this book, is far from perfect. But it does importantly insist on the connections between our ruptured social worlds and our damaged psychic lives. Perhaps reckoning with its stories can offer some intellectual resources for our urgent need to move from the acknowledgment of injustice to the actualization of justice.

The sections on Conrad, Kipling, Sarduy, Head, and Salinger appeared in earlier form in the following publications. My thanks to each journal for allowing republication: "Buddhism and the Postmodern Novel: Severo Sarduy's *Cobra*," *Twentieth Century Literature* 62, no. 1 (2016): 32–55; "Buddhism Between Worlds: Contested Liberations in Kipling, Salinger, and Head," *Religion & Literature* 49, no. 3 (2017): 23–47; "Empires of Enlightenment: On Illumination and the Politics of Buddhism in *Heart of Darkness*," *Journal of Modern Literature* 40, no. 2 (2017): 1–21.

A PARTIAL ENLIGHTENMENT

INTRODUCTION

In the late nineteenth and early twentieth centuries, a revolution in the history of Buddhism occurred. As European and U.S. imperial interests in Asia advanced, Buddhist communities were forced to grapple with both territorial encroachments and the claims to greater rationality that these foreign powers brought with them. Aligned with sympathetic Westerners (Orientalists, anticolonialists, and mystics), Buddhists across Asia began to reinvent Buddhism in response to this epochal shift. Buddhism, they said, was not to be found in the folk practices of ritual, recitation, magic, and worship that visitors were witnessing. The true Buddhism, though perhaps not immediately evident, was to be found in its rich scriptural history. And what would be found there not only was as philosophical and rational as modern Western philosophy but also had achieved these insights millennia earlier. Further still, it had a method—meditation—that could close the gap between our claims to rationality and our still unruly emotional lives. As Buddhism continued to update itself over the century to come, claims would also be made that it was now and had always been pacifist, egalitarian, feminist, democratic, and antiracist.[1]

What is perhaps most remarkable about this reinvention of Buddhism is how well it worked. Based on the strength and eloquence of its supporters as well as the truly powerful insights to be gleaned in the scriptural canon, modern Buddhism became the dominant way of understanding what it meant to be Buddhist. Buddhism went from despised other to universally applauded emancipator in a matter of decades. But its success has recently come under fire. For many critics, this modern global Buddhism is an inauthentic, Westernized invention that ripped Buddhist practices and histories out of their variegated local contexts and denied the power, meaning, and logic of the aspects that did not conform to Western ideals about rational living. In many ways the criticism is true, and this history has resulted in widespread ignorance of Buddhist life and even provided cover for the rise of new, militant Buddhist nationalisms in countries like Sri Lanka and Myanmar.[2]

Nevertheless, as scholars in Buddhist studies have noted, simply discarding global, modern Buddhism as a false accretion is itself a rather inaccurate way to approach the history of Buddhism. After all, it developed as a missionary religion that spread throughout Asia over centuries. In so doing, it was constantly grafted to local traditions, transformed through encounters with other ways of belief, and forced to reform itself as other traditions surged or encroached. By the time Europeans began to really study Buddhism in the nineteenth century, they encountered a history so diverse that most Buddhists would not have even recognized each other as being part of the same tradition.[3] Indeed, in some ways analogous to the rise of Pan-Africanism, it was only in the face of the European onslaught that diverse Buddhists would begin to recognize their connections and develop a Pan-Buddhist, anticolonial, pro-peace, pro-meditation agenda.[4]

This is a book about twentieth-century novels that incorporate this modern global Buddhism. Its argument is that we[5] can learn a lot from the novels about the complexity of this new era in the history of religion, and, more broadly, what that complexity teaches us about how to structure our desires, relationships, and activities in ways that can best promote human flourishing while still recognizing the inevitable dissatisfactions of human experience. In briefest form, I think that what we learn from this literary history of global Buddhism is that we live in a world where our hopes for some other way of thinking to save us have been destroyed. There is no absolute enlightenment coming from Buddhism or anywhere else. But this is precisely the lesson of modern Buddhism: once we move past the desire for complete resolution, we can begin to appreciate the minor insights and partial enlightenments—what Joseph Conrad called "spectral illuminations"—that light a path to lives of greater liberation and authenticity, even as we know full well that new problems will always arise.

In a sense, this is itself a spectral illumination of classical Buddhism. The canonical teaching was that life was unsatisfactory and that our only path to overcoming it was a course of righteousness that would eventually allow us to escape the cycle of reincarnation. This broad soteriological goal has largely fallen away from modern Buddhism. But a specter of its insight continues to illuminate something about our existence. Samuel Beckett (who picked up a pessimistic strand of Buddhism from the philosopher Arthur Schopenhauer) said it succinctly: "You're on earth, there's no cure for that!"[6] Some modern Buddhists had promised something like a cure. They promised that we could live in this world without anxiety or fear, and with tremendous generosity and presence. Modern Buddhist literature contains the spectral illumination of classical Buddhism's response: you cannot live in such a complete way. The world runs beyond you. There is no cure for all the complexity and anxiety of life. But though we cannot fully overcome, we can still ameliorate our condition. Beckett again: "Try again. Fail again. Fail better."[7] Modern literary encounters with Buddhism offer their own spectral illuminations about how to fail better from within this incomplete state.

I began writing this book because, outside of Buddhist studies, recognition of the complexity of what modern Buddhism is has been very slow. For many literary and cultural critics, philosophers, and those generally interested in the humanities, Buddhism is primarily a philosophical and meditative practice.[8] Indeed, one of my concerns here is that critics, theorists, and philosophers have so abstracted Buddhism that a caricatured vision of it now freely circulates among even the most sophisticated critics.[9] In my first draft, I thought of my task as simply disabusing my fellow literary critics of their inaccurate ideas about Buddhism. But after a few colleagues read my several hundred pages of annoying finger-wagging, they encouraged me to think again about the purpose of this book. Through these conversations, I realized that I had something else to say about what we can learn through the study of modern Buddhism in world literature.[10]

This realization began with a simple insight: even modern Buddhism remains "embedded" in complex social systems and ways of life.[11] That is to say, however much we have come to think of modern Buddhism as an abstraction of the lived experience of Buddhists, this abstraction is itself necessarily part of other social fabrics. Literature discloses to us how Buddhist practice has become embedded in global modernity in unpredictable ways. And studying Buddhism from this vantage teaches us that novels are not merely sites displaying the potential realization of philosophical ideas. They are not—or at least not always—moral fables. Rather, they can be social indices of how ideas are unevenly embedded in the world. Or, in simpler words, fiction can show us how ideas whose theoretical meaning we take for granted come to play out in surprising ways in our lived experience.[12]

As we will see, for example, the Buddhist ideal of dedicating one's life to meditation does not mean removing oneself from the social world. Rather, it means creating the conditions in the social world that allow for some to undertake such rigorous meditations. These conditions may be as simple as time off from work or as complex as an entire monastic-political system dedicated to renting land to laypeople, using slaves to grow food, and collecting taxes in order to feed and house the monks. What we find in literary accounts, in turn, is a recognition of this whole interactive system that may escape modernizers, theorists, and meditative enthusiasts. The novels show how the ideals of Buddhist practice play out in the diverse situations of modern life.

In this study, I focus on four primary themes—enlightenment, reincarnation, liberation, and authenticity—that predominate in the novels considered. While these ideas have appeared as philosophical concepts removed from everyday concerns or actual histories of Buddhist lives, I show how novelists explore their embeddedness in the difficult details of daily reality. Joseph Conrad's *Heart of Darkness* (1899/1902), for example, considers the links between the desire for enlightenment and the practice of colonialism. The radical Tibetan secularist Jamyang Norbu, a century later, mines esoteric ideas about reincarnation for material paths to overthrowing Chinese colonization. Across this book, I consider ten novels that explore these themes and relations. The novels I have chosen tell a particular story about the embeddedness of Buddhism in modern literature. In brief form, it is as follows: deciding that total enlightenment is unachievable and personal identity is inescapable, these novelists embrace partial enlightenments as the most one can hope for within the accelerated conditions of global modernity. In so doing, they find themselves condemned to reincarnating failed historical processes, which they in turn seek to appropriate and reclaim for liberatory ends. This leads them to negotiate how their twin aspirations for spiritual and political liberation both coincide with and contradict each other, and how the irremovable suffering of being human requires an authentic way of being that embraces both humanity's hopes and failures.

Part of what I think blinds us to understanding this complexity of Buddhism in the modern world is that the desire for Buddhism to be special is incredibly strong. In a world of terror and suffering, modern Buddhism has presented itself as a realistic possibility for making life better. And modern Buddhists have indeed created new ways of being in the world that align with our highest aspirations. Mindfulness meditation for laypeople, which, as I discuss below, was practically invented in the early twentieth century, has had some documented success in decreasing anxiety and increasing awareness and joy.[13] Engaged Buddhism, meanwhile, is a school of thought that developed in such contexts as Vietnamese responses to French and American colonization and Dalit critiques of caste Hinduism. Leading innovators—Thich Nhat Hanh in Vietnam and B. R. Ambedkar in India—reinterpreted everything in Buddhism, all the way down to the Four Noble Truths themselves. For Nhat Hanh, for example, old age, sickness, and death "are old ways of describing the First Noble Truth." Speaking of suffering today, we should focus on "tension, stress, anxiety, fear, violence, broken families, suicide, war, conflict, terrorism, destruction of the ecosystem, global warming, etc."[14] Ambed-kar's version is similarly revolutionary, offering a vision of the ideal Buddhist not as a "perfect man" but as a "social servant."[15] Scholar Christopher Queen offers a synthesis of Ambedkar's four *new* Noble Truths as follows: "For Ambedkar, the *first noble truth* for the present age was the widespread suffering of injustice and poverty; the *second truth* was social, political, and cultural institutions of oppression—the collective expressions of greed, hatred, and delusion; the *third truth* was expressed by the European ideals of 'liberty, equality, and fraternity'; and the *fourth truth* was the threefold path of Ambedkar's famous slogan [taken from the international labor movement], 'Edu-cate! Agitate! Organize!'"[16] As these are ideals that developed in a global matrix of the modern striving for justice, they read-ily speak to the kind of world that many of us want to see today. And the idea that Buddhism has thousands of years of experience bringing peace, nondomination, and equality into the world gives it an unmatched pedigree.

But while there are certainly brilliant moments of insight and justice in premodern Buddhist history, the idea of an unbro-ken continuum of Buddhist perfection is simply not true. What we should learn from Buddhism's history is not that it has time-tested ways to overcome suffering and create ideal worlds. Rather, it is that the creation of ideal worlds is an ongoing struggle with the conditions of one's times that must constantly be updated. We run several risks in seeing things otherwise, including stereotyping Buddhists and ignoring the lessons of just how difficult it is to evenly embed our ideals in the founda-tions of society. And when Buddhists act like other humans and commit atrocities, we risk growing frustrated and abandoning what we can learn from the historical and modern forms of Buddhism altogether. After all, we should remember that

Buddhism's modern global reception was not always so rosy. In *The British Discovery of Buddhism*, Philip Almond records one reaction from a little before 1900: "Sirs and ladies, I venture to ask you if any people on the face of the earth seem to be more utterly indifferent to the shedding of blood and to human suffering than the followers of Buddhism."[17] More than a century later, when Buddhist monks were part of the genocidal campaign against the Rohingya in northern Myanmar, it was almost inconceivable to many onlookers that any Buddhists, let alone monks, could have done such a thing.[18] It would be as wrong to think that the original British conception is correct as to hold that Buddhists are uniquely wonderful humans.

Nevertheless, I recognize this story of enchantment and disenchantment, this rapture with the possibility of Buddhism that gives way to tremendous disappointment, because it is the story of my own engagement with Buddhism, which began in enthusiastic embrace and suffered a sharp decline in the face of learning this history. Each of these positions was mistaken, because what makes Buddhism worth thinking through is neither its perfection nor its failure, but rather how its remarkable ideals and practices have struggled to confront the everyday realities of human interactions and social orders. As I take the reader through this literary history, I will also share parts of my own story of learning, unlearning, and relearning Buddhism.

This choice may surprise some of my academic colleagues. Personal accounts are not typical in professional literary criticism or exegetical religious studies, which tend to focus more on the texts being explicated than the author writing about them. Even a recent (and very interesting) book on the relationship between modernism and self-help, subtitled "searching for advice in modern literature," does not reflect on the author's own search for advice in what she is reading.[19] Personal accounts are, however, relatively common in scholarly studies of modern Buddhism. Authors like Georges Dreyfus, Ann Gleig, and Evan Thompson weave their own experiences with Buddhism into their scholarly works.[20] Why take this different approach?

Often it is because they, like me, found the gap between the Buddhism they imagined and the Buddhism they encountered to be so remarkable. Thompson relates, for example, that he set out to learn about Buddhism as part of a "transformative path of rational liberation." It promised not only what he had learned from Western philosophy—ideas about the meaning of life and the functions of the mind—but also a dedication to actually embodying that meaning through a meditative practice leading to "'awakening.'"[21] But while he certainly found elements of this in his study of Buddhism, he also found that meditation communities could be annoying and cliquish, meditation teachers could be sexual harassers, and Buddhist enthusiasts could overlook damning evidence about the history of Buddhism and the limits of meditation to advance its aims.[22] While most scholars have personal narratives about why they got into their scholarship, with Buddhist modernism that narrative often *is* the scholarship: it's the story of why we thought one thing about Buddhism, realized it was something much more complex, and then continued to probe this complexity. Indeed, for the most part, the initial disappointment did not chase people away: it is estimated that up to half of Buddhist studies scholars are also practicing Buddhists.[23] (I am not one of them.) However, it did lead some of them, like Thompson, to become full-on critics of modern Buddhism. Part of my story is about how literature and my own experiences led me in a different direction: from this criticism into a new appreciation of what modern Buddhism offers.

Another reason for the prevalence of personal narrative is that many studies of modern Buddhism come from the anthropology of religion.[24] Anthropologists, much more than other scholars, tend to reflect on their own participation (or lack thereof) in the practices that they write about. As Ann Gleig notes in her ethnography of contemporary Buddhism in the United States, this is part of a tradition within anthropology of identifying with what one is writing about rather than keeping it at a critical distance.[25] I have learned a lot from ethnographies like Gleig's and personal accounts like Thompson's to think about how something that seems so personal and abstract as the ideals of modern Buddhism could become re-embedded in communal practice. They helped me to reflect on my own experience of embedding myself within diverse Buddhist communities and to see how my experiences connected to the broader narratives of modern Buddhism—in both life and literature.

As with many not born into the Buddhist tradition who have become fascinated by it, my story begins with a mundane feeling of loss and alienation. My interest began when I was a high school student in the suburbs of Philadelphia. Like many intellectually adventurous youths, I felt no sense of identification growing up. The problem was not so much with those around me, who were as hope-worthy and dismaying as any other set of human beings, as with the fact that the world I sought to be a part of—a world of creativity and ideas, of an openness to strangeness and fragility, of a deep and abiding care for social justice—simply did not exist around me. Indeed, I had no language even to express what I was looking for. Like an infant learning vision, I assumed that what I could not see did not exist.

A reaction to this kind of alienation from the options life appears to present to us is, at least for the philosophically inclined, to abstract our feelings onto a metaphysical plane. Mistaking my alienation from the world around me as alienation from the world, I began to wonder if perhaps there was a simple mental cure that could connect me to the flow of things that everyone else seemed to be in.[26] Maybe if I could just stop thinking all the time, analyzing everything all the time, then I could be part of the world. I chanced across a line from Wallace Stevens that spoke to this feeling, and that I have memorized to this day: "It may be the ignorant man, alone, / Has any chance to mate his life with life." But I wanted a chance to become one with life without falling into ignorance. For a time, I came to believe that Buddhism offered this path.

I arrived at this belief through a series of coincidences, or at least what seemed like coincidences.[27] In the late 1990s, my mother, a rabbi, had gone on a meditation retreat held at Insight Meditation Society (IMS) in Barre, Massachusetts. She went there because of a wave of Jewish interest in Buddhism spurred by the publication of Roger Kamenetz's 1994 best-seller, *The Jew in the Lotus*, which first coined the term "JUBU" (now more commonly rendered as JewBu). Kamenetz's book is about accompanying eight Jewish spiritual leaders on a trip to meet the Dalai Lama in exile in Dharamsala, India. Kamenetz popularized a phenomenon that had begun at least a century earlier, when in 1893 a man named Charles Strauss became the first U.S. Jew to convert to Buddhism. The engagement between the religious traditions really took off, however, in the late 1960s and '70s, when a group of young, alienated Jews (perhaps not too dissimilar from my teenage self) made their own discovery of Buddhism through study and trips to Southeast Asia. The principal four—Sharon Salzberg, Jack Kornfield, Jacqueline Mandell (neé Schwartz), and Joseph Goldstein—would go on to found IMS.[28]

While as a healthy skeptic my mother remained somewhat aloof from this trend, she still found the experience quite meaningful. I remember her telling me on her return how food had never tasted so good as when one had been silently meditating for days, since you finally were present enough to focus on it. This description of thinking less and feeling more intrigued me. She paid for me to go on a four-day youth retreat as a high school graduation present.

During the very first "Dharma talk," the leader of the retreat told us about an experience she had had meditating. One day while walking silently through the woods she stopped to look at the scenery around her. As she looked up to see the tree leaves in the sunlight, she realized that she had never *really* seen leaves before. She had always seen them with a million other thoughts in her mind. But that day, through the focus gained in her years of meditation, she was finally seeing the trees as they were, without the cloud of words and concerns. I was listening to someone describe the experience I had always sought but never knew was possible—the feeling of absolute, unmediated connection.

After leaving the retreat, I began to devour popular works in Buddhism, especially by D. T. Suzuki, Alan Watts, and Nhat Hanh. When I read Watts's claim that there was a moment in meditative practice when "the peculiar anxiety which Kierkegaard has rightly seen to lie at the very roots of the ordinary man's soul is no longer there," I became convinced not only that Buddhism was the path to the experience of the world I wanted but also that that experience would be linked to my liberation from alienated anxiety.[29] Buddhism, through its techniques of meditative practice, would be the thread to suture me to the world. I never thought to "take refuge" in (convert to) Buddhism, but I did think of meditation and Buddhist philosophy as keys to the way of being I most cherished.

Once in university, however, I largely delayed academic study of Buddhism until a planned third-year semester abroad in Dharamsala. By the time I left, I had read a fair amount of postcolonial criticism. I was familiar with the idea that Western scholars had a long-standing fascination with an "unchanging East," whose lived complexity was masked by Orientalist fantasy. And like many people caught in an ideological trap, I could see perfectly well how it applied to others but not to myself. The idea that my vision of Buddhism might be distorted by Orientalist desire never crossed my mind. Buddhism was the true path, and I was finally about to encounter it in the real world.

On that point, at least, I was right: in Dharamsala I did encounter Buddhism in the real world. But that did not mean that I somehow found a community of enlightened people who *really* saw trees, had dissolved their false sense of self, and didn't experience anxiety. Instead I met Tibetan laypeople who struggled day by day to make a living, monks who had been dropped off in the monastery as toddlers because their families couldn't afford to feed them, and a whole trove of Westerners like myself, who were asking this people in exile to show them spiritual truth. I felt wretched in my ignorance and ashamed of my desires. How had I been so wrong? How had I not seen that the suffering of the world was political, not just spiritual?

Perhaps, I thought, it was the Chinese colonization of Tibet and the resulting condition of exile that was at fault. But as I began to read about the history of Buddhism, I discovered I had been misled there, as well. The Buddhist philosophical system was as full of disagreement about nitpicky issues as the Western one I thought I was fleeing. I had wanted Buddhism to free me from the anxieties of self-consciousness, but of course "anxiety" was hardly a canonical topic in Buddhist history, which was more concerned with the problem of how to end the cycle of transmigration. The focus was more (though not exclusively by any means) on how to get out of living, not how to be peaceful while living. And although there were certainly exemplars of progressive Buddhist communities, the direct link to liberation I had read about in writers like Thich Nhat Hanh turned out to be another modern invention. Historically, Buddhists have been about as prone to war, slavery, and domination as any other people.[30]

But at least, I thought, the technique was pure; meditation would work. And in some ways, it does. As I mentioned above, the anecdotal evidence for meditation's capacity to help us be more present and less anxious is relatively strong. Meditation, however, is not really an ancient Buddhist technique cultivated for these purposes. Before the twentieth century, in fact, there were almost no lay Buddhists who meditated and very few monks who did. Most monks spent their time in daily monastery upkeep and the performance of rituals. The reason that laypeople and monks began meditating was, in large part, British colonialism. As monasteries and texts were destroyed and Buddhism persecuted, an innovative group of Burmese Buddhist leaders found a new way to protect the Dharma: by embodying it in the general population. Similar movements sprang up in Thailand. It was the second generation of teachers—most prominently S. N. Goenka—who would welcome the first generation of JewBus to Southeast Asia.[31] As I was leaving Dharamsala, however, I was not aware of this particularly anti-colonial history of meditation. All I could see was that I had become part of a group of Orientalizers who were seeking their own spiritual salvation at the price of another people's political devastation.

For some years, overwhelmed by disenchantment, I abandoned my study of Buddhism, or at least directly. I continued studying philosophy, especially Jean-Paul Sartre and his critical descendants in French thought (Foucault, Derrida, Deleuze, and others). But while mostly focused on unpacking these difficult writings, I often thought about their connections to modern Buddhism. So much of what I read at that time was asking what struck me as very similar questions to those the Buddhists were asking: How can one be an authentic individual in the midst of an inauthentic world? How can we understand a world that lacks essence and is constantly transforming? How can we develop and ground an ethical system if there are no normative values given to us? How can individuals flourish in a world of such intense misery? And should they even aspire to happiness while others are so miserable?

This overlap is not surprising. In part that is because these are generally perplexing human questions that can be found across global philosophy. And in part it is because of mutual influences across philosophical traditions that span the centuries. But perhaps most significantly, modern Buddhist thought was partly shaped by the horizon of existentialism. This often meant showing how philosophers like Kierkegaard or Sartre had correctly seen the existential anguish of life but not understood the path out of it that Buddhist meditation offered. We can see this, for example, in the citation from Watts above, in which he says that Buddhism helps us overcome the anxiety that Kierkegaard only diagnosed. D. T. Suzuki similarly suggested that Buddhism went beyond what existentialism could offer: "The existentialist looks into the abyss of *tathatā* [suchness] and trembles, and is seized with inexpressible fear. Zen would tell him: Why not plunge right into the abyss and see what is there? The idea of individualism fatally holds him back from throwing himself into the devil's maw."[32] Modern Buddhist luminaries were not above scholarly one-upmanship!

There is something interesting about this particular relation between Buddhism and existentialism, however, beyond a standard debate about truth claims. Two of the watchwords of existentialism in this era were "anxiety" and "authenticity." Part of what made Kierkegaard, Sartre, and others so appealing was the relation that they drew between them. The authentic self was not the calm individual who managed to function day by day. Nor was it the fearless subject who had overcome their anxiety. Rather, it was the existential hero who had understood that there was no life beyond anxiety. To be authentic was to come to terms with the fact that our life was absurd and full of despair, that we were hopeless and abandoned, a paltry figure in an uncaring universe, *and yet* to still be able to make meaning, take stances, and passionately engage with this very indifferent universe.

What Watts and Suzuki were basically saying was, to put it colloquially, "Nice try, pal." Existentialism tore through the idea that we could be authentic according to god-given or nature-given ideals, and it forced us to reconcile the fact that any beliefs we had were solely the product of the human imagination. This was a good start, Watts and Suzuki responded, but it missed the final step. The flux of the universe does not render it meaningless; flux itself is the meaning. Zen offered a different kind of authenticity: one that found a path to overcome anxiety by seeking out an experience on the other side of this realization about flux. When we let go of the self, when we let go of all the language and concepts and strivings we use to try to make sense of the world, *then* we pierce through our personal anxiety into the impersonal experience of enlightenment.[33] To be authentic in this sense is to have had an experience of enlightenment, and then to radiate that experience in everything one does.

The irony of the whole situation is that while Suzuki and Watts gained an edge on the question of authenticity, they would eventually lose it on the same grounds. They claimed a path to authenticity that could itself be authenticated through the experiences of adherents and historical figures. The trouble was that as scholars began to do ethnographies and dig through Buddhist archives, they did not find much of anything like what Suzuki described. You could, to be sure, read admonitions to achieve perfected states, but if you actually spent time with monks, you found that many of them did not put much effort into trying to surpass anxiety and reach enlightenment. Instead they often breezed through the texts as part of elaborate rituals, not attempts at liberation. This was the devastating claim made by Robert Sharf in his landmark essay, "Buddhist Modernism and the Rhetoric of Meditative Experience" (1995): "scholars read ideological prescription as phenomenological description."[34] In other words, the texts that Suzuki relied on to define his version of Zen were about not what was authentically achieved, but what was textually imagined.

Essays like Sharf's had seemed to settle the matter for me. But as I kept progressing through French thought, I eventually arrived at the late lectures of Michel Foucault. These lectures, I was surprised to see, more or less repeated Suzuki's thoughts about medieval Japan with respect to ancient Greece and Rome. According to Foucault, modern Western thought had lost its way because it divorced truth claims from the actual practices that might help one realize the truth. We might, for example, think that the truth of ethics was generosity, but what methods did we have to actually make ourselves be more generous, beyond will power? Foucault argued that this separation lay at the heart of many impasses in modern life and thought. We had become helplessly inauthentic because we kept holding ideas we had no methods to enable ourselves to actually practice. He called these missing elements "practices" or "techniques of the self," and he worked to excavate them from writers like Seneca and Aurelius.[35]

I thought it surprising that Foucault was starting to sound a lot like Suzuki. And then I discovered that this was no coincidence: Foucault had been reading works on Zen—including one with an important introduction by Suzuki—while he was working on these lectures.[36] It suddenly seemed as if my journey away from Suzuki had come full circle. And it made me begin to wonder: How much did it really matter if his Zen was not "authentic"? He had certainly made incorrect claims—and we owe a lot to Sharf and others for shaking up the hagiographic picture of him—but it was still the case that he, Foucault, and others were doing something very interesting with the archives that they were, in a sense, inventing. As the anthropologist Marshall Sahlins has written, maybe it's time we move beyond noting that traditions are invented and begin to think about "the inventiveness of tradition."[37] If we accept that modern Buddhism is an invention, then what can we learn from its inventiveness?

My return to Suzuki led me to ask questions about the general dismissal of modern Buddhism. Could it really be the case that so many people were wrong about Buddhism for so long? If meditation really worked, did it matter that none of the monks I met in Dharamsala did it? And what were we to make of all those modern writers from Asia—D. T. Suzuki, Anagarika Dharmapala, Taixu, the Dalai Lama, B. R. Ambedkar, and many others—who were arguing as vociferously for modern Buddhism as the Western Orientalists? And especially, how did it matter that some of them, like Nhat Hanh and Ambedkar, were so committed to equality and justice through Buddhism? Indeed, this has long been one of the main critical concerns about Orientalism: that in its fascination with what is wrong about Western knowledge of the East, it allowed very little room for how thinkers in other parts of the world thought about themselves.[38]

Why, then, is this not a book that explains the globalist, Buddhist worldview via the Asian philosophers who outlined it? Because, while I think such an account of modern, global Buddhist philosophy would be useful, the overwhelming focus on Buddhism as a philosophy was what got me—and most Orientalists—into trouble in the first place. Buddhism first appeared in the West in primarily two ways: as an exalted philosophy and as a degraded practice. Western writers upheld the marvelous philosophical insights of Buddhism at the same time that they excoriated its present condition in Asian countries.[39] I learned in Dharamsala that this division was precisely what was occluding our understanding of Buddhist actuality. One cannot understand Buddhism as a pure philosophy or as a specific set of practices; one has to understand it, like most things, as part of an articulated and socially embedded web of relationships among different actors, ideas, and historical facts. And one of the best ways to do this is and has always been through stories.

Donald Lopez, one of the main critics of our impoverished understanding of Buddhism, puts the point precisely in his *The Story of Buddhism*:

> Most Buddhists throughout history have not engaged in meditation. Many monks have not known the four noble truths. But everyone, monk and nun, layman and laywoman, knows stories about the Buddha, about the bodhisattvas, about famous monks and nuns. These stories, sometimes miraculous, sometimes humorous, sometimes both, have provided the most enduring

means for the transmission of the dharma, more enduring even than grand images carved in stone. Each retelling of a story is slightly different from the one before, with embellishments and omissions, yet always able to be told again, its plot providing a coherence to the myriad constituents of experience, from which we may derive both instruction and delight.[40]

What I have set out to do in this book is to show how modern novelists from around the world—from Botswana, Cuba, Japan, South Africa, Tibet, the United Kingdom, and the United States—have told the story of modern Buddhism. I have tried to understand and rearticulate the instruction they provide, the ways they have used Buddhism to make sense of the world around them and their place in it.

I argue that one of the most intriguing things we learn from this study of Buddhism in world literature is that no attempt to extract Buddhism from the complexity of its life-worlds is possible or even meaningful. It is not possible, as I have already mentioned, because every attempt to do so has inevitably found that even the most abstracted claims can only be based on and respondent to material frameworks. And even if it were possible, it would not be meaningful because to have a philosophy, as Foucault argued, is not to have a simple vision of the way the world works that may or may not be liveable. It is to think through how our ideas about the world succeed or fail to coincide with what we are able to make possible. It is thus equally about how we create the practices and institutions in which to effectively embed our ideals. My literary history of global Buddhism is the story of this ongoing dynamic between the promised ideals of Buddhism and their embedded histories.

Here's a story, for example. At the turn of the twentieth century, a powerful and well-connected Tibetan monk leaves his home on what appears to be a religious pilgrimage. The timing is somewhat suspicious, since there is no particularly good reason for him to be on pilgrimage now, especially since it is an extremely intense moment for his country. It is, after all, the height of the "Great Game" of empire, and Tibet is being threatened by both Russia to the north and Britain, via India, from the south. Tibet's fraught relationships with Mongolia and China—whose patronage powerful Tibetan religiopolitical figures have sought for centuries—also continues.[41] Along the way, the monk has a surprising number of contacts with the British and their imperial agents, and an outside observer—at least one savvy enough to know that monks are political figures—might begin to wonder if his trip is indeed just a religious pilgrimage, or somehow a covert excursion related to geopolitics.

Readers of British literature may recognize the plot I've described as more or less that of Rudyard Kipling's *Kim* (1900/1901), and in a sense, it is. But it's also a description of a 1905 journey by the Panchen Lama (the second most powerful figure, after the Dalai Lama, in the Geluk sect of Tibetan Buddhism) who went to India on a pilgrimage to Buddhist holy sites. The trip was certainly in part a genuine pilgrimage for the lama, who by all accounts found it profound and moving, but it also functioned as "'religious cover'" for covert political meetings with the British.[42] That such a political context for the lama of *Kim* might underlie his trip to India has not, so far as I know, been broached by another literary critic, although, as I will argue in chapter 1, there is ample evidence for this within the text of *Kim* itself. Indeed, the lama figure in *Kim* is based on this very lama.

Such a critical lapse has occurred because we take the lama to represent only our own ideas about Buddhism. Because literary critics assume Buddhism to be otherworldly, they take it at face value that the sole purpose of his journey is to find a mystical "river of the Buddha's arrow," where he will find salvation. Because they assume that Buddhism and politics don't mix, they take it that the interesting political plot of the novel has to do with British imperialism in India, and ignore the obvious Tibetan context. If we change such assumptions, we learn something about both modern Buddhism and modern literature. We learn that modern Buddhism has never been otherworldly or removed from everyday concerns, but has always been embedded in the politics of its time. And we learn that literature, far from simply representing Orientalist fantasies, in fact often registers a complexity that the critics have tended to ignore. This is even the case, as we will see, with Edward Said's own writing on *Kim*.[43]

This is the kind of reading I do throughout this book. I want to show how what we have taken for Buddhist abstraction is in fact embedded in modern life-worlds, and to discuss the lessons that begin to emerge once we pay attention to this. While I will primarily focus on the thematic lessons we may learn, I will also discuss what this teaches us about the formal aspects of these novels in greater detail in each of the chapters that follow. It includes, for example: the meaning of the frame story in Conrad's *Heart of Darkness*; the way literary language and characters are reincarnated in Jamyang Norbu's *Mandala of Sherlock Holmes* and J. M. Coetzee's *Elizabeth Costello*; the interpretation of seemingly nonsensical phrases or plot twists in Severo Sarduy's *Cobra*; and the structuring power of parables in Zadie Smith's *The Autograph Man*. In these and other instances, the application of vague ideas about what Buddhism is stops us from understanding how these novels formally operate. Once we know how Buddhism has informed these novels at a complex, formal level, we will see their composition in a new light.

Like all stories, my global literary history of global modern Buddhism has to begin and end somewhere. This is *a* literary history; not *the* literary history. Some of the choices I have made in telling this story may surprise readers. You will not find in what follows a discussion of Herman Hesse's *Siddhartha*, James Hilton's *Lost Horizon*, Jack Kerouac's *Dharma Bums*, the stories of Jorge Luis Borges, or any other fictions generally associated with modern forms of Buddhism. Part of the reason for this is precisely that they are expected, and I have tried to discuss Buddhism in authors and countries generally less associated with it. This includes Buddhism's often unremarked appearance in canonical works like *Heart of Darkness* and writers like Coetzee. And it also includes a greater diversity of writers than are often considered in studies of Buddhism and literature: novels like Bessie Head's *A Question of Power*—a novel about founding a new kind of Buddhism in the midst of insanity and domestic abuse—and Severy Sarduy's *Cobra*—a wild narrative about magic potions, sex changes, and drug dealers spending time with Tibetan monks in India.

The diversity of these selections matters a great deal for the literary history I am telling here. Too often, it is presumed that modern Buddhism is mostly for middle-class, bourgeois white people who have time to meditate and possessions to abandon. There is some truth to this. But focusing on it too heavily erases the many experiences with Buddhism that we find across lines of race, class, gender, and sexuality.[44] And factoring in these experiences presents us with a richer tapestry of modern Buddhist novels. It allows us to understand how seemingly abstract themes like authenticity, liberation, and enlightenment become embedded differently depending on the subject and their identity (or identities). At the same time, it helps us understand how such themes are shared in spite of the remarkable diversity of the authors. That's why I have grouped these novels by their shared themes. Across their diversity, they help to illustrate a singular history of global Buddhism: one in which we give up the hope for total salvation and instead focus on spectral illuminations that can help us work through the burdens of history and identity in our quests for liberation and authenticity.

In each chapter I will also relate the novels to chapters from my own story of learning, unlearning, and relearning global Buddhist history. While some academic readers may be less interested in my personal story, some general readers may find these sections more entertaining than the literary criticism. I have done my best to make the criticism as available and interesting as possible, within the conditions of scholarship, to readers coming from different backgrounds. I situate each novel's encounter with Buddhism at the nexus of authorial intentions, linguistic and narrative choices, and historical and philosophical contexts. I believe this methodological pluralism better explores the complexity of what Buddhism does in these novels than any particular school of interpretation.[45] One tip to readers who do not frequently engage with literary criticism: it is much more enjoyable to read about novels that you have read, so I encourage you to read as many of these wonderful books as you can.

Whatever your background, I hope this book leads you to take critical Buddhist studies more seriously—not just for accuracy but also because factoring in Buddhism can give you a greater amplitude and understanding for dealing with suffering, liberation, history, oppression, and other themes pertinent to our lives today. It may at first be disappointing that in the story I tell about these themes, spectral illuminations of Buddhism cannot save the ruins of modernity, any more than the revelations of modernity could save the ruins of Buddhism. But perhaps the study of the global interactions of Buddhism, literature, and modernity may teach us something about how to appreciate the genuine values of existence in such a fraught and damaged world. And it may remind us of the immense joys and gifts that not only surround but also come through the damage. We may not find absolute enlightenment, the type of blazing revelation I wanted as a teenager, but the spectral illuminations may yet light a path to the world that the best aspects of Buddhism have always imagined.

1

ENLIGHTENMENT

WORLDLY ENLIGHTENMENT

When I arrived in Dharamsala, I was looking for enlightenment, even though I was not quite sure what that meant. I had a
vague idea that being enlightened would end my anxiety, recon-
nect me to the world, and give me a feeling of calm, ease, and
perspicacity. I thought often of a line I had read by the twelfth-
century Zen master Dōgen: the "Buddha of Great Compassion"
acts "like a man reaching behind him in the night searching for
a pillow."[1] I thought of what it would mean to exist in a chaotic
world with such clarity, as if every action were as straightforward
as reaching for a pillow in the night. I imagined living as a compassionate being who knew in each instance what had to be done
to diminish suffering, and who thought only of this and never of
himself. And I believed that meditation and philosophical study
among the Tibetans would bring me to that point.

It's a strange idea for many reasons, not least of which is that
this ideal was as foreign to most Tibetans as it was to me. Not
only were most of the people I met in Dharamsala more focused
on eating and reclaiming their country than on perfecting their
compassion, but also the main schools of Tibetan Buddhism are

opposed to Dōgen's Chan/Zen thinking. (Chan is the Chinese name for Zen.) Although I, like many newly interested in Buddhism, did not take its doctrinal divisions all that seriously, there is a real gap between the Buddhism of Dōgen and the Buddhism of Tsongkhapa, the fourteenth-century founder of the Geluk sect of Tibetan Buddhism and leading philosophical light of the current Dalai Lama. In fact, one of the defining myths of Tibetan Buddhism is its explicit difference from Chan Buddhism. As the story goes, there was a debate in the eighth century between Heshang Moheyan, representing Chan, and Kamalaśīla, representing a version of Indian Buddhism. The basic difference was a question of whether enlightenment was sudden and could happen at any instant (the Chan position), or whether it accrued gradually over millennia of practice cultivating wisdom and compassion.[2] It is said that Kamalaśīla handily won the debate, and Tibetan Buddhism has followed the Indian path ever since.[3] While very few people I met were concerned with achieving enlightenment, there was no shortage of Tibetans who told me that this story was one more nail in the coffin of any Chinese claim to long-standing sovereignty over Tibet.

This was all somewhat hard for me to process. I knew perfectly well that, with some exceptions, enlightenment did not refer to the feeling of calm and ease that I wanted, but rather to the ability to end the cycle of transmigration—that is to say, to achieve nirvana and go out of existence entirely. (Classically nirvana is *not* a state of bliss, as many imagine, but rather the end of the enchainment to living altogether. This is not to say that Buddhists lack visions of heavens or states of eternal bliss. Like all things in Buddhism, the idea of the afterlife is heavily contested.) But I accepted the modernist claim that what enlightenment would mean today *would* be something quite like what I was looking for.

What was perplexing to me about the sudden versus gradual debate was how much it had to do with politics and colonization in the present day. The debate was not so much about what enlightenment was, but about whether it proved a relationship between Tibet and India or Tibet and China. It turned out that searching for enlightenment could not be extricated from taking a position on very worldly, political matters. As I would go on to learn, the relationship between enlightenment and politics hardly stops here. Throughout Tibetan history there have been fights—literal bloody fights—over securing the patronage necessary to allow one to pursue enlightenment.[4] Here, as in so many other places, modern literature seems to have understood modern Buddhism's embeddedness better than its philosophical expounders. This, at least, is the argument I will be making about Rudyard Kipling's *Kim* (1900/1901), where the quest for enlightenment simply cannot be extricated from the politics of empire.

In Sarat Chandra Das's *Journey to Lhasa and Central Tibet*, a text based on the Indian pundit's travels in 1879 and 1881–82 at the behest of British imperial forces in India, we find the following prophecy: "It is universally believed in Tibet that after two hundred years the Tashi lama will retire to Shambala, the Utopian city of the Buddhists, and will not return to Tibet, and that in the meantime the world will succumb to the power of the . . . Russians and English."[5] The "Tashi lama" is the name Das and many others used for the political and spiritual leader we now know as the Panchen Lama, who is today second in power only to the Dalai Lama within the Geluk sect of Tibetan Buddhism.[6] The prophecy recorded by Das shows that we don't need to be scholars of Buddhism to understand how ingrained it is in everyday politics. Just by talking to people he learned that the enlightenment of the Panchen Lama would mean that there was no longer a worldly force to hold back the interests of two empires then competing for sovereignty over Tibet.

The Panchen Lama is important for those interested in literature because he is the inspiration for Rudyard Kipling's "Teshoo Lama," whom Kipling might have learned about in large part by reading about Das's travels. Das himself, after all, was the inspiration for Kipling's character Hurree Chunder Mookerjee.[7] It is difficult to say what exactly of Das's travel notes Kipling might have incorporated into the novel. It has been suggested that he took the use of code names (R25, C17, etc.) from the pundit.[8] It also seems likely that he learned the technique of using rosary beads to secretly mark distance from his account. (In this practice, each seemingly religious movement of a bead in fact represents a measurement of distance.)[9] There are also, I will suggest, reasons for seeing this prophecy as an unspoken structure of the narrative. The brief prophecy recorded by Das contains a fascinating claim: that when the Tashi Lama achieves spiritual liberation (becomes unbound by earthly conditions), it will result in conditions of political domination for the Tibetan people he leaves behind. This is a potentially significant context for *Kim*, since a lama seeking liberation from this world while the Russians and English fight over colonial control is precisely what happens. Reading the novel from this perspective will help us understand more about the often underappreciated role of the lama in the story, as well as something about the modern meaning of Buddhist enlightenment.

The narrative begins in Lahore, where a seemingly befuddled lama meets Kim, an orphaned Irish boy living a wild life on the streets. Kim agrees to join the lama on his mystical quest for the "river of the arrow"—a pilgrimage site where the lama expects to find salvation.[10] On their journey, Kim is also roped into

being a British imperial spy and charged with a mission to stop
Franco-Russian engagements with local kings in the hill regions
along the northern border by stealing the foreigners' maps and
letters. In the climactic scene, the lama is explaining a drawing
of the "Wheel of Life," which is a visual representation of Buddhist soteriology.[11] The lama refuses to sell his version of the
diagram to a Russian spy unless the latter proves himself a true
adept. The Russian tries to take the diagram by force and rips it.
In the ensuing fight and confusion, Kim and Mookerjee (the
Das character) manage to steal the Russians' bags and so complete their mission. After this, Kim and the lama return from
the hills, and while Kim recuperates from an illness, the lama
finds his river, achieves enlightenment, and decides to remain a
while longer in his mortal body in order to initiate Kim. The
novel closes with his offer to his potential disciple, who has
meanwhile also been invited to join in the Great Game of
empire on a more permanent basis. We are not told how Kim
replies.

Literary critics who have discussed Buddhism in the novel
have tended to do so in an abstract way that ignores the specificity of the lama's position in Tibet. Edward Said, who more
than perhaps any other critic has helped generations of readers
(myself included) to see the colonial politics of literature, derides
what the lama says as "mumbo jumbo," and reduces his painting
of the philosophically complex "Wheel of Life" to a "talisman-
like chart."[12] Focusing only on the India-Britain colonial relation and reading the lama as an archetype of the religious
pilgrim (akin to Chaucer's or Bunyan's characters), Said misses
the specificity of the lama's geopolitics in the narrative. Srinivas
Aravamudan's reading is more sympathetic, but it still denies
the specifics of the lama's role: "[In *Kim*] Buddhist philosophy
[has been] stripped of its Tibetan particularities and rendered

in terms of the larger picture of an 'Indian' religion."[13] William Dillingham has also attempted to add nuance to our understanding of the character, but only at the expense of simplifying what Buddhism is. Thus he claims, "the Lama is . . . as far from being an ordinary Buddhist monk as Kim is from being an ordinary teenager," but what it would mean to be an "ordinary Buddhist monk" (peaceful and apolitical) is taken for granted.[14] Most recently, Jeffrey Franklin has given a reading of the novel from the standpoint of nondualist Buddhist philosophy. Franklin suggests that Kim in fact does not have to make a choice at the novel's close: the point is not whether he becomes a monk or an imperial agent, but rather that he uphold the virtues of either position through "disinterested and compassionate" action. (How one can do so as an imperial agent is itself left as something of a mystery.)[15]

In all of these readings Buddhist philosophy takes precedence over Buddhist actuality. This results in the impression that Buddhism is an abstract philosophy that only accidentally engages politics. Thus in Dillingham's reading, even if a Buddhist were to get involved in politics, she would be betraying her faith and would not be an "ordinary" Buddhist. But as I've already mentioned, a lot of what ordinary Buddhists have done in Tibetan history is to find patrons who can materially support their monasteries. The history of the relationship between the Dalai Lama and the Panchen Lama is largely about fights over political patronage from either the Mongols or the Qing Dynasty.[16] These kinds of fights continue today in debates among Tibet, China, India, and the United States. It even continues in the realm of reincarnation in an ongoing dispute between the People's Republic of China and the Tibetan government-in-exile over where the Fifteenth Dalai Lama (the next reincarnation) will be found (in Tibet or in China; or,

indeed, whether he will reincarnate at all). What is unique to
modernity is that readers would think of lamas as philosophical
treatise writers and pilgrims wholly removed from the world of
politics. Once we see that this is not now and has never been the
case, we can read the lama's character, and the novel's understanding of the relationship between empire and enlightenment, differently.

One way to see the Buddhist conditions that inform *Kim* is
to read it in the context of Das's prophecy. The novel takes
place at a time when the actions of the spiritual ruler of Tibet
overlapped with the machinations of imperial power. In this
context, the interesting choice is arguably less Kim's and more
the lama's. Perhaps this is why we never see Kim choose empire
or enlightenment: Kipling is illuminating their connection,
not their difference. He rewrites Das's prophecy so that the
lama, rather than leaving the British and Russians to fight over
Tibet, decides to stay in this world *in order to choose the British*.
Revising Franklin, then, we can say indeed that whether Kim
chooses the lama's path or the Great Game does not matter,
but this is not because of nondualism. Rather, it is because the
lama has already wedded his path to Britain's imperial power.

To my knowledge, no reading of the novel exists in which
the lama is himself an active player in the Game.[17] Critics find
it inexplicable, meanwhile, that he puts his spiritual journey on
hiatus for three years and pays for Kim's education in colonial
schools earlier in the narrative. Such an act makes perfect sense,
however, if we understand Kim as part of the lama's search for
a patron: he is testing both the boy and the British system. This
reading also coheres with the novel's climactic scene, which
revolves around the Russians' limited knowledge of Buddhism.
(Russian Orientalism was in fact quite advanced.[18]) What
Kipling refers to as the lama's consistently childlike behavior,

ignoring the conventions of men and even lecturing in Hindi to the Franco-Russian spies—who he has just been told by Mookerjee likely don't speak very much Hindi—can be seen less as his ignorance of reality or his insistence on a Buddhist path in the face of political danger and more as his playing the holy fool as part of his search for a new patron.[19] The Englishmen speak his language and listen to his teachings on Buddhism, as the Mongols and Chinese had done with previous Panchen Lamas. The Russians, at least in Kipling's chauvinistic rendering, are ignorant of the language and defile the teachings. Having witnessed all this, the lama decides that rather than seeking Shambhala and letting the British and Russians fight over Tibet, he should remain in this world in order to choose the British. In so doing, he reveals something otherwise hidden in modern Buddhism: becoming enlightened does not mean pursuing spiritual perfection and abandoning your people to empire; it means making correct political decisions about how to deal with the power of empires.[20]

What, after all, is the lama doing in India in the first place? The novel begins with the second most powerful figure in Tibet wandering in pilgrimage from Lahore to Benares at the height of the Great Game that might have determined Tibet's future. While some have read this as the quixotic lama's disinterest from politics and focus on enlightenment, this does not help us make sense of the novel or its historical context. As noted in the introduction, seeing the lama as a political actor in his pilgrimage accords with what actually happened a few years later. In 1904, the British invaded Tibet, fearing growing Russian power in Lhasa. The Thirteenth Dalai Lama fled into exile in Mongolia for protection. A few months later, as historian of Tibetan pilgrimage Toni Huber has related, the Panchen Lama took a pilgrimage tour of modern India. Huber writes, "It is clear the

British intended to use the prospect of pilgrimage to the Buddhist holy places as a lure to secure the Panchen's acceptance of
the invitation, and perhaps also as a necessary 'religious cover'
for what other parties would undoubtedly consider a political
visit."[21] Huber notes that we shouldn't read the lama's visit as
purely or cynically political. Indeed, he was very interested in the
pilgrimage tour as such. And that's the point: Buddhism and politics are not separated. The lama can earnestly seek his enlightenment at the same time that he seeks a political patron. Indeed, at
some level, for the preservation of the very conditions of life that
make enlightenment possible, he must do so. *Kim* in this context
does not just borrow Das's recorded prophecy, it repudiates it, and
then turns out to be more prophetic. The Panchen Lama *did* put
off Shambhala and went to India under the "religious cover" of
pilgrimage in order to find new patrons in the British.

In so doing, he was certainly not unique in Tibet's history.
Tibet had long been part of international trade on the Silk
Road. The continuity of this in the present is signaled in *Kim* by
an offhand reference to "Tibetans hurrying down . . . each
laden with a bag of borax."[22] The book's editor tells us that borax
is a "mineral found in Tibet," which is true, but undersells the
point.[23] Borax had for centuries been transmitted west from
Tibet along the Silk Road. It had a significant role in the domi-
nance of the Venetian glass industry through contacts secured
by Marco Polo. However, by the mid-nineteenth century, new
deposits had been found in Italy and the United States, replac-
ing Tibetan dominance of the trade, and so Kipling's reference
is anachronistic. But this may just as well signal that while some
may forget Tibet's links to the world of commerce and empire,
there are material traces everywhere.[24]

The "Spencerian" Hurree Chunder Mookerjee (our Das
character) seems to be aware of this as he periodically voices his

understanding of the lama's complexity in the novel. At various points in the narrative, he questions whether otherworldly assumptions about the lama make sense, going so far as to say that he is "totally devoid of releegiosity." After interrogating the lama on "releegious points and devil-worship," Mookerjee deduces that "He is pure agnostic—same as me."[25] These are signs that the lama is a modernist who rejects certain practices but continues to care about enlightenment all the same. And then there is Mookerjee's even more curious remark, in the same conversation with Kim: "Now suppose you go with the lama, or with me, I hope, some day, or with Mahbub."[26] The language seems to imply that going with him or the lama or Mahbub (another imperial agent) is all the same. There is some ambiguity, and this could just be a list of options, but it could also be a list of choices for Kim as agent of empire.

Mookerjee/Das, in any event, has good reason to doubt the pure religiosity of the lamas in the sense believed by the other characters. As he remarks later, "I remember once they wanted to cut off my head on the road to Lhassa."[27] This is no mere rumor. The Lama who gave Das hospitality at Tashilunpo was not the Panchen Lama, but the Sengchen Lama (possibly the origin of "Such-zen," the name of the monastery in *Kim*). Due to changing political tides, the Sengchen Lama was executed by drowning some four years after Das left, on orders from Lhasa, because he had "'given refuge to foreigners in his monastery and betrayed the secrets of lamaism to the envoy of a foreign power.'"[28] Whether or not Kipling was aware of the specifics, he clearly inscribes the historical relation between Buddhism and politics into the heart of the text.

But the embeddedness of Buddhism does not just mean that enlightenment is related to politics. It also means that politics is related to enlightenment. Buddhism, even if it interacts with politics, is not reducible to it, even in this very political novel. After all, this is still a story about a man who finds a mystical river that can provide enlightenment. And, as we have seen in the historical context, the politics of Buddhism are not cynicism, but part of the difficult effort of creating the material conditions necessary for Buddhist practice. Indeed, the story of the lama's enlightenment is crucial, but not in the way most readers have understood it to be. Thinking through what enlightenment might mean in the text shows both the narrative's attempt to instantiate Britain's imperial order and its inability to do so.

Let's return to the lama's "Wheel of Life" and its depiction of suffering, its causes, and its possible cessation. The philosophical idea embodied here is that of "dependent origination"— the idea that if all things arise dependently on other things (down to the subatomic level), then entities have no essence, no fullness, no presence from their own side, and thus they always succeed each other and produce new causes and conditions. To achieve nirvana, to become unconditioned, is to escape this cycle of dependent origination.[29] The key difference between the stereotypical idea of nirvana as a kind of oneness with the universe (such as Kipling articulates in *Kim*) and what is happening here in philosophical Buddhism is the meaning of this succession of time.[30] The goal is not the *experience* of eternity, in which there is bliss, but rather to end the state of being conditioned by life and time. As Steven Collins, one of the leading scholars of Buddhist philosophy, puts it, "the temporal event denoted by [achieving nirvana] is not anything directly occurring in or to nirvana, but rather the ending-moment of the conditioned process. Unlike all other such moments . . . this has a relation to the past, but not to the future."[31] In this understanding, past earthly conditions make nirvana possible, but nirvana has no effect in the world, and it is not an experience for the subject who achieves it. It is simply the ending of an entity as such. To be unconditioned is not to be at all.[32]

The lama states to Kim near the novel's close that if not "for the merit I have acquired in guiding thee upon the Way," he would not have had the possibility of escaping reincarnation.[33] As evidence of this causal chain he points to the diagram torn by the Russian spy. What is left after the tear shows an explicit connection across the links of dependent origination from the image representing the six senses (intellection is considered a sense in Buddhist philosophy) to the one representing the birth of a child from desire. With some degree of creative interpretation, the lama seems to be suggesting that what spared him returning to sensate life was his connection to the child, Kim. It is Kim who breaks the links that lead from sensation to desire.[34] Now that he has Kim, now that he has secured a patron for his people, as I read it, he need not worry about the life of the senses.

At the last minute, however, he has doubts about whether the young Kim is truly ready.[35] Kim has helped him achieve enlightenment, but he's unsure that the boy himself will go on to do the same. Thus, he offers to continue teaching him. In the final scene of *Kim*, the Lama tells his *chela*, "I have wrenched my Soul back from the Threshold of Freedom to free thee from all sin."[36] Christianizing language aside, the lama here is fulfilling the bodhisattva ideal of putting off enlightenment in order to help others. He is doing what the current Dalai Lama is said to have done now for centuries: returning to the world in order to help more people achieve liberation. By having the Teshoo Lama make this offer to Kim, Kipling seems to want him to put his faith into the British empire as the true protector of the Dharma.

There is one final twist, however: the irony that seems to have been beyond Kipling's reach. The lama may temporarily accede to the British, but ultimately he puts the entire imperial project into question. Although empire conditions the possibility of enlightenment, enlightenment creates the possibility for all things to become unconditioned. The lama returns to lead all things, including the empire itself, to extinction. Perhaps here Kipling's attempt to force the lama to choose the British over the Russians outruns his creative power, since the lama does this only to create the conditions through which the British themselves might eventually go out of existence. *Kim* dramatizes this struggle between empires of "enlightenment": the worldly British seek to bring light to the "dark places of the earth," while the otherworldly nirvana seeks to extinguish the very flame of existence. In the Great Game of empire, the Teshoo Lama is playing the long game.

When I sought out my Tibetan lama figure to guide me to enlightenment, I had no idea about any of the complex history of Tibetan Buddhist politics. Even if I had read *Kim* at the time, I would most likely not have gained any new understanding, as the many critics who ignore the complexity of the lama show. It is very easy to see the charming Teshoo Lama as precisely the embodiment of an enlightened existence seeking only compassion that so many want him—and Buddhists in general—to be. Buddhists themselves have cultivated this image, and with great success. The present Dalai Lama (in spite of a recent instance where he was "canceled" because he said his reincarnation, if a woman, would have to be beautiful) is a shining example of this achieved cultural meaning.[37] Indeed, one of the things that drew me to Dharamsala was that the program I was on promised a private group meeting with the Dalai Lama as part of the experience (more on that in chapter 3).

This vision of Tibet is one of the instances where our critical sensibility has failed to keep up with what the literature records.

I had such a fixed idea of Buddhist monks separated from politics that I could only think it a travesty that a debate about the very nature of enlightenment and how to achieve it had become politicized. But the real travesty was that I could not see that my desires for Buddhism to be something were part of a very different political matrix that trapped Tibetans in a Buddhist box and refused to recognize their claims as universal human expressions of resistance to oppression. This should be heeded not because they are perfect or are repositories of ancient wisdom, but on the precise political grounds on which their claims are articulated: as a human right not to be dominated, whether by a monastic elite or by a foreign power.[38]

Perhaps this in-retrospect obvious realization captures something of what enlightenment means today. Like the sudden enlightenment school, it suggests that we are already enlightened and simply have to realize it. But like the gradual enlightenment school, it insists that even obvious facts require a radical reorientation of our perspective and a long learning process. And it means that enlightenment may not quite look like the Watts-inspired vision I had of a life free from anxiety. Instead, following more Nhat Hanh and Ambedkar and the present Dalai Lama, it would be linked to overcoming the political suffering caused by oppression. The lama in Kipling's narrative does not directly tell us any of this. He is more a tragic figure illustrating the kinds of difficult political situations enlightenment seekers are pushed into when they must carry out work between empires. But he should thus teach a discerning reader that thinking of his quest for enlightenment as an otherworldly or antisocial pursuit barely comprehends his labors. Finding his river and its bending path is a political struggle. There may be reasons to doubt how he plays the game. Indeed, the conciliatory path of the current Dalai Lama has produced a number of critics, including

Jamyang Norbu, who I discuss in the next chapter. But whether or not we agree with his methods, we have to recognize that it is a very worldly game he is playing. When the Teshoo Lama puts off his escape to Shambhala in order to tarry with empire, he is teaching us something fundamental about modern Buddhism: the grand strategies of enlightenment are inseparable from smaller revelations about how to survive in the chaos and turmoil of the modern world.

ANOTHER KIND OF ENLIGHTENMENT

In *Heart of Darkness,* Joseph Conrad takes this point one step further: it's not just that modern life only offers minor revelations; it's that claiming anything other than a minor revelation poses potentially catastrophic risks. Buddhists, after all, are not always the ones being dominated in the games of empire. One thing we learn from the history of Buddhism is that focusing single-mindedly on the conditions of enlightenment for some (a monastic few, or today a wealthy few who have the time for self-care[39]) can become a cynical logic of oppression, as it was at times in Tibet and elsewhere: Because we need food for the monks to be able to meditate around the clock, we need you to give your life and labor for free to feed them. But don't worry, the merit you accrue for doing so will help you become enlightened yourself in a future cycle of existence. We might call this the trickle-down theory of enlightenment.

The basic idea of a forced education program "for your own good" is not exclusive to repressive Buddhist regimes. It is also part of the story of the liberal ideal of enlightenment, whose famous mission was to "civilize the savages," no matter how much savagery was required in the process.[40] The possible terror of enlightenment—in both its liberal and Buddhist forms—is, I will argue in the rest of this chapter, a central theme of Joseph Conrad's *Heart of Darkness*. This may be surprising to some readers, because we often forget that one of the obscurities we come across as we make our way to the horrors of that novel is the twice-made comparison between the protagonist, Marlow, and the Buddha—once in the opening pages and again in the closing paragraph. Interspersed throughout the story are references to meditation and reincarnation as well. The Buddhist elements are perhaps perplexing in a story largely focused on Belgian imperialism in the Congo.[41] But Conrad, I will argue, stages these two moments together based on a singular vision: to question any worldview that claims absolute knowledge through enlightenment.[42]

In so doing, the narrative offers a possibility for modern readers focused more on this life than on the endless games of enlightenment. This possibility is contained in Conrad's vision of "spectral illumination"—a less satisfying, murkier, but ultimately more honest and less imposing mode of human understanding.[43] To fully understand what is meant by spectral illumination, we will need to work our way slowly through Conrad's narrative. But the phrase may generally be understood to refer to the kind of insights into the world we have after we stop looking for perfect knowledge. They are momentary insights that enable us to reorient our understanding of a situation or phenomenon. For Conrad, a kind of gradualist, this insight is not sudden, but occurs through the difficult work of interpreting reality, and it is often aided by a story. Moreover, it is an insight that can at times be so faint—so spectral—that we might not even discern it. For example, I had no absolute illumination about the true nature of Buddhism. Rather, I slowly pieced together the narrative of my understanding to realize a spectral illumination: that even as Buddhism modernized into abstraction, it could not and should not be understood beyond the modern worlds it remained embedded in. While there are certainly objectionable elements in Conrad's presentation of Buddhism, we may still glean some insight about Buddhism today by closely reading his philosophical and highly symbolic novella.

The plot of *Heart of Darkness*—read in countless high school English classrooms—will be known to many readers, but a brief summary may be helpful. The novella is a story within a story. Several travelers are waiting for the tide to go out. The narrator tells us that while they wait, another man, Marlow, begins to tell a story about his time working for an ivory trading company. Marlow traveled to the Congo to investigate some problems the company was having at its Inner Station. Once there, he began to be led into the mystery of a man named Kurtz, a cultlike figure who seemed to have gone mad in the Congo. Conrad's criticisms of colonialism are stark, but so are his descriptions of the Africans there—something that drew him a famous rebuke from Chinua Achebe.[44] As Marlow makes his way to Kurtz, he realizes how the voraciousness of colonialism and the terror of the jungle have led to his demise. Kurtz's famous last words to Marlow are "The horror. The horror."[45] Marlow manages to escape Kurtz's fury and returns to Europe, where he meets Kurtz's fiancée, his Intended. She asks what his last words were, and he lies—your name, he tells her. The original narrator then takes over and remarks on the pale gloom that Marlow's story has cast on the world around them.

When considering the role of Buddhism in *Heart of Darkness*, it is important to remember that Marlow is carefully and specifically described as distinct from the Buddha himself. In the first comparison: "Marlow sat cross-legged right aft . . . He had sunken cheeks, a yellow complexion, a straight back, an ascetic aspect, and with his arms dropped, the palms of hands outwards, resembled an idol."[46] Then: "he had the pose of a Buddha preaching in European clothes and without a lotus-flower."[47] The narrator is careful to the point of excess to separate his buddha from the historical Buddha: Marlow has an "aspect"; he "resembled"; he is in a "pose"; he is "European"; he lacks the symbolic "lotus-flower."[48] This differentiation is central to understanding Buddhism's role: it marks for us that at this juncture, European Buddhism is the concern. More specifically, it is that "European Buddhist" who so interested Conrad: the philosopher Arthur Schopenhauer.[49] To understand the role of Buddhism in Conrad's book, we need to know something of Schopenhauer.

One of the main routes of Buddhism's migration into modernism was through Schopenhauer's two-volume work, *The World as Will and Representation* (1818/1844). The part of Schopenhauer's complex argument that concerns us here can be summarized as follows: the world is an interconnected whole, which, as it objectifies itself in space and time, takes on the form of individuals. These individuals, blindly striving to maintain their meaningless individuality, egotistically assert themselves and their needs. Schopenhauer thus approvingly cites Thomas Hobbes's idea of nature as a war of all against all.[50] While for Hobbes this conflict can be overcome through politics, for Schopenhauer there is only limited respite through modes of aesthetic appreciation and an uncompromising morality. There is no political cure for our woes, which are everlasting. We may at best be ethical by seeing past the illusion of individuality and realizing that to do good we must do good for all. Schopenhauer famously found this belief in accord with the Hindu concept of the veil or *maya*.[51] He denied the influence of "Orientalism" on his thinking. Rather, he suggested that this overlap gave proof of his transcendental insight into the human condition. (One of Nietzsche's main critiques of Schopenhauer was that he fails to see the *historical* dimension of humanity, and that who we are is not a transcendental given but a historical state to be overcome.[52])

What is particularly important about Schopenhauer in this context is that he understood this movement against natural strife as the contribution of religious thought. The blind struggle of natural life, as well as the savagery of so-called civilized society (Schopenhauer singles out "Negro slavery" as an example of how human beings treat each other in order to get the things they want[53]), led him to propose asceticism—whether Christian, Hindu, or Buddhist—as the only possible path to salvation.[54] The fact of a primitive human nature of violence meant that our moral task as humans was to let the world die: "Therefore that great fundamental truth contained in Christianity as well as in Brahmanism and Buddhism, the need for salvation from an existence given up to suffering and death, and its attainability through the denial of the will, *hence by a decided opposition to nature*, is beyond all comparison the most important truth there can be."[55] Once I am enlightened and pierce the illusion of the need to live, my sole aim is to bring about the end of the will to live. This could not occur for Schopenhauer through war, which only stirred up more misery, or suicide, which demonstrated a too passionate distaste for life. It was possible only by the individual's refusal to continue the world through celibacy or "accidental" starvation caused by a loss of the will to live.[56]

Schopenhauer's pessimistic version of Buddhism was celebrated by some writers in Europe, creating what John Bramble calls a "Schopenhauer vogue" that spread across the continent.[57] His influence would reach from Conrad to Virginia Woolf,

Samuel Beckett, and, later, Jorge Luis Borges, among many others. Schopenhauer's interpretation of Buddhism is not bad considering the state of Indological scholarship, but still generally discredited. Even David McMahan, whose *Making of Modern Buddhism* is very open to the legitimacy of transformations of Buddhism in modernity, writes of Schopenhauer's "famously inadequate reading of the words of Gautama."[58] But however deficient his understanding at a textual level may have been, it still spurred interesting new forms of modern Buddhist thought. In Conrad's fiction, we will encounter two: Kurtz's and Marlow's. (There is also an anti-Schopenhauerian Buddhism in the text to which I will return—that of an unnamed Congolese laborer.)

Heart of Darkness begins with a warning to readers about the difficulty of interpretation. In the narrator's oft-cited but cryptic words:

> The yarns of seamen have a direct simplicity, the whole meaning of which lies within the shell of a cracked nut. But Marlow was not typical (if his propensity to spin yarns be excepted) and to him the meaning of an episode was not inside like a kernel but outside, enveloping the tale which brought it out only as a glow brings out a haze, in the likeness of those misty halos that, sometimes, are made visible by the spectral illumination of the moonshine.[59]

This is a dense but not inexplicable passage.[60] Meaning is neither hidden in the depths of things nor merely on their surface, but rather is found in some vague space outside them. Moreover, meaning is not hard like a kernel but soft like a mist. Whereas the hardness of a kernel cannot be missed when we bite into it, we may walk through a haze completely unaware. Our only hope to see it is for a bit of moonlight to suddenly shine and give us "spectral illumination"—partial enlightenment. Such revelation is again not like a kernel. It does not perdure safely in its shell, awaiting the opportunity to grow and reproduce. Rather, "we live in the flicker," the brief moment in which a story may bring out for us the meaning that otherwise lies hidden in plain sight.[61]

There is something odd, however, in the fact that this is the primary exegetical clue given for a work with the title *Heart of Darkness*, which would suggest that it is in the center, the heart, where we would find meaning.[62] There is in a sense a double warning here: we will not find the meaning where we expect it but will be led to seek it there nevertheless. Marlow is atypical in his geography of meaning, but, the narrator warns, still typical in that he spins yarns. Like the current of the river or the destiny of the fabric, we will be pulled along *as if* into meaning. We must remain vigilant to see how the story is about a hermeneutical relationship between inner and outer.[63]

I mark this moment not only because it is important for any reading of the novella and because of its invocation of "illumination" but also because it is primarily on the *outside* of the text that we find the references to Marlow as a buddha. Readers have tended to look for the meaning of the book in the kernel—in the heart of darkness. However, the "spectral illumination" that the narrator offers consists in how the story about imperialism brings out the meaning of Europe's turn to Buddhism. This is not at all to claim that the story of colonial atrocities in the ivory trade should be downplayed. To the contrary, I argue that the function of the narrative is to call into question the nature of our interpretation of those atrocities and the geographic space—the supposed darkness—in which they take place. What is at stake is the very idea of a "heart of darkness," a savage core to the universe, a Hobbesian war of all against all, which we, like Schopenhauer,

Kurtz, or Marlow, might respond to with a desire to bring about the end of life as such.

We can see this by looking at a few moments in which the exegetical logic of spectral illumination is operative in Marlow's own narration. As the ship approaches Kurtz's station, a fog sets in—"a white fog, very warm and clammy, and more blinding than the night."[64] We are in the midst of a haze without spectral illumination, and no insight can be gained. Then the fog clears, "as a shutter lifts." A photograph, claiming to represent objective reality, is about to be taken. What we see is "a glimpse" of "the towering multitude of trees, of the immense matted jungle, with the blazing little ball of the sun hanging over it—all perfectly still—and then the white shutter came down again."[65] The picture is taken. The jungle is picturesque, indeed—full of interlocked sinews illuminated by a warm light. And it is stilled in a moment of time.

But once the photograph is taken and the fog revokes the vision, the power of description is returned from image to language, in the form of a "very loud cry as of infinite desolation . . . modulated in savage discords." These are the Congolese subjects, whom Kurtz has sent to attack the ship, announcing their presence. But lest we presume that this battle cry holds the meaning of the scene, Marlow states, "it seemed as though the mist itself had screamed."[66] If the mist is where we are looking for meaning, then neither the photographic image of the pacific jungle nor the sonic image of war (that is, the inner kernels) is our concern. Rather, the key is the interpretation—decoding what exactly the mist is screaming.

It turns out that the meaning of this episode for Marlow is not in the "savage" scream at all, but rather in the interaction it produces with one of his shipmates, the leader of a group he is traveling with, who it turns out are sometimes cannibals. The unnamed man asks him to catch those who have screamed so that he and his comrades may eat them. Marlow reflects and realizes that the conditions of these men's employment have made it nearly impossible for them to eat anything on their voyage to the Inner Station. Suddenly realizing the situation his inattentiveness has created, he wonders why they have not already eaten the rest of the crew. What enables them to show "restraint"—a word he repeats three times?[67] He wonders if it is "superstition, disgust, patience, fear—or some kind of primitive honour?" but quickly rules out each of these possibilities in turn.[68] In the face of hunger, "these chaps had . . . no earthly reason for any kind of scruple."[69] This leads Marlow to a formulation of the same kind of claim that the narrator has made about his general style: "But there was the fact facing me—the fact dazzling, to be seen, like the foam on the depths of the sea, like a ripple on an unfathomable enigma, a mystery greater— when I thought of it—than the curious, inexplicable note of desperate grief in this savage clamour that had swept by us on the river-bank, behind the blind whiteness of the fog."[70] As before, the work of the tale is not to contain the meaning but to illuminate it.

In this instance, the main part of the narrative—the attack on the ship—illuminates the more important meaning found in the conversation. Marlow realizes that the seeming savagery of the jungle is not in any sense primeval. One may have the restraint of his shipmate or the insanity of Kurtz. Most likely these men refuse to eat their fellow passengers because they, like most who practice cannibalism, would only consume enemies from battle or other specific situations, not just because they are hungry. And there is "no earthly reason" to explain which values would emerge at a given place or time. What is interesting, then, is not the darkness at the core of the world as signified by the attack, but only the surprising way the sheer being of the universe can manifest in humane interactions at any given time and in any given place. Thus the meaning we should expect to find—the terror in the face of savagery—is replaced by a new illumination: that there is no such ontological fact as savagery. We are products of a variable combination of possible human dispositions, not determined by some singular nature. Hence our concern is less with human nature, which is plural, and more with how humans have built their worlds in relation to one another and the indeterminacy of the universe in which they find themselves.[71]

As Marlow approaches Kurtz, however, he still leads his listeners to believe that what is fascinating about Kurtz is his hollowness—that his emptiness has allowed the darkness to "echo loudly" within him. But we soon learn again that there is no core to Kurtz, light or dark. There are only the choices he has made because he *believes* in the universe's essential darkness. When Marlow first espies Kurtz's compound, he notices some ornaments adorning poles around it. When he looks with his binoculars he sees that the "round knobs were not ornamental but symbolic."[72] In fact, they are severed heads strung up on stands. As with all the other symbols in the novella, the key is to interpret them with regard to the light they cast on the haze surrounding them.

Marlow puts the binoculars down and the severed heads recede into an "inaccessible distance." Just as the shutter had to close before the meaning of the jungle scene arose, so here it is only when the device of technological vision is put away that the storyteller lets us see something else. Kurtz's "admirer" begins to describe how people would ritualistically approach the compound by crawling. Marlow cuts him off:

"I don't want to know anything of the ceremonies used when approaching Mr. Kurtz," I shouted. Curious, this feeling that came over me that such details would be more intolerable than those heads. . . . After all, that was only a savage sight while I seemed at one bound to have been transported into some light- less region of subtle horrors, where pure, uncomplicated savagery was a positive relief, being something that had a right to exist— obviously—in the sunshine.[73]

What is fascinating about Kurtz is not that he is hollow or that he lacks restraint, although both may be true. What is fascinat- ing is that *even though* he lacks restraint, he still has wits enough to control the outside. The horror of his enlightenment about the horror of the world is that it threatens to dispel even spectral illumination, creating a "lightless region." Now savagery appears less savage to Marlow than the thought that Kurtz could reflectively inscribe his terrible acts in ceremonies and rituals.

Throughout the narrative, Marlow has wanted to believe there is a darkness *only* at the core, an "inner truth" that we can avoid through the creation of public order—the space "between the butcher and the policeman." When that is gone, he claims, there is only "your own innate strength [and] . . . capacity for faithfulness."[74] This is equally the lesson of the cannibals: what is interesting in his dialogue with their leader is not the clamor from the wilderness but the possibility that there extends across humanity a kind of faithfulness that preserves certain modes of the social contract, even when it no longer seems to apply. What is most disturbing to Marlow now is his discovery that the meaning on the outside is not necessarily enlightenment. Kurtz's inner savagery is in the skulls, and these, like all inner meanings, Marlow is able to comprehend. It is the *outer* savagery that he cannot handle. How can it be that a rational, ceremonial order is created around it? This is what constitutes for the first time the "lightless region," the fog so thick that no faithfulness can penetrate and make a halo of meaning. And this is also the logic behind the repetition of Kurtz's final words, "The horror! The horror!" For what is horrible is no longer just the darkness at the center but also the darkness that surrounds it. Neither nature nor culture can be relied on to guarantee values.

It is not a coincidence that the language describing the scene in which Kurtz reveals this affirmative negation is decidedly Schopenhauerian. Marlow tells us first that it "was as though a veil had been rent." This is perhaps the veil of *maya*, the world of illusion in which we live. And he reinforces the image perhaps as strongly as he can without naming his source: "Did he live his life again in every detail of desire, temptation, and surrender during that supreme moment of complete knowledge?. . . He cried out twice, a cry that was no more than a breath: 'The horror! The horror!'"[75] The idea of living again, of desire and surrender at the moment of "complete knowledge," the truth expressed in that moment being a "breath"— these are all elements of the enlightenment of the Buddha as figured in both classic and modern representations. Also here is Schopenhauer's strange emptying of the meaning of that moment by transforming it into a complete negation of all life. Kurtz, like Schopenhauer, senses that life is suffering at its core, but rather than attempting to overcome suffering, he insists that there is only suffering, and so life, all life, must end. That double negation is the essence of the double horror.[76]

Kurtz, we might say, is Schopenhauer run amok. This is why, when he writes in his final manifesto, "Exterminate all the brutes!" (a line that may well apply to all of humanity), he does so in the context of a "moving appeal to every altruistic element."[77] That we are all brutes beneath the surface, that we all need extermination, is Schopenhauer's basic philosophy. Kurtz, in his mania, takes this wild suggestion for self-sacrifice and turns it into a program for murderous action. Kurtz perverts Schopenhauer: Conrad's character became completely engrossed in his desires, whereas the philosopher sought to end them.

It is left to Marlow to take on Schopenhauer's more literal role and develop a philosophy of pity and compassion in the face of his knowledge of the horror of the natural and human worlds. This happens in one final occurrence of the halo imagery in the novella, when Marlow goes to visit Kurtz's unnamed Intended. He describes her face as "surrounded by an ashy halo from which her dark eyes looked out at me."[78] Unlike the "misty halo" of the book's beginning, this one has been covered in the ash of Kurtz's manifesto. Ultimately, Kurtz's enlightenment continues to dispel all insight, and the encounter with the Intended produces not spectral illumination, only "a feeling of infinite pity."[79] The message that Marlow brings, that he speaks at the end, is not of the darkness but of the need to confront it with pity. Thus instead of telling the Intended what Kurtz's last words in fact were, Marlow says that he spoke her name.[80]

Marlow foreshadows this lie earlier in the text, saying that he would not fight for Kurtz, "but I went for him near enough to a lie." Lying is no mean feat for Marlow, as testified in his famous line: "You know I hate, detest, and can't bear a lie. . . . There is a taint of death, a flavour of mortality in lies—which is exactly what I hate and detest in the world—what I want to forget."[81] Thus, by his own logic, in lying out of pity, Marlow sacrifices himself for the Intended. The need to sacrifice ourselves out of pity for others is precisely what an ascetic priest is said to believe in. Not surprisingly, right after recounting his lie, the narrator compares him again to someone "in the pose of a meditating Buddha."[82]

The narrator had stated at the beginning of the story that Marlow's claims often came from what were in fact "inconclusive experiences."[83] By the end, however, the narrator *appears* to agree with his vision of the world: "the tranquil waterway leading to the uttermost ends of the earth flowed sombre under an overcast sky—*seemed* to lead into the heart of an immense darkness."[84] But this apparent agreement is little more than a mirage. The waterway in itself is "tranquil." It only "seemed" to lead to the darkness. This is an imposition onto an indifferent material reality from a mood—an ashy halo—cast by the story. Marlow's vision of the world is an idea, not a reality. Only because he believes in the inner depravity of the world does he believe that self-sacrificing pity is the necessary response.[85]

This interpretation is supported elsewhere in Conrad's writings. That we need not assume the darkness of the world is suggested by juxtaposing Marlow's ideas of world history with those of the narrator of the roughly contemporaneous story "Falk: A Reminiscence" (1901). For Marlow, the darkness he finds has always been there: "Going up that river was like travelling back to the earliest beginnings of the world, when vegetation rioted on the earth and the big trees were kings."[86] But a different interpretation is possible. The narrator of "Falk" offers this contrasting take on "the earliest beginnings": "I don't mean the worn-out earth of our possession, but a young Earth, a virginal planet undisturbed by the vision of a future teeming with monstrous forms of life and death, clamorous with the cruel battles of hunger and thought."[87] For this narrator there is an undisturbed time before human existence: the time of real stillness, real calm, not "worn-out" by our greed and possessiveness. Because Marlow interprets the world as he does—because he sees savage violence at the core of the world and that that violence is with us still—he develops a philosophy of life that works against a pacific vision. His story of darkness, his interpretation of life *as* darkness, only brings out the ashy halo of nihilism and death.

This choice of interpretation provides the intimate connection of the novella's depiction of colonialism and its interrogation of (European) Buddhism: the "enlightened" preaching about the sickness of the world leads either to the destruction of the world (Kurtz) or the denial of it (Marlow). Marlow senses the inner proximity when he states that lying is dying, since, in his sense of existence, by lying one denies the true darkness of this world and so turns toward death. This is what he does when he lies to the Intended. But he fails to see that he has lied *twice*. The second lie—the turn to pity—is only because he has told himself an original lie (consciously or not), that the world is dark. This is equally true of Kurtz's two lies, about the horror of nature and the horror of our attempts to confront it. In this double lie, both Marlow and Kurtz insist on the kernel and deny spectral illumination. In their Schopenhauerian Buddhism, they fail to make any positive transformation of the world. Kurtz breaks with Schopenhauer to an extent, asserting his will to destruction. Marlow, full of pity and the ascetic ideal, remains a follower to his last words. But one essential connection between them remains: Marlow, in effect, *does* say Kurtz's final words to the Intended—there is the horror at the core of the world, and the horror that we must sacrifice ourselves to deathlike lies in order to keep on living. Once embedded in lifeworlds, Schopenhauer's Buddhism conscribes us to perpetual darkness.

This is not the end of our story, however. Another Buddhism emerges briefly in the text, so briefly that most readers will miss it. Indeed, as with Kipling, it seems that Conrad himself may have missed it. Near the beginning, on his arrival in the Congo, Marlow describes a scene of abused laborers "dying slowly . . . in the greenish gloom." At the end of his description is a haunting passage:

> Near the . . . tree two more bundles of acute angles sat with their legs drawn up. One, with his chin propped on his knees, stared at nothing in an intolerable and appalling manner. His brother phantom rested its forehead as if overcome with a great weariness; and all about others were scattered in every pose of contorted collapse, as in some picture of a massacre or a pestilence. While I stood horror-struck one of these creatures rose to his hands and knees and went off on all-fours towards the river to drink. He lapped out of his hand, then sat up in the sunlight crossing his shins in front of him, and after a time let his woolly head fall on his breastbone.[88]

There are many remarkable things about this passage—including Conrad's impressionistic cubism of description and the reduction (by Marlow? by Conrad? by colonial power?) of these humans to shapes and "creatures." It is particularly significant that a parallel is being drawn between Marlow's Buddha pose and "every pose of contorted collapse" that these figures strike. Marlow has his perfected pose, meditating deeply on the nothingness of the universe, while these men are too weary for such concentration. They do not look into nothingness; they "stare at nothing." They do not take the proper posture but rather sit at acute and exhausted angles. But then one figure breaks the mournful stillness of this scene and goes for a drink of water.

Afterward he takes up the meditative posture for a time—
"crossing his shins in front of him"—until he does not have the
strength to hold the position and his head collapses.[89]

Conrad had recorded a vision like this in his Congo diary of
1890, writing, "Saw another dead body lying by the path in an
attitude of meditative repose."[90] Some thirty years later, he
would write of himself as such a decrepit figure in a letter about
how he had been in the "blackest depression." Conrad remarked
that if one were to enter his study, one would see him "sitting
absolutely motionless, like a crabbed, un-Asiatic-looking
Buddha—and not even twirling my thumbs—all day long."[91]
Meditative stillness appears in all of these instances as a false
repose. There is nothing that resembles a positive or profound
stillness. There is no sense in which meditative calm is anything
but the end of an intolerable and enforced exhaustion. What has
been drained from these men is not only their labor but also
their ability to be attentive to life at all. The stillness in this
scene appears very much like the stillness of Marlow the buddha at the end of the book: it is not merely the presence of death
in life but an actual death that somehow keeps on living. The
European Enlightenment wreaks havoc, and Buddhist enlightenment, at least in this form, offers only a false and unachievable respite.

Conrad himself may have had reasons to be as skeptical of
Buddhist institutional practice as he was of Schopenhauer's
philosophy. We can find the traces of this by turning again to
"Falk," which is set in Siam (Thailand), where Conrad had been
as a sailor. Early in the story, the narrator tells us: "There was a
shallow bar at the mouth of the river which ought to have been
kept down, but the authorities of the State were piously busy
gilding afresh the great Buddhist Pagoda just then, and I suppose had no money to spare for dredging operations."[92] This

scene nicely, if unintentionally, encapsulates the complexity of Buddhism in this time: however positive a moral force it may be, Buddhism is also an instrument of power. After all, the gold to gild the temples did not come from the merit of the monks alone! At the same time, Buddhism is seen in the equally ambiguous service of disrupting the (often perilous) path of commerce and development.

Whether or not Conrad was aware of it, the scene also hints at one of the darker aspects of the history of Thai Buddhism. Providing centralized manpower for defense and for agricultural production was essential to Buddhism's relations to the state. As Somboon Suksamran, a scholar of Buddhism and politics in Thailand, writes: "The building of the wat [Buddhist temple-monastery complexes] . . . served the practical purpose of drawing together additional labour."[93] Fleeing conscription and taxes, many people had self-exiled to the hills, outside the reach of the central government. Others found another way: "One method of avoiding becoming an outlaw was to register with the government as a kha phra (monastery slave)." These monastery slaves provided protection to the monasteries and worked their arable land. The monasteries thus also served the purpose of "collecting a population in permanent settlements within easy political reach" of centralized state power.[94] This appropriation of agricultural power, along with a tithing system, is likely the origin of the gold for the temples.

By the time Conrad was writing *Heart of Darkness* in the late 1890s, he had traveled to both the Congo and Southeast Asia. He had seen both the brutality of European imperialism and the complexity of political Buddhism. I do not believe it is a mere coincidence that both these geographies find their way into the novella. But the meaning of meditation is not circumscribed by these contexts alone, and this is certainly not the only way to

understand the relationship between monastic practice and politics. It is worth putting the moment of the laborer's meditation
in *Heart of Darkness* into the context of what other Buddhist
communities were doing with meditation at the time. As noted
above, meditation became standard in Buddhists' self-conception
in large part as a response to colonial missionaries' attempts to
eliminate Buddhist practice. Modern Buddhists (re)discovered
lay meditation as a means of both spreading and preserving
Buddhism in peoples' minds and practices, outside its perishable
embodiment in texts and monasteries.[95] The rise in meditation
around the turn of the nineteenth century and into the twentieth was part of a broader movement to return to "original Buddhism," constructing a new image of Buddhism as a worldview
imbued with science, peace, meditation, and rationality.

This was an explicitly self-conscious process in Buddhist
countries at the time. Already in 1870, Henry Alabaster, a British diplomat in Siam, published a book on how "modern Buddhists" were reforming their present beliefs to meet the new
world of both imperial domination and rational skepticism,
along with the nihilism that both produced. He wrote: "The
'Modern Buddhist,' in his endeavours to justify his religion in
the eyes of Europeans, has enunciated a form of Buddhism
which must be of considerable interest to many who, in these
days of criticism and doubt, have lost all the faith and hope that
was in them, and search in vain for some foundation on which
to rebuild their belief."[96] Many of these reforms were led by
King Rama IV, and they created dramatic shifts in the history
of Thai Buddhism.[97] This reformed Buddhism, in Alabaster's
view, offered a new foundation for life in a cynical world forced
together by the power of imperial rule.

One might at first read the anticolonial act of meditating in
the same way that Conrad reads "European Buddhism": as a

merely spiritual response to colonialism that has negligible or even negative political effects. Here another dimension of meditation's politics comes out if we consider the work on peasant resistance by the political scientist James C. Scott. Scott argues that we need to rethink and revalorize the small and even seemingly petty acts of resistance that make up peasant struggle, both because they are actually what happens and because they have surprising effects.[98] Showing the resistant logic of acts like desertion, pilfering, and loitering, Scott argues that by focusing on organized struggle as the only kind of politics, we have ignored the lived conditions in which tyranny renders such struggle nearly impossible. He suggests we understand the "infrapolitics" of minor actions as "vehicles by which, among other things, they [the powerless] insinuate a critique of power while hiding behind anonymity or behind innocuous understandings of their conduct."[99] Such actions are often considered to be "hollow *posing* that is rarely acted out in earnest."[100] He shows how, historically, these seemingly minor acts have had an equal or greater efficacy than the more visible forms of insurrection. The point is not to argue against large-scale insurrection or organized fights against colonial power but that we should not dismiss seemingly nonpolitical activities like meditation as lacking value. In the language of this book: we should look for not just the absolute enlightenment of revolution but also the spectral illuminations of resistance.

We can reread the scene from Conrad from this point of view. Here are humans who have been brutalized and reduced to abstraction by colonialism. They have literally been beaten into the landscape. But then one man stirs and uses what strength he can still muster to get a drink of water. His final act is to assume a meditative posture and seek some calm dignity beyond enforced labor. As his head falls back down, he never achieves enlightenment. But he does offer a brief moment of spectral illumination. Instead of some absolute transformation, as in a revolution, or some transcendent resistance, he illuminates a kind of weapon of the weak: a simple moment in which he says, *This is not the end of the story; I am more than the sum of colonial horror.* This Congolese man modernizes meditation as an act of resistance, countering Marlow's acquiescence to darkness. And so his meditative moment becomes an activity of meaning-making. His stillness shows that he still matters, over and against all the activity that has been forced on his body.

To be sure, this is a minor redemptive fragment in a vast space of ruins. Sometimes such fragments are the cracks in empire. Sometimes they are just acts that salvage a degree of humanity in the face of it. Sometimes they go on to produce profound meaning for others, as when meditative stillness is embodied in progressive political communities as a means of preparation for nonviolent struggle. And sometimes spectral illuminations can perpetuate ruins, as when they become a salve to cover over the pain of simply "letting it go," even when the "it" is life itself.

Thus while the question of enlightenment is the predominant problem in the engagement with both classic and Schopenhauerian Buddhism, it does not circumscribe the totality of what enlightenment (Buddhist and otherwise) can mean in this work. Nearly concurrent with the writing of *Heart of Darkness*, Buddhist communities across Southeast Asia were reinventing meditation as an anticolonial tool. Marlow's Buddhism springs from a desire to impose enlightenment on the world's inner depravity. This other Buddhism presumes no such permanent darkness, and rather insists on the capacity of human communities to interpret and reinterpret their worlds. In moments of grief and dismay, it offers a spectral illumination that may light the way beyond the absolutism of claims to enlightenment. There is certainly no guarantee that these new interpretations of enlightenment will yield a better world, as they too will have to wrestle with the relationship of insight and institution. But at the very least they keep us from becoming permanently conscribed to the darkness.

2

REINCARNATION

I f we are unable in modernity to achieve full enlightenment, then, classical Buddhism would say, we are bound to rein- carnate. Although I went to Dharamsala seeking enlight- enment, I did not give much thought to improving my future lives. Like most modernizers, I think that the current Dalai Lama being the fourteenth reincarnated leader of Tibet, who is also an incarnation of the Buddha of Compassion, is about as likely as Santa Claus existing. Even most Buddhists outside Tibet would agree, since as Bernard Faure notes, reincarnation as the specific return of individuals is a "purely Tibetan institu- tion." It transformed the general doctrine of transmigration based on one's personal karma to a capacity of highly advanced monks to choose where and how they would reincarnate due to questions of political control.[1] (Because "reincarnation" is often the more familiar term, I have used it as a synonym for "transmi- gration" throughout this book.) In a canonical image of transmi- gration, the flame of a candle is passed to a new wick. Although the first candle goes out, the flame continues in a new form. (Enlightenment is when no new wick is lit.) Reincarnation, as I imagine it, is more like the chute to John Malkovich's head in

Being John Malkovich: you slide through a tunnel into a chosen person.

Reincarnation may seem outside the pale of a modern global Buddhism. The concept is a frequent target of attacks by those sympathetic to Buddhism's philosophical message but wary of its lingering "superstitious beliefs."[2] These proponents of Buddhism want to see it purged of the baggage of the afterlife and refocused on its lessons for living a decent and happy existence in the here and now. But to accurately understand modern global Buddhism, we again do better to look to the literary accounts than to the modernizing proselytizers. The reincarnation that we find in literature is neither banished nor preserved as it was. Rather, it is reimagined as a way of understanding the social and historical forces that recur across generations and continue to condition the here and now of which secular Buddhism wants so badly to be mindful. Real attention to the present moment means understanding our lives as bound up with the multitudes of generations that have preceded us and those potentially infinite ones that will come to take our place. The possibility that something will *not* take our place, that at least some part of the horrors we reincarnate through our injustices might end, is one of Buddhism's great contributions to religious and philosophical history.

Anthropologist Gananath Obeyesekere has shown that the doctrine of reincarnation is nearly universal across the geographic spaces of human history.[3] Most cultures have historically had different versions of reincarnation (and often internal disagreements about how it works), but what emerged in India and Greece and among some Amerindian peoples is what he calls "ethicization," or "the processes whereby a morally right or wrong action becomes a religiously right or wrong action that in turn affects a person's destiny after death."[4] What is often considered the signature move of Buddhism in its historical context was to shift the question of the soul and its postmortal destiny. In Upanishadic thought, after "ethicization" occurred, broadly speaking, the *atman*, or essence of self, could break with the cycle of reincarnation and achieve *moksha*, or unity with the ultimate power of the universe. Buddhism posited the idea of *anatman*, or selflessness, and that liberation was not to join a greater entity but to go out of being altogether.[5] Buddhism, from our vantage today, may thus be said to have emphasized a key possibility in the history of thought: the aspiration to liberation as cessation rather than fulfillment.

It is a stark idea, and one whose power and novelty no doubt helped to create Buddhism's historical reception as a nihilistic school of thought.[6] But it is also, ironically perhaps, a supremely secular and rational ideal: the possibility that the dreaded things we have lived with—inequality, oppression, domination—can come to an end once and for all. In this sense the disappointments of liberal rationality and contemporary Buddhism are tightly related: ending things is not so easy as we had hoped. That enlightenment fails and reincarnation continues is one of the guiding threads of the history I am telling. My suggestion is that as we continue reincarnating negative elements from our past (whether through the failure of revolution at a macro level or repeating our mistakes at a personal one), we might learn something from Buddhist modernism's spectral illuminations about how, as Beckett might say, to keep failing better.

I will argue in this chapter that potentially liberatory visions for surviving failed conditions mark a primary concern of the novels of Yukio Mishima, Jamyang Norbu, and J. M. Coetzee. Their aim is not to end existence as such, but to ask how we can stop reincarnating a past that perpetually overdetermines our existence. As they shift from the total illumination of nirvana to the spectral illumination of history, these novels present the critique of *atman* as a critique of all essences that claim to pre-ordain the path of human existence. Reincarnation becomes one of the questions of the good life: how to live completely as a temporal being in touch with but not determined by their historical present.

The reinterpretation of reincarnation in modernity was not confined to Buddhists. Ralph Waldo Emerson, for example, argued that "The transmigration of souls is no fable. I would it were; but men and women are only half human."[7] Emerson would that it were a fable because then we would be autonomous and self-reliant from birth. But as the world is, we must make ourselves self-sufficient. For Emerson this means using our ability to overcome the "facts" of natural existence: "Those men who cannot answer by a superior wisdom these facts or questions of time, serve them. Facts encumber them, tyrannize over them . . . [In them] a literal obedience to facts has extinguished every spark of that light by which man is truly man."[8] Knowledge of the facts of the world enables one to break with the cycle of human folly. Or so, at least, it is hoped.

Emerson links the theory of reincarnation to the then-burgeoning field of evolutionary science. He suggests that the doctrine of transmigration indicated in the form of the fable what science was then proving: that our existence is made of the "vestiges of the natural history of creation," as Robert Chambers put it in 1844.[9] This kind of reinterpretation of reincarnation as evolution was also picked up by modernizing Buddhists. As David McMahan notes in an essay on Buddhism and secularism: "Attempting to explicitly assimilate Darwin's theory of evolution to the doctrine of rebirth . . . Taixu [a Chinese reformer of the early twentieth century] described evolution as 'an infinite number of souls who have evolved through endless reincarnations.'"[10]

We can find similar ideas in the works of T. W. Rhys Davids and Thomas Huxley, both of whom found reincarnation to be a certain kind of explanation of character and heredity.[11]

Reincarnation in this sense is not only about understanding the human place in the natural world but also about political institutions—in both positive and negative ways. Just as evolution was appropriated by eugenicists, so reincarnation can be used to justify someone's low social status as a determinate effect of past karma. Buddhism's history offers an uneven response here, and its position on caste and class offers more subjects for ongoing debate than clear ethical positions.[12] This is true for modern literature as well. In this chapter, for example, we will see that reincarnation accommodates Mishima's imperialism as much as Norbu's critique of empire. But the point that comes across in each of their reckonings with reincarnation is that we cannot so easily remove it as a concept from our view of the world. Or, more strongly put, that we can only do so at the expense of failing to understand what the world is actually like—overdetermined by a past whose impact we only barely register before the future arrives. Across these narratives, as I understand them, the question is not so much whether or not there is to be reincarnation, but, given the place of reincarnation in our world, what can be done with it?

REINCARNATION AS A SOCIAL EXPERIENCE

Mishima criticism in the Anglophone world is, perhaps not surprisingly to those familiar with him, dominated by his life story. Thumbing most library shelves, one finds few complete works of literary criticism but a seemingly endless stream of biographies.[13]

And even the criticism that exists cannot help but address the sensational story of Mishima's decision to commit ritual suicide after a failed attempted coup d'état in 1970. This overlap of life and criticism is especially apparent when dealing with the *Sea of Fertility* tetralogy (1965–1971), since one of the characters (Isao Iinuma of *Runaway Horses*, the second novel in the series) commits ritual suicide after he assassinates a high-powered figure. Other elements of Mishima's life may help to illuminate other aspects of the novel, perhaps even to explain the utility he found in the idea of reincarnation. Certainly a man so interested in the power of history, and himself so full of multiplicity—at once nationalist traditionalist and cosmopolitan modernist, a man with wife and kids and an ardent investment in gay subculture, a frail figure who later in life began to exercise relentlessly—would have understood the idea of many lives within one human as well as anybody. "The purest evil," the narrator of *Runaway Horses* maintains, can be found in "men who went against the pattern of life's diversity."[14] Reincarnation in *Sea of Fertility* is bound up with this idea of diversity, especially as it manifests in social life. By following a brief reference to the seventeenth-century Italian philosopher Giambattista Vico's theory of reincarnation that appears in the tetralogy, I will argue that Mishima's vision of reincarnation is concerned with diversity because it shares with Vico an essential claim: that reincarnation is not strictly personal, but takes place at the nexus of the individual and the social.

The Sea of Fertility is an epic narrative of Japan in the twentieth century, from just after victory in the 1904–05 war with Russia to the post-U.S. occupation condition. It includes four novels: *Spring Snow* (1969), *Runaway Horses* (1969), *The Temple of Dawn* (1970), and *The Decay of the Angel* (1971). The first novel, *Spring Snow*, tells of the youthful friendship between Honda

Shigekuni and Kiyoaki Matsugae. It centers on the story of Kiyoaki's downfall due to his ill-timed and ill-fated romance with Satoko Ayakura. Their affair ends after being discovered. To save face, she renounces the world and joins a convent. He tries repeatedly and unsuccessfully to see her there. Eventually he dies from a fever brought on by spring snow falling as he tries to gain entry one last time. Honda, perhaps envious of Kiyoaki for both his friend's passion and his own love of Satoko, fails to save his friend from this cruel fate. Over the next three novels, he lives out the rest of his life and becomes a very successful lawyer and judge. But his own path is constantly interrupted as he follows a unique birthmark of Kiyoaki's to find his reincarnations: the ardent nationalist Isao Iinuma, the young Thai princess Ying Chan, and the seemingly fraudulent and certainly petulant orphan Tōru Yasunaga. As Honda goes to absurd lengths to help these reincarnations, he seems mostly to be attempting to come to terms with this failure and envy—an envy that he does not even realize he feels till near the end of his own life.[15] Indeed, one of the versions of reincarnation that Mishima intimates is melancholia, in Freud's sense of a loss that always returns since it never finds a new object of desire: "[Honda] saw that what had been reborn in all likelihood was not Kiyoaki himself but merely his own sense of loss."[16]

In such lines we begin to glimpse the many meanings of the concept of reincarnation in the *Sea of Fertility*. Just as it is the "purest evil" to deny the pattern of diversity in humans, so it is an act against the text to insist on singular meanings. There is evidence that Honda's belief in reincarnation is based on objective evidence *and* on a misguided desire for something beyond mere existence, *and* that it's just a symbol for the various mundane reincarnations of history and emotions. It may also function, as Roy Starrs suggests, as a national allegory of Japan's declining fate across Kiyoaki's increasingly inept incarnations, or it may, as Susan Napier has it, express Honda's desire for a secret knowledge.[17]

Mishima's take on reincarnation in the tetralogy offers itself as an extensive metaphor for the multiplicity of meaning generated by any phenomenon that is a social concern. Leveraging the concept of reincarnation in this way, he writes of human beings as what we all know them to be—inheritors of a past they did not create and the bequeathers of a future they cannot control. Mishima offers a vision of the possibilities for an ethical life that are bound up with recognizing the multiplicity of the individual. Even those like Kiyoaki and Isao who attempt to find singular meanings for life (romance, the imperial state) are still bound to remain unfulfilled and their souls to be reborn. This is because rebirth is tied to the social in the form of the lover or the state. And as these beings and historical units persevere, so does the individual who sought completion through them.

Mishima thus probes not only the metaphysics of rebirth—what it is, whether or not it "actually" happens, how the "selfless" individual of Buddhism could even reincarnate—but also its ethics. Mishima's ethicization is not the same as we see in Obeyeskere's overview. It is not about how the individual's ability to live up to moral codes affects their destiny in the afterlife. It concerns, rather, the individual's relationship to the social, and how one who is connected to a social world can be said to live a good life in bad times. Honda expresses the pessimistic vision of this condition: "Honda's theory, unchanged since his youth, was that history could not be advanced by human volition, but that the intrinsic nature of human will was to become involved in history."[18] He resigns himself to the fatalism of the individual in the face of the social, in the face of historical power beyond the individual's force. What he does not recognize is the power of the social—of individuals bound together—to change history.

Starrs's interpretation of the role of reincarnation in the novel picks up on this relation between the social and the individual. But he, like Honda, concludes with an excessive dose of pessimism: the "cumulative effect of these various forms of decline is an overwhelming sense of life itself as a process of ineluctable decay—given time, everything ends badly."[19] But this assumes that the end of the novel is the end of the story. Why should it be the case that the successive changes we witness across the narrative come to an abrupt halt? Should we not imagine that in the future the tragicomic existence we all experience will reemerge in an upswing? Indeed, by handing his novel to the publisher on the same day he attempted his coup, Mishima linked the narrative to life, to the nation, to its declines and advances. Given time, in fact, nothing ends well, or badly, or indeed at all. Developing an ethics in such a chaotic and cryptic world is far from easy.

There is an occasional idea in Buddhist practice that not all historical eras offer the possibility of escaping reincarnation and achieving enlightenment. It is written in the *Jātakas* (the collected stories of the Buddha's previous lives), for example, that "four countless aeons . . . and one hundred thousand kalpas" passed between the enlightenment of Siddhartha Gautama and that of the previous Buddha, Dīpankara.[20] And there are Buddhist sects who believe that we live in the *mappō*, or the age of the decline of the Dharma, in which we must wait for its true return in a new enlightened figure.[21] These ideas map onto certain Buddhist cosmological systems that understand the world to be in a continual process of birth and disappearance, with humans always occupying a short cycle of time during the countless eons of the universe going in and out of being.[22] There can be no enlightenment except in specific times and places.

This understanding of the relation between the individual and the social within a context of vast historical changes is what the Buddhist tradition shares with Giambattista Vico. Vico comes up only briefly in the tetralogy when Honda is studying various global theories of reincarnation.[23] Honda's interest in Vico is primarily theological, focusing on the relation between a creator god and the created. But if my suspicion is correct—that Honda focuses on interpersonal relations at the expense of understanding his place in a broader social world—then this focus too is something of a red herring. It is, after all, not something that Vico is known for. In some sense it is the opposite. At the center of Vico's *New Science* (1725) is the claim that we need to move past a theology that studies the God-human relation to a "new science" that comprehends the relationship between universal laws and the specifically human characteristic of forming civic life: "No philosopher has yet contemplated God's providence under humankind's most characteristic property, which is its essentially social nature."[24]

One of the curious aspects of Vico's theory is what he calls the "*ricorso.*" Though generally translated "recurrence," the term also means a "review," especially in the legal sense of an appeal, and also a "recourse," as in a venue for action.[25] Vico's idea is sometimes understood to imply a mere repetition of history as it cycles endlessly through stages of birth, growth, and decline. But it is equally concerned to show the possibility of historical change that is not—as other moderns contend—a clean break with the past. Giuseppe Mazzotta puts it poetically: "Vico places modernity's coil within the ancient spirals of universal history."[26] He goes on to offer this complex definition: "The *ricorso* . . . is the simultaneous figuration of closure and openness of a circle that repeats itself with a difference, is always out of place and is eccentric to the other circles in the series. But the *ricorso* is for Vico also a mode of writing and reading, and, more importantly, it is itself a new way of thinking and seeing . . . It is history's second chance or appeal."[27] In other words, the *ricorso* is, like Mishima's concept of reincarnation, many things at once. It is a theory of historical continuity and change, of how to see the world's transitions, how to write in such a way as to capture this flux and flow, *and* a suggestion that by reviewing our history, we can appeal the result that has led us to where we are and, through our poetic recourse, invent a new future. And while there is a veritable chasm between aspects of Vico's theory and Buddhist ideas of reincarnation, there is also a certain parallel, attested to again in the *Jātakas*: that each life is an opportunity to repeat the past with an accumulated knowledge that allows for a different outcome.

Although Honda does not speak of these concerns in his brief thoughts on *The New Science*, he does pause to cite Vico's remarks on Japan, which not coincidentally appear in his chapter on the theme of "recurrence."[28] It is also curious that, in order to defend Isao after his first assassination plot is discovered, Honda quits his position as an appeals court judge. He then manages to get Isao a guilty verdict but with no penalty and hopes that there will not be an appeal against this ruling.[29] The fundamental irony of Honda's character is that he has the power to make social appeals in his position as judge, but he squanders it by focusing on a singular, personal reincarnation. He avoids seeing the connection between reincarnation and the social toward which his reading should be pointing him.

It is also here that we can see one potential attraction of Vico's theory for Mishima himself. In the conclusion of *The New Science*, shortly after the mention of Japan, Vico writes:

"The nations mean to dissolve themselves, and their remnants flee for safety to the wilderness, whence, like the phoenix, they rise again. That which did all this was mind, for men did it with intelligence; it was not fate, for they did it by choice; not chance, for the results of their always so acting are perpetually the same."[30] These lines condense Vico's general historical theory, which works to navigate between ideas of pure contingency and pure determinism.[31] This is what Honda, with his fatalist theory, fails to grasp: that he is bound up with history and although he alone cannot change it, he can work with others to transform its condition. Even as things recur, they return, as Mazzotta puts it, with a difference. Honda's tragedy is that he becomes so focused on a single interpersonal relationship that he never cares about the broader changes happening in the world around him, discarding his social and familial power in his relentless quest to save Kiyoaki. In so doing he loses the whole point of his quest: the appeal, the possibility that he could redeem his failure to save his friend by acting differently this time. To do this would require a vision of social power that he cannot grasp.

In the last volume, *Decay of the Angel*, Honda finally takes a logical step in his process of appeal: reinterviewing witnesses. In the novel's closing pages, he goes to visit Satoko at the monastery, something that he has not done since Kiyoaki's death. He has just received a likely fatal diagnosis at the end of several unpleasant years dealing with Kiyoaki's final (and perhaps false) reincarnation. He looks upon this trip as his "last pleasure . . . last effort . . . last good look . . . with an unoccupied heart."[32] What he finds instead is an utterly inexplicable response from Satoko: that she does not know him, nor Kiyoaki. She even asks him if he is sure that Kiyoaki ever existed, and Honda is forced to ask whether he himself exists at all.[33] His final thought is that "he had come . . . to a place that has no memories, nothing."[34] So the story ends, and, it would seem, his life as well.

Is it possible that Honda has managed to bring the cycle of reincarnation to an end, in a moment of what could be considered "sudden enlightenment"? Possibly, but it seems more likely that Honda simply has fallen out of history. We have some reason to think this will happen from earlier moments in the cycle, such as when the narrator states: "Since the dawn of history [Honda] had been alone in his study, and he would still be alone in it when history came to an end."[35] And here is Honda alone, with no memory (no history), and thus with nothing at all. But this nothingness is not the result of overcoming reincarnation. It is more likely a signal that he is now himself trapped in it. Honda realizes that he was never in fact part of human history, only of the very specific history that Satoko denies: their triangular relationship. Once Satoko denies it, Honda is no longer bound to anything that he can comprehend, and so he has "no memories, nothing."

By thinking that he could exit history, Honda feels that he has made it possible to exit reincarnation. He has not learned that reincarnation, in Mishima's Buddhist modernism, is a political question, a social concern, a matter of being able to face up to the struggles of one's times. By personalizing reincarnation, Honda fails to connect with its broad social implications.[36] He manages to go out of his triangle of existence, but he fails to change the social world that was meant to be affected by his transformation. This is the same mistake that modern critics often make today: we understand reincarnation only as a superstitious religious question, not as a fraught issue embedded in our everyday social and historical worlds. In so doing, we risk being as disconnected from history as Honda himself.

REINCARNATION AS
A POLITICAL NECESSITY

If Jamyang Norbu has a solution to this problem, it may in part come from his decision to use reincarnation for social purposes in spite of his personal rejection of the idea. Norbu is not the kind of Tibetan writer one hears about most often in the West. He is radical, secularist, militant, and steadfastly opposed to the image of Tibetans as "the baby seals of the human rights movement," as Tibetologist and propagandist Robert Thurman (father of Uma) once put it, (apparently unironically).[37] Norbu has repeatedly questioned the "mystical" image of Tibet, which, he argues, has "trapped" Tibetans in an odd place between image and reality. Speaking of a time someone died from rabies because they went to a shaman instead of taking the required shots, he writes: "in the exile Tibetan world in which I have lived most of my life, even a moderately progressive position runs up against not only the conservatism of the older genera-tion and the church, but often against the whimsies of western dharma-types, enamoured with everything 'traditional' or 'mystical' in Tibet."[38] That is, against annoying travelers like my young self. He is also an outspoken critic of the Dalai Lama and especially the Tibetan government-in-exile in Dharamsala. He sees the government as having taken too conciliatory a stance, failed to recognize China's true ambitions for absolute domi-nance, and thus vitiated any coordinated fight for Tibetan independence.[39]

Given that Norbu is not the stereotypical Tibetan writer, it is perhaps surprising that he wrote a novel called *The Mandala of Sherlock Holmes* (1999). In addition to the stereotypical man-dala in its title, the story turns Holmes into a reincarnation of a mystically powerful Tibetan monk. As the plot unfolds, we learn that he must defeat the similarly powerful Moriarty, who is also a reincarnation but turned to the dark side and aiding the Chinese. Holmes must use a secret mandala to connect to the mystical kingdom of Shambhala in order to save the life of the Thirteenth Dalai Lama (the prior incarnation of the current and better-known Fourteenth).

All these mystical elements would not seem to be Norbu's style. This may be why he attached an appendix (unfortunately cut from the U.S. edition) pleading that his novel be understood in "symbolic rather than literal terms . . . [so that it] not become another source of indulgence for those, all too many, cultists and crackpots drawn to Tibetan and Indian esoterica."[40] His academic critics have mostly obliged.[41] But not always. Kristin Guest, for example, writes, "Norbu aligns the two enemies [Holmes and Moriarty] with forces of light and darkness central to Buddhist spirituality. Unlike western frames of reference that privilege one term in the pair over the other, however, Norbu's Buddhist frame of reference connects the clash of light and dark with the worldliness one must transcend in the quest for spiritual enlightenment."[42] As we have seen, such general claims about "Buddhist frames of reference" rarely hold up—light is often, in fact, a metaphor for enlightenment.[43] And Norbu, I will argue, is less interested in transcending the fight than he is in winning it in Tibet's favor. Similarly, David Damrosch asserts that "Tibetan Buddhism is shown to be a moral resource for the whole world, transcending greed and the quest for domination, in an ideal blend of religion and science, ancient and modern, East and West together."[44] This is strange to hear from Damrosch, who also notes Norbu's skepticism toward Tibetan Buddhism—and especially the idea that it blends religion and science.[45] This is what happens so often when Buddhism is in the mix: the critical desire for it to have a transcendent morality overcomes the histories and texts before our very eyes. As we saw in the previous chapter, and as Norbu himself notes in his critical writings, Tibetan Buddhists, far from surpassing greed and the quest for domination, have themselves been very tightly bound up with material concerns.

In terms of the material politics of reincarnation, these controversies continue today in the debates over whether and where the current Dalai Lama will reincarnate. The Dalai Lama has said that he will not do so, while the Chinese government maintains that he will reincarnate in China.[46] Interestingly, Norbu himself has argued *for* reincarnation in this context: "I have long come to realize that this particular institution, and indeed the whole business of lamas reincarnating has served its spiritual and historical purpose and should 'cease one day' as His Holiness quite rightly told the BBC. It's just that at this pivotal moment in our history, for reasons of pure political strategy, we absolutely must safeguard this institution for one last future incarnation."[47] In other words, he thinks the Dalai Lama is strategically necessary as part of fighting back against Chinese colonization—or at least one more Dalai Lama is. These comments are very revealing about the use of religious symbolism in *The Mandala of Sherlock Holmes*. I would suggest that Norbu is attempting a very complex—and risky—strategy of reclaiming and asserting the political history of Tibetan Buddhism. He is willing to risk the misunderstanding of his text as some strange mysticism in order to show the sources of political power within that tradition.[48] To understand reincarnation and other elements of Buddhism in the novel is to understand them in this context. The novel works to, in effect, reincarnate the political potential of Tibet that, like the monk in Holmes's body, is buried in the unconscious of the nation. To do so, Norbu will reincarnate into his fiction certain characters from the literary past.

Conan Doyle gave Norbu the thread for the narrative that sets this recovery in motion. As is well known to all Holmes aficionados, after the detective's death at Reichenbach Falls, fans clamored for his return. When Conan Doyle finally gave in a few years later, he explained Holmes's absence by having him say that he had spent a few years in Tibet and even met the "head Lama" there.[49] Norbu then couples Conan Doyle with another figure reincarnated from British literature—Hurree Chunder Mookerjee from Kipling's *Kim*. The choice is not mere whimsy since, as discussed in chapter 1, the erasure of Tibet from our understanding of *Kim* is one of the blind spots of postcolonial literary criticism.[50] Mookerjee, playing the role of Watson and narrating the story, joins Holmes on his adventure into Tibet.

Mookerjee is directed to keep an eye on Holmes, who at the time he believes to be a Norwegian explorer named Sigerson. On their first encounter, he feigns being a mere travel guide and notes, "It is always an advantage for a babu to try and live up to a sahib's preconception of the semi-educated native."[51] Holmes quickly sees through the mask and refuses his services, but there is also a clue for the reader here. The game afoot in the novel is that Norbu will try to live up to certain preconceptions of what Tibet is, with the hope that readers (both foreign and domestic) can, like Holmes, see through the veneer to the other aims of the novel. And lest the readers drop their guard, Holmes acts as a constant metacommentator, enjoining the other characters not merely to see, but to "observe."[52]

The initial encounter between Holmes and Mookerjee underscores one of the key elements in this novel: the constant structure of inversion. This not only takes place at the general level of the plot, with the revelation of Holmes's and Moriarty's true identities, but also is carefully woven through the narrative. For example, when Holmes tells the story of his journey from Reichenbach Falls to Bombay (where he meets Mookerjee), he pauses to note that he passed through Florence, "the city of Dante—who when he remarked '*Nel mezzo del camin di nostra vita*,' could have been describing my own life at the moment."[53] Norbu has Holmes quote from the opening lines of *The Inferno:* "When I had journeyed half our life's way, / I found myself within a shadowed forest, / for I had lost the path that does not stray."[54] *The Inferno*, of course, is the story (written by an exile) of a passage through Hell that eventually arrives at restoration. And as critics have noted, Dante, like Norbu, uses the extraworldly for overt worldly purposes.[55] Further still, like Holmes, Dante's character requires a literary guide—Virgil. It is no coincidence then that Mookerjee ends his narrative with a paraphrase from Virgil—*sic itur a mons ad astra* (so we go from the mountains to the stars)—and that this phrase, *"ad astra"* is also how Dante ends each of his three volumes—with the stars.[56]

At a basic level, Norbu's use of Dante is obvious—it is a literary parallel for his own religious allegory of having to pass through Hell (exile) in order to recover one's own place in the world. And its scholasticism helps him shore up his relation to Conan Doyle, whose Holmes stories are scattered with such tidbits of canonical knowledge. But there is also something very specific about the line of Dante's that Norbu cites, a more literal translation of which would be, "In the middle of the path of our life." The "middle path" or "middle way" is the name of the signature philosophical gesture of the historical Buddha, who sought a "middle path" between the extremes of asceticism and hedonism. And it is also the official stance of the Tibetan government-in-exile, first announced by the Dalai Lama at the

European Parliament in 1988, where he officially declared that Tibet would seek a "middle path" between Chinese rule and full independence through a structure of "autonomy." In this proposal, Tibet would regulate its internal affairs and China its foreign affairs.[57]

Norbu has strenuously objected to this approach across his writings as he continues to call for full independence.[58] But he has also argued that it is an incredibly clever marketing campaign:

> Just the name "Middle Way" confers on this "approach" a deeply spiritual aura. It makes its proponents seem moderate, sensible and tolerant, and those opposing it extreme and radical. All this happens reflexively, as a matter of course, sometimes without even the need for any explanation, since Tibetans, and indeed, almost all those who have been raised Buddhist, are conditioned to accept the Middle Way as infallible and perfect. Naming the policy of surrendering Tibetan sovereignty to Communist China the "Middle Way" was a stroke of genius. It was also a deeply dishonest, perhaps even a sacrilegious act.[59]

Norbu is applying this strategy of using Buddhist ideas to his own ends. Like Mookerjee, he appears in the expected guise—a mystical Buddhist—but his aim is to invert the meaning of this mysticism. The Dalai Lama in Europe "lost" the Middle Way, just as Dante did in Florence. Norbu is trying to restore the Middle Way to its proper place as a method of philosophical discrimination for discerning the inconvenient truths about the world, not a theory of capitulation and diplomatic strategy.

Indeed, throughout his writings he is concerned that certain formations of Tibetan Buddhism mask its critical side. In *Mandala*, Holmes cites the concept of "dependent origination" (discussed in chapter 1) as a "chain of reasoning."[60] In his essay

"Trapped by Buddha," Norbu notes that in the past such "popular Tibetan saints as Drukpa Kunleg, Agu (Uncle) Tompa and Milarepa essentially taught people to disregard appearances, ritual, superstition and even conventional thinking and to seek spiritual (and sometimes worldly) truths through good sense, direct experience and their own efforts."[61] He also notes, of relevance for reading the novel, that he is "no absolute advocate of Victorian-style rationality and progress."[62] His point, then, is not that all tradition must be discarded in the name of rationality, but rather that we need to understand tradition as itself plural and evolving, and that "to be Tibetan" can mean to use logical discrimination as much as mystical power, just as the reverse can be said of "being Victorian."[63]

As Guest rightly notes, the cosmopolitan representation of "old Lhasa" is therefore pronounced in Norbu's narrative.[64] And this is not just Norbu's wish for there to have been a more complex past; it is an accurate description. Janet Gyatso has even noted evidence of this cosmopolitanism going as far back as medical texts from the seventh century CE. "The Tibetan medical histories list, page after page, the titles of scores of works on Greco-Arabic, Indian, and Chinese medicine that were brought to Tibet at this time."[65] The cosmopolitan impulse was furthered by the powerful Fifth Dalai Lama, who instigated something of a modernization period in the seventeenth century. Tibet did mostly close to the outside world until the early twentieth century, though it always maintained contact with regional powers and traders.[66] This reality of interconnected histories is one of the key functions of reincarnation in the novel: not just selves but also cultural histories are reborn in a manner of endless mixing. Dante is part of Norbu's birthright, as Milarepa is of mine. Reincarnation, then, is inverted from superstition and is revealed to have important political ramifications, even possessing a rational kernel as a symbol of humanity's layered historical formation and internal multiplicity.

Perhaps the major inversion of the novel is where Norbu engages the most prevalent narrative of reincarnation within the exile community—the use of the *Kalachakra Tantra* (The Wheel of Time Tantra). Like Dante, the tantra speaks of the downfall and exile of Buddhism for many centuries until (apparently in 2425 CE) the armies of Shambhala will sweep out of their mystical abode and establish a global Buddhist order of peace and tranquility. The mandala of Sherlock Holmes, it turns out, is a representation of the *Kalachakra Tantra* and, along with a riddle penned on the back of the mandala by the First Dalai Lama, is the key to unlocking the gate to Shambhala. At this gate Holmes and Moriarty's epic battle will take place.

The *Kalachakra Tantra* has assumed a new importance since 1959, as it has become a fundamental narrative by which certain Tibetans and Tibetophiles justify the logic of history. According to Robert Thurman, Tibetans view history on two levels— ordinary and extraordinary.[67] On the ordinary level, Thurman suggests, Siddhartha was simply a rich prince who joined some ascetics, but on an extraordinary level he was someone who had been planning his reincarnation for countless eons. The destruction of Tibet also has an ordinary history—terror, loss, exile— and an extraordinary one. Thurman says that the "most compelling . . . if somewhat dramatic" version of the extraordinary-level explanation is the following: "Vajrapani [the Lord of Power] emanated himself as Mao Tse-Tung and took upon himself the heinous sin of destroying the Buddha Dharma's institutions, along with many beings."[68] One of the reasons Thurman says Vajrapani would do this is "to scatter the Indo-Tibetan Buddhist teachers and disseminate their teachings through the planet among all the people, whether religious or secular, at this apocalyptic time when humanity must make a quantum leap from violence to peacefulness in order to preserve all life on earth."[69] Thurman thus inverts the narrative of destruction, making it into a hopeful moment for the redemption of all humanity. This is the kind of inversion (or perversion) of Buddhism that Norbu is reacting against.

Thurman further claims that "This all happens within the context of the advent of Shambhala upon the entire planet, according to the prophecy originating with the *Kalachakra Tantra*."[70] According to that prophecy, whatever external manifestations happen in the world, the "extraordinary" truth is that we are simply progressing toward the moment when Shambhala will save the planet from its path of destruction. In this Tibetan version of Dante, the several-hundred-year hell of exile is part of this process. Moreover, exile is necessary in order to build the armies of Shambhala, since all who see the mandala of the tantra, as well as all who receive the initiation, are beginning their path toward reincarnation as part of these armies.[71] It is not just Thurman who is pushing this narrative. As Donald Lopez notes, the Dalai Lama himself has given the Kalachakra initiation dozens of times, to audiences exceeding 250,000 people. Lopez concludes his book, *Prisoners of Shangri-La*, by quipping wryly that the Dalai Lama may have found the best way to populate Shambhala for this future fight: "It is the Dalai Lama's prayer, he says, that he will someday give the Kalachakra initiation in Beijing."[72] In the continuation of Thurman's assertion, even those who dispelled the Dharma from Tibet will eventually fight for it.

Mookerjee, in his role as Tibetan ethnologist, faithfully records the Kalachakra story in the pages of the novel.[73] Norbu's characters do not, however, have much time to go around showing the mandala to others, nor do they give any initiations. Rather, they realize that the power of the mandala is not mystical but real; that history does not move by the extraordinary forces of ordered destiny, but by the ordinary struggles of extraordinary people against frailty and tragedy. Bringing the tantra and its mandala into his novel, Norbu attempts to appropriate the mythic narrative. He *uses* the mysticism in order to show that Tibetans must fight for independence against the Chinese imperialists (Moriarty), not wait for some vague compromise (the Middle Way), which is no more likely to be realized than the prophecy of Shambhala. In this context, as Gauri Viswanathan notes, it is significant that the passage to Shambhala is found in an ancient ice cave.[74] The glacial time of the Teshoo Lama in *Kim* or the Dalai Lama in real life in their long games to overcome empire is unjustifiable in Norbu's vision. We need to go into the cave right now—to leverage all the powers stored in the deep time of history to create a profound transformation in the present.

Thus, while magical powers from Shambhala are used in *The Mandala of Sherlock Holmes*, Norbu wants to be sure we do not misunderstand his intentions. This is the purpose of the appendix. After his "Editor's Note," Norbu gives the reader some excerpts from C. G. Jung's *Flying Saucers: A Modern Myth of Things Seen in the Sky* (1958), which, he notes, appears in volume 10 of Jung's collected writings (more on this volume below). Not only does Jung there relate UFOs to mandalas, but he also offers some germane words about how to understand human interest in seemingly unbelievable ideas. He writes: "It depends on us whether we help coming events to birth by understanding them, and reinforce their healing effect, or whether we repress them with our prejudices, narrow-mindedness and ignorance, thus turning their effect into its opposite, into poison and destruction."[75] In other words, the point with UFOs, as with mandalas and prophecies, is not merely to decry their absurdity. Rather, it is to see what they are expressing that might contain a "healing effect." And what Jung sees in UFOs is the same basic point he finds in the mandala symbolism: "the 'protective' or apotropaic circle . . . which organises and embraces the psychic totality."[76] Jung continues: "In so far as the mandala encompasses, protects and defends the psychic totality against outside influences and seeks to unite the inner opposites, it is, at the same time, a distinct *individuation symbol* [Jung's italics]."[77] To understand why Tibetans turn so strongly to mysticism, Norbu seems to be saying through Jung, we have to understand what the mysticism actually expresses. And what it calls for is not waiting in vain for the realization of a prophecy but uniting around a symbol that can restore the nation. The mandala of Sherlock Holmes is just such a symbol—securing the individuation of the Tibetan people against a foreign attack.

And yet, Norbu is too smart a writer to simply let Jung explain the whole logic of his novel. It is not a coincidence, I think, that Norbu cites volume 10 of Jung's collected works, rather than the more readily accessible separate volume on flying saucers. For in volume 10 we also find Jung's infamous essay, "The State of Psychotherapy Today." It is infamous because of a few pages Jung dedicates to understanding the role of Jewishness for the dominant figures in psychotherapy then: Freud and Adler. He makes some not too flattering remarks, such as, "The Jews have this peculiarity in common with women; being physically weaker, they have to aim at the chinks in the armour of their adversary, and thanks to this technique which has been forced on them through the centuries, the Jews themselves are best protected where others are most vulnerable." He continues: "Because . . . of their civilization, more than twice as ancient as ours, they are vastly more conscious than we of human weaknesses, of the shadow-side of things, and hence in this respect much less vulnerable than we." Jung goes on to compare the Jewish consciousness to the Chinese, and then to note that the ' "Aryan' " consciousness, because it is so young, is more volatile and dangerous.[78]

I have only circumstantial proof, but I believe that Norbu may have chosen to cite Jung's collected works precisely because of these words. My main evidence is that this explains what is otherwise a seemingly random moment in the novel: when Mookerjee and Holmes are fleeing Moriarty's men and on their way to Tibet, they believe they are being ambushed by a "ferret-faced" man who seems to be among the henchmen. But he turns out to be Jacob Asterman, a nomadic Jewish trader who is acting as the emissary of the Dalai Lama, and whose excellent shot saves Holmes's life.[79] Not only does Norbu thus refute the myth of the weak, feminized Jew (something also applied to Tibetans—the "baby seals of the human rights movement"), he also establishes a connection between the destiny of the Jews in exile and the Tibetans. Norbu, sympathetic to the Palestinian cause, if critical of some of its tactics, is not suggesting Israel as a kind of beacon of hope for Tibetans.[80] He is performing another inversion, now of Jung: the true strength of an individual is not formed by closing off from the outside and claiming to embody the singular essence of a culture but by making global connections with the exiled and oppressed.

Unlike Jung, with his sweeping claims about different cultures, Norbu is what I would call a "radical pluralist"—someone who bases their radical politics not on absolute cultural difference but on a demand to respect the plurality of all.[81] Thus, the mandala in Norbu's hands becomes a symbol of a radically plural whole—a historically emerged and real culture, Tibet—that has of course become what it is *through* interactions with others. This is the logic of the novel's insistence on the cosmopolitanism of all spaces, even "closed" Lhasa. It is also why Norbu, as Guest brilliantly observes, makes a connection between his novel and the protests in Tiananmen Square by inscribing the date of the novel's composition as the same day as the height of the protests.[82] And it is perhaps the main logic of reincarnation in the novel: that we are all literally part of one another, even as we individuate.

Tibet is not to be fought for because it is some magical repository, but rather because it is a meaningful historical formation that has benefited from years of interaction. Jung's purity, which maps onto certain mystical defenses of Tibet, is in fact the problem. The mandala of Sherlock Holmes, by contrast, is a symbol of nonexclusive, radically plural wholeness. In his preface, Norbu writes, "even such a strange fragment of history as this . . . may contribute to nailing at least a few lies of the tyrants."[83] In a broken world, he does not attempt to re-create some mythic whole that can put it all back together, such as the narrative of the Kalachakra. Rather, he seeks to learn from the damage how to build a new kind of whole, one that respects the fragmentary nature of all our souls—how we are all patchworks of each other, bound together on a wheel of time. Liberation is not to exit the cycle of reincarnation. It is to reincarnate the elements of the past that can create the conditions for political liberation.

LEARNING NOT TO RETURN

Elizabeth Costello (2003) consists of eight "lessons" in which the titular character lectures, loves, fights, and (probably) dies on a quixotic journey in search of an embodied ethics. The roots of these fictions are in talks that J. M. Coetzee himself gave over a period of several years in which, rather than giving a standard lecture, he would read a story about Costello—often in similar circumstances to where he found himself—speaking on topics including human-animal relations, the humanities, and evil. The "lessons" would encase the lectures within a story about their context: the dinner after, the amorous encounters, the troubled familial relations. While many critics question Coetzee's seeming unwillingness to take a position, others (myself included) praise him for understanding that positions are relational, and that ideas are only interesting, powerful, or meaningful in the worlds they come to, fail to, or only partly manage to inhabit.[84]

Some, like James Wood, have taken the key idea that Coetzee wants to see his characters embody as the realization that they will die. The "key" to seeing this heart of the novel is what Wood claims is a reference to Tolstoy's *The Death of Ivan Ilyich*. Costello, speaking of the lives (and deaths) of animals in slaughterhouses, argues that her opposition to our treatment of animals is based more on sensation than ratiocination. She states, "The knowledge we have [of death] is not abstract—'All human beings are mortal, I am a human being, therefore I am mortal'—but embodied."[85] Wood suggests that this recalls the "celebrated" syllogism found in Tolstoy's novella: "Caius is a man, men are mortal, therefore Caius is mortal," and, more specifically, Ilyich's recognition that this applies not just to Caius but to him.[86] Costello's salvation, for Wood, is bound up with this recognition.

What is strange about Wood's assertion is that it rests on tracing the origin of Costello's use of the syllogism and then asserting that it is to be found in Tolstoy. This is particularly curious since in Tolstoy's work the reference is traced back to "Kiesewetter's logic," a 1791 logic textbook.[87] Indeed, the syllogism is hardly a reference to Tolstoy so much as a literal textbook example of the syllogism. The more common form involves not Caius but Socrates, and any Google search will quickly demonstrate that it is a form so general as to be practically untraceable. One early version appears in Sextus Empiricus where, interestingly, the syllogism is about Socrates's animality, not mortality, and the whole point is to suggest that syllogisms are incoherent because of their circular reasoning. After all, one must use the particular example of any individual's mortality in order to secure the supposedly universal claim—humans are mortal—which is meant to secure the truth of mortality of the specified individual in the first place.[88]

In short, if Wood wanted to trace an idea to anchor the meaning of Coetzee's fiction, then he could hardly have picked a less reliable base. Nevertheless, the untraceability of this particular quote and the doubt around its logical coherence seem to me to point to a rather intriguing possibility for Coetzee's novel: that it is about not the confrontation with death so much as the confrontation with reincarnation, which is to say, the unknowability of where we come from and where we are going, and thus our unclear indebtedness to the past, to the future, and to the myriad forms of life with whom we share this world. *Elizabeth Costello* is about the difficulty of understanding these unfolding and unsure relations, and, I will suggest, it develops an ethics around these concerns.

There is more than ample evidence of this thematic throughout the novel, even though very few critics of this much-written-about book, so far as I can tell, have made reference to it.[89] To begin with, there is the strange beginning of the novel: "There is first of all the problem of the opening, namely, how to get us from where we are, which, as yet, is nowhere, to the far bank. . . . Let us assume that, however it may have been done, it is done. . . . We have left behind the territory in which we were."[90] Now we are in the story: "Elizabeth Costello is a writer, born in 1928 . . ." The "problem of the opening," which threatens to stop the story even before it begins, is dealt with somewhat abruptly. There appears to be a difficult problem of how to begin, but then we just do it. Stephen Mulhall suggests that this is the general experience of reading—we are in one place, our lives, and then suddenly we are just reading a story and somewhere else.[91] Eduardo Viveiros de Castro, in a rather offhand but interesting remark, suggests that this is the movement of Coetzee himself "just before he transforms himself into Elizabeth Costello."[92] These are both plausible and also both speak to the broader possibility of what may be happening here: (re)incarnation. Given the book's ending, in which Costello, apparently deceased, waits before a gate in a certain "nowhere" before perhaps going on to a new territory, it seems perfectly reasonable to assume that in the beginning we were in a space after death and before life. Hence, the first sentence of the novel is about Costello's birth, in 1928.

Then there is the curious fact that Costello's most famous book, *The House on Eccles Street*, is a retelling of James Joyce's *Ulysses* from the perspective of Molly Bloom. Costello thus gains recognition as a writer through her ability to reincarnate another writer's work. And not just any writer or any work, but *Ulysses*, itself a rewriting of *The Odyssey*, and, moreover, a book in which "metempsychosis" plays a recurring role. Indeed, it is the very first thing that Leopold and Molly Bloom discuss.[93] And the origins of Joyce's interest in the concept have been traced not only to its obvious Greek sources and Joyce's abiding interest in Vico but also to his readings in Gaelic myths and "esoteric Buddhism."[94] When, in the book's closing pages, Costello is trying to get the judges before the gate to appreciate what she understands by identity and belief, she says, "*I am an other.* Pardon me for resorting to words that are not my own, but I cannot improve on them." She does not give the citation perhaps because there are too many. She is directly quoting a famous line of Arthur Rimbaud, but by not naming it as such she suggests that there are others who have said similar things of the self. For example, Joyce's Stephen: "I am other I now," and his Leopold: "Or am I now I?"[95] Characters and words reincarnate throughout the book, and in so doing, throw identity into question. The point, I will be arguing, is that this leaves us not in a "postmodern flux" but in a very specific ethical situation with regard to others who we may or may not be or have been or be part of in the future.

Further evidence for these claims is provided by a litany of moments throughout the narrative, including:

- A character named Moebius (as in the recurring figure, also central to Joyce's circular text, *Finnegans Wake*)
- Costello's desire that her memory fade and cease to be a burden for future generations[96]
- Her son John's saying that she "can think her way into other people, into other existences"[97]
- John's suggestion that his mother "is not in the Greco-Roman mould. Tibet or India more like it: a god incarnated in a child, wheeled from village to village to be applauded"[98]
- Costello's rejection of the ethical doctrine of karma, as she affirms that there is no punishment for our evil deeds, which just live on[99]
- Her sister's critique of "a secular vision of salvation. Rebirth without the intervention of Christ"[100]
- Costello's concern with Paul West's (real) novel about the execution of failed Hitler assassins: "what has Paul West

done . . . but bring to life, bring back to life, the history of what happened in that cellar in Berlin?"[101]

- Her final realization of what she believes: "Yes, that she can believe in: the dissolution, the return to the elements; and the converse moment she can believe in too, when the first quiver of returning life runs through the body and the limbs contract, the hands flex. She can believe in that, if she concentrates closely enough, word by word"[102]

- That the novel begins with the hope to reach "the far bank" and ends with Costello's attempt to imagine "the far side," as if she is in the space where she began, trying to figure out how to get to the other side—the problem that was skipped over—as if the novel, like *Finnegans Wake*, is about to begin again, to be reincarnated in the next reading (this may also explain the simplistic reversal of dog and god that pops into her head in the book's closing lines—suggesting recurrence, reversal, and rebirth, perhaps as an animal)[103]

- And finally, the implicit suggestion in the postscript that she herself is a reincarnation of another "Elizabeth C." from 1603[104]

There is also the extratextual evidence from Coetzee's critical writings, such as:

- His remark in reference to the novels of Italo Svevo: "From Socrates to Freud, Western ethical philosophy has subscribed to the Delphic *Know yourself*. But what good does it do to know yourself if, taking your lead from Schopenhauer, you believe that character is founded on a substrarum of will, and doubt that the will wants to change?"[105]

- And on his own being and writing: "Let me add, *entirely* parenthetically, that I, as a person, as a personality, am overwhelmed, that my thinking is thrown into confusion and helplessness, by the fact of suffering in the world, and not only human suffering. These fictional constructions of mine are paltry, ludicrous defenses against that being overwhelmed, and, to me, transparently so."[106]

- And his essay on Nadine Gordimer, published in 2003, the same year as *Elizabeth Costello*, in which he remarks on her story "Karma": "The soul has knocked at the gate but been barred from entry: for its own sake, the women who guard the gate have decided not to admit it into the world as the world presently is." And again, noting about Gordimer what Costello's son has noted about her powers of entering other characters: her use of reincarnation is "metafictional: participating in one life after another, reflects the soul, is much like being a novelist inhabiting one character after another."[107]

This compilation of moments and remarks can tell us quite a bit about the themes of reincarnation in *Elizabeth Costello*. They suggest that Coetzee's concern, like Norbu's and Mishima's, is with the reincarnation of languages and narratives as much as persons, and, moreover, that they are linked in the figure of the human and in the study of the humanities. As Costello puts it, "If the humanities want to survive, surely it is those energies and that craving for guidance that they must respond to: a craving that is, in the end, a quest for salvation."[108] And if it is true what Coetzee says of himself, that his fictions are but thinly veiled meditations to forestall the problem of suffering, then the quest for salvation in his works, as in Buddhism, is (at least in part) about the ability to overcome suffering through an engagement with the histories, languages, and other beings who constitute every individual.

Of course, Elizabeth Costello does not study Buddhism, meditate, or participate in any of the lay practices or rituals.

And besides scattered references—to India/Tibet, to Schopenhauer, to suffering in general—there is little to tie Coetzee's
ideas to Buddhist thought any more than to, say, the resurrec-
tion of Christ or the Greek histories of metempsychosis. It is
not my particular concern to argue that Coetzee is secretly
engaging Buddhism, so much as that he shares its concern with
the question of reincarnation, and that further, thinking about
Elizabeth Costello with these Buddhist themes in mind may tie
together the otherwise disparate strands of the text. For across
these eight "lessons" is a fundamental suggestion that the act of
reincarnating stories—sifting through other lives, learning to
see things differently, whether from the perspective of another
gender, race, or species—is part of learning what it means to be
human. This is not, for Coetzee, so far as I can tell, a matter of
possible "success," that is, a guarantee or philosophical assur-
ance about life and its purpose. It is rather a kind of Pascalian
wager. If Pascal wagered that it would be better after this life
had ended to have believed in God, Coetzee might then be suggesting that we are better off believing in our interconnectedness and infinite replication. The question of salvation, in such
a scheme, is not about my personal death or my philosophic
relation to it, but about the capacity of a dependently originated
and nonsubstantial emergent being—a human—to end some
small bit of suffering.

Steven Collins has insisted that this vision is always singular
in Buddhism—that, unlike in Christianity, there is no possible
vision of an end of history, no collective finale. Similarly, in
Buddhism there is no "Let there be light" origin. The universe
simply is, and it will always continue to be. Suffering can be
diminished but not ended. "Buddhist dramas of humankind as
a whole are never-ending: only privatized, individual time can
end, not public."[109] Nevertheless, this does not mean (or at least

does not necessarily mean) that Buddhism becomes a purely individual practice, as Collins explores over hundreds of pages about the Buddhist political community. Furthermore, reincarnation creates an unclear network among individuals. Collins writes:

> The world of samsara represents . . . a four-dimensional throng of "individualities": some of these happen to be connected with "him" in a linear temporal series, and so represent past and future "selves"; some are not thus connected, and so remain forever "others." The crucial point is this:. . . *any given individual cannot know which of these are which.* Accordingly, the rationale for action which acceptance of Buddhism furnishes provides neither for simple self-interest nor for self-denying altruism. The attitude to all "individualities," whether past and future "selves," past, future, or contemporary "others," is the same—loving-kindness, compassion, sympathetic joy, and equanimity.[110]

Buddhist ethical theory here is not about absolute interdependence, or the "connectedness of all things," as is sometimes asserted.[111] Nor is it about some authenticity that I achieve through comprehending my mortality, as in Tolstoy. Rather, it is about an ethics derived from the fact that *I do not know* how I am connected to the universe and the people, plants, animals, and bacteria I share it with, and thus—here is the Pascalian wager—it is best that I act kindly and calmly toward it.[112]

Like all ideas that get embedded in our lives, this one has its limits. Costello, for example, certainly does not fulfill the ideal of equanimity. She is, for lack of a better term, a nervous wreck. In one of the most heartfelt scenes in the novel (after the awkwardness of her animal ethics lectures with their comparisons of factory farms to Nazi concentration camps), she tells her son that although she sees around her "human kindness" and keeps telling herself to "calm down," she feels as if she lives in a world of absolute butchery, and she simply can't "come to terms with it." All that her academic son can offer her by way of emotional balm is a lukewarm hug and the cringeworthy: "There, there. It will soon be over."[113] But of course, the novel is only halfway through, and in any case, if my suspicion is correct, it will not soon be over; indeed, it will never end. Unless, that is, Costello can figure out a way, a means, a path, to taking this emergent self out of existence.

Perhaps part of Costello's problem is that she does not have access to the very way of thinking she inhabits; in other words, that she does not study Buddhism. I take this to be the rather large wink we are given in the book's first lesson, cited above, when her son John (the author's own name) tells us that although his mother may be a "mouthpiece for the divine," she "is not in the Greco-Roman mould. Tibet or India more like it: a god incarnated in a child, wheeled from village to village to be applauded."[114] There is a bit of harsh criticism here, a sense of bitterness at his mother's need for veneration. But there is also a suggestion that Costello is trapped not just in a cycle of reincarnation but in a cycle of history that does not offer her a way of being that speaks to her understanding of things. The secular life, without belief, without anchor, has done little for her, leaving her with the empty feeling of that moment in the car. Perhaps this is why she is so taken with Franz Kafka's character Red Peter, an ape forced to speak to an academic conference. He tells his audience that he wanted not "freedom," but only "a way out."[115]

The way out that secular, disenchanted life should offer Costello—death—seems only to be a continuance and confirmation of her difficulties. Secular humanism has not prepared her for the afterlife. To her judges there, she enters a heartfelt plea that she lacks an essence, which is met with mockery and derision by those who weigh the balance of her life: "First they titter like children, then abandon all dignity and howl with laughter."[116] She never manages to articulate aloud the realization she has come to: that what she believes in, the only thing she can say she believes in, "word by word," is the process of rebirth. Rather, she only thinks this, and her train of thought is interrupted by the bailiff.

In the unbearable afterlife in which she finds herself, forced to recount her beliefs, it is as if the same idiots who made life on earth so insufferable have taken over. They are forcing her to speak Greek, even though she does not believe in *psyche*, the soul. She is thrown into a new social world as unjust, incomprehensible, and vaguely unfamiliar as the one she thought she had left behind. We have no reason to believe that the afterlife was *always* this way. We have no reason to presume that these judges are not actually just themselves stuck in purgatory, and, as wayward humans do, have installed themselves in a position of power in a world without a supreme arbiter of justice. Or perhaps these really are her judges, and she really must just confess what she believes: that she believes in rebirth, renewal, the fact that she must return. If the final chapter, as the writer (Costello? Coetzee?) admits, is almost too "Kafkaesque," perhaps it is less because the novelist feels ashamed to reincarnate another's vision than because it remains unbearable to her, or him, that Kafka was right: we live in an unjust world in which we are not always quite sure if we are the victims, the perpetrators, or merely idiots.[117]

Should we then dedicate our lives to ending the cycle of reincarnation, the infinite burden of these unbearable pasts on the living? Costello seems to think this at one point: "There must be some limit to the burden we impose on our children and grand-children. They will have a world of their own, of which we should be less and less part."[118] Or should we strive, like the frogs that she finally comes to believe in, to be reborn after the flood, to return to the earth from our little tombs, again and again, if only to be drowned, again and again? We do not know. Or at least we do not have the vision to see when each task is called for—what we are to bring to an end and what we are to continue and bequeath.

Whatever ethics we might have in such a space must come from this very doubt about who we are, where we are going, and what we will affect. Such an ethics does not provide salvation in the classical sense—it does not free our souls to an afterlife, nor to our dissolution. It leaves us, as it leaves Elizabeth Costello, unsure, in limbo, confused as to whether or not we are real or merely characters in a story, playing out a role handed down to us by the bounded and interpenetrating burdens of our history. But perhaps it does provide salvation in another sense: a salvation from knowingness, from the impudence of judges who would bind souls to a single belief, idea, or identity and deny the richness of the many lives that they inhabit and which, in turn, inhabit them. If reincarnation is to be taken seriously, it may be on this level: the recognition that we cannot but believe in it, that we cannot but constantly reincarnate the words and the stories and the histories that precede us, and that we make our history, as Marx put it, not on conditions of our own choosing.[119] The eight lessons of *Elizabeth Costello* add up to this grudging recognition that we are trapped in a nightmare called history in which our ideals must confront their rocky situated-ness in sometimes hellish social worlds. If we do not take that fact seriously, we will continue on this path forever. Perhaps we will be stuck here even if we *do* take it seriously, but it's hard to see what hope we might have otherwise. This is another lesson of our unknown relation to others: that we do not know is no reason not to act.

At the novel's close, Costello engages in a conversation with the recorder of the courts. She asks him if he sees others like her, trapped as she is. The final lines of these lessons are: "The man behind the desk has evidently had enough of questions. He lays down his pen, folds his hands, regards her levelly. 'All the time,' he says. 'We see people like you all the time.' "[120] It does not seem a far stretch to assume that *this* is Coetzee, who, tired of dealing with the questions his characters provoke, puts down his pen and stops writing, and thus the *fiction* ends. And then the only truth, the only nonquestion to appear in these passages, is the fact of timelessness, endlessness, ceaseless repetition. This is the situation of humans, "all the time." Will Costello's story now just begin again? Is there no hope for change?

On one of my last nights in Dharamsala, I went to the tourist bar at the top of the hill. As the disillusionment of my time there sunk in, I had been frequenting the bar and drinking too much of India's much too sweet Kingfisher beer. I had become friendly, or at least chatty, with one of the waiters, an Indian man. Toward the end of the night he looked around at me and my friends and shook his head with a smile. I saw this and felt self-conscious. I walked over and asked him what he was thinking. He said, "I don't know what you did in a previous life to get so lucky, and what I did in a previous life to be so unlucky." I thought there would be more, but he just gave a surprisingly genuine laugh and walked off to keep working. I was glad he walked away, because I did not know how to respond. I never saw him again.

I think that modern Buddhism has something profound to say about reincarnation, about how taking it seriously should lead us to foreground interdependence and social relations in our ethical systems. But in a moment like this, when confronted with such a disheartening expression, it is not so easy to actually do the right thing because what that would be remains opaque. Should I have expressed my critique of the idea that reincarnation is what determines our fate and insisted that this is a political question of inequality instead? But wouldn't that just have been to reincarnate the patronizing attitude of colonial benevolence ("we know better than you about your own beliefs")? And didn't he probably already know that—weren't his words less a statement of his belief and more a safe vessel in which to hide a devastating criticism of me? Indeed, if I really thought that global inequality was the issue, then what was I still doing spending all this time and money in India rather than taking up the kind of political work I had come to understand was necessary? What more could I be doing to end these cycles of reincarnating unequal lives? I can imagine a version of the conversation with the waiter where I bring up all of these issues and at some impasse, in a fleeting egotistic moment, I ask him if I am at least better than the rest of the tourists—if my self-conscious anxiety about colonization and class sets me apart; if, indeed, he has ever met someone like me. And then I think of how Coetzee might describe his response: The waiter has evidently had enough of questions. He lays down his tray, folds his hands, regards me levelly. "All the time," he says. "We see people like you all the time."

3

LIBERATION

In a world so burdened by layers of global history, how might we go about achieving the old dream of combining personal and political liberation? When I arrived in Dharamsala, I thought I had an answer: that we should overcome personal and national divisions and embrace an ethic of global oneness. You deal with complexity by melting it away, by dissolving the self, by becoming one with others. I had not yet realized the obvious response: once we are all one, what are we supposed to do next? In the very instant after connection, we become distinct individuals confronted with a new existential choice.

During our group's meeting with the Dalai Lama, I was lucky enough to be able to ask him a question. I thought at length about what to ask and decided to see if he agreed with my solution. Given Buddhism's ideal of selflessness, I wanted to know if he thought Buddhism might help overcome other essentialist forms of identity, especially nationalism. My earnest query was something like this: How does the Buddhist critique of identity apply to forms of collective identity, like ethnicity or nationality? I realize in retrospect that I might have seemed like a Chinese spy, trying to find a contradiction between the Dalai Lama's Buddhism and his nationalism. But my question was earnest: If Buddhism critiques the idea of a personal substance, should it not also critique broader categories of identity, such as race, gender, or nationality? And, the Tibetan-Chinese context aside, would the abandonment of identity not in fact be what liberates us to be equally human?

The Dalai Lama's answer was short but devastating: "You have not understood the two truths." He went on to explain further, but as my ears rang in nervousness, I did not follow what he said. The point, I later understood, was this: I was imposing the ultimate truth—the emptiness of identity, its lack of essence—onto the conventional truth—the ways identity functions in everyday existence, such as the fact that chairs can be sat on or groups can be identified. This is the moment after insight, well expressed in a classic Zen aphorism: "Before enlightenment mountains are mountains and rivers are rivers. During enlightenment, mountains are no longer mountains and rivers no longer rivers. After enlightenment, mountains are mountains and rivers are rivers." Mahayana Buddhism does not, in this reading, transcend identity; it merely shows that identity is not itself transcendent. In other words, identities are real; they're just not permanent. And thus the Dalai Lama's answer was not just a pragmatic defense of Tibetan nationalism but a genuine philosophical response.

In some ways my question was a product of my identity as a left-leaning white male who has little time for nationalism, but whose nationality and the protections it affords are relatively secure. And it was also a product of what I felt the few times I experienced anti-Semitism: a desire to just be treated as any other human—to flee the encasings of identity, not embrace them. In this respect, I wonder if the Dalai Lama's answer might have been different had I phrased my question as about not Tibetan but Chinese identity. Might he then have placed more emphasis on the lack of ultimate existence of any given national form?

The relationship of identity to liberation is of course not unique to Buddhism, and today there is a great resurgence of concern about identity politics, ranging from claims that it is absolutely essential to political mobilization to critiques of its propensity to create new elite formations divorced from the very constituencies they claim to support.[1] If modern Buddhism has something to say in these debates, it may be about the sheer indeterminacy of the whole problem. The critique of identity can be liberating as much as it can undercut a liberation movement. And the praise of identity can be liberating as much as it may disable positive forms of alliance. The point, in the end, is less about identity itself than about what virtues one brings to the question.

The radical feminist and committed Buddhist bell hooks, for example, has suggested that overcoming the self can be too white a desire (like my question to the Dalai Lama) because it ignores that oppressed people must build up their dominated identities. But at the same time, she insists that this very claim can keep others from recognizing their selfishness. One must tread the critique of self carefully. Being black or a woman or poor might mean that liberation requires establishing an identity, but not just any identity. It must remain committed to liberation for others as well.[2]

This difficult gap between identity, ideology, and practices appears throughout modern Buddhism. As another example: in an overview of recent work on "queer Buddhism," Ann Gleig has pointed to a gap between theoretical descriptions of modern Buddhism and its actual practice. Theorists of queer Buddhism have suggested that Buddhism's critique of essence and dualism should be naturally aligned with queer practice, even if this has not been the case historically. They—somewhat problematically—oppose regressive Asian Buddhist practices, which have often (but not always, as we will see) been homophobic, with philosophical Buddhism's potential to be more inclusive. They suggest that a philosophical belief system that critiques duality between the sexes could potentially be open to any number of dispositions and lifestyles. But ethnographers like Gleig have shown that there is no necessary progress being made in modern Buddhism, where critiques of discussing identity tend to reinforce rather than undermine heteronormativity. This is because, in a situation analogous to what hooks critiques, the concept of selflessness leads to people being told simply not to talk about being gay.[3] The point is not ultimately the philosophy or the geography, but how practitioners anywhere "utilize non-essentialist philosophy" to either "reinforce" or "subvert."[4] Gleig's ongoing research has suggested further complications in that the desire to either announce or downplay queer identity varies from practitioner to practitioner, thus again underscoring the plurality of what may count in a politics of identity.[5]

Like my experience in Dharamsala, or hooks's with black Buddhism, or Gleig's with queer Buddhism, the novels considered here show how the hope for Buddhism to liberate us from our burdensome identities can become embedded in surprising and even troublesome ways. Looking at queer and trans identity in Severo Sarduy, feminism in Bessie Head, and race in Charles Johnson, I suggest that the ambivalence between ethnography and philosophy is part of the subject matter of these novels about Buddhist liberation. For each of them, moreover, the politics of identity and liberation cannot be confined to these categories but must also be understood within broader circuits of oppression: the Chinese occupation of Tibet for Sarduy, the lingering effects of English colonialism in Southern Africa for Head, and the legacy of the enslavement of African Americans for Johnson. In linking the personal and the political, each novel suggests that the scope of liberation that Buddhism demands is total. At the same time, the fractures of the narratives continue to ask whether such a total demand could actually be fulfilled in our world. What we thus find across the struggles is that modern Buddhism, rather than setting itself against identity, has instead learned to think of liberation as a process of negotiating identities, finding where they are useful and where they ought to be overcome. It encourages us to respect our self-ascriptions at the same time that it gently asks us to move past them in the name of more universal causes. In other words, it calls on us to understand the two truths.

REWRITING THE SUFFERING BODY

A Cuban exile in Paris from 1960 to 1993, Severo Sarduy was among the first writers to integrate the rising tide of poststructuralism and its critique of the idea of a substantial self into his fictions. Roland Barthes, Hélène Cixous, and Philippe Sollers were among his most ardent supporters. And Sarduy, like many writers in both Paris and Havana, developed a lifelong interest in Buddhism. In his middle period, particularly in *Cobra* (1972) and later in *Maitreya* (1978), the question of how to engage the culture and ideas of Buddhism became a central preoccupation. In this section I will focus on how *Cobra* explores the difficult relationship between personal liberation and political liberation, as it simultaneously explores questions of the transformation of self—especially sex and gender—and the politics of colonial rule.

Cobra is notoriously difficult to read. The plot, confusing at first, diverges into quasi-poetic fragments by the end, and anyone trying to map the transformations of the characters or narrators is bound to get lost along the way. Not only that, but we must suffer Sarduy's scorn should we falter: "Moronic reader: if even with these clues, thick as posts, you have not understood that we're dealing with a metamorphosis . . . abandon this novel and devote yourself to screwing or to reading the novels of the Boom, which are much easier."[6] Nevertheless, some general structure of a plot emerges.[7] In brief, it begins in The Lyrical Theater of Dolls, where Cobra, the Madam's star, has everything perfect except for her overgrown feet. Various attempts to shrink them fail, until a combination of drugs results in disaster, shrinking both the Madam and Cobra and rendering them little "white dwarfs." It turns out, however, that the dwarfs are not in fact the Madame and Cobra, but only their miniature doubles, since normal-size Cobra finds them one day under the bed.

From here the actions split in various ways. First the Madam leaves Cobra with the dwarves, and Cobra goes through various activities in an attempt to convert Cobrita, her miniature (soon to be called Pup) into her mimetic double. Then the Madam returns, Cobra leaves, and the miniature Mademoiselle falls out of the picture while Madam spends her time trying to turn Pup into a full-sized Cobra. But then Cobra herself comes back, only to leave again, taking Pup with her on a journey to find Dr. Ktazob (according to Rubén Gallo, Sarduy learned on a trip to Morocco that this meant "'penis slasher' in Arabic"[8]). She catches up to him in Tangiers, where he performs a rather cruel operation during which he attempts to transfer Cobra's pain to Pup. The first part of the novel closes in a subway station, where Cobra reappears, and the narrative voice begins to dissolve as the character transformations become unclear.

The second part transports us into the lives of four drug pushers from Amsterdam who had appeared earlier in relation to Ktazob. In a somewhat unclear order, Cobra is brutally initiated into their gang, there is a raid, various rituals are performed, Cobra dies and is reborn (perhaps), they smuggle drugs inside cracked Buddhist sculptures, a Guru answers their questions about life, a parody of Columbus's conquest diary is inserted into the text, and a series of prayers/rituals/declamations from an indeterminate (or at least multiple) narrator punctuate the rest of the text. It ends with various images of the destruction of temples in Tibet after the Chinese invasion, the commercialization and loss of faith that follow, and finally a prayer for a better tomorrow, ending with a variation of the famous Indo-Tibetan chant, *Om mani padme hum*. (It is usually translated as "The Jewel in the Lotus," "Hail the Lotus Jewel," or some variant. Sarduy's version, "May the Diamond come to the lotus flower," is an important variation to which we will return.[9])

In most criticisms of the novel, Buddhism is assumed to be used as either an apolitical philosophy or a mere trapping for some larger point about harmony or desire.[10] Such readings do not seem to me to accord with what takes place in *Cobra*, even if the novel tempts us to such conclusions. Consider, for example, what appears like a "Zen" moment in the second part of *Cobra* as the drug pushers query a Guru. Tiger asks, "What's the quickest way to liberation?" to which the Guru responds, "Don't think about it."[11] This is a typically paradoxical response that aligns with modern understandings of Zen. Most people don't think about exiting the cycle of reincarnation, and that, according to most Buddhist texts, is why they are stuck in it. The point should be to effactually do something to end the cycle of suffering. But this is the place of the Zen paradox. As D. T.

Suzuki writes, "According to the followers of Zen, its apparently paradoxical statements are not artificialities contrived to hide themselves behind a screen of obscurity . . . they are to be experienced in the inmost soul when they become for the first time intelligible."[12] This appears like just such a paradoxical statement meant to provoke a deeper understanding.

But consider this passage in the full context of the fiction. These characters are not in a monastery, but in something more like a nightclub or den of thieves, driven there both by their own greed and by their exile from Tibet. After the Guru finishes his lesson about not thinking, the scene is narrated as follows:

> (Sighs. Interjections of approval.) (Shirley Temple comes out of the men's room.) (The narcotics squad comes in: polyurethane muskets, shields of expanded epoxy.) (A black man takes the backboard off a pinball machine: hides a kif ball in each light bulb. . . . Another black hides a diamond in the inside pump of the toilet and then swallows a list of Buddhist maxims, another one containing the names of the members of the Supreme Soviet . . . and still another, in color, containing top secret designs of the new winter fashions.)[13]

The wisdom of the monk has been reduced to a kind of theatrical display met with sighs and approval, like in a game show or live television. U.S. pop stars float into the scene as if it were to be expected. Then there is a drug raid, and cocaine is hidden along with Buddhist maxims, political secrets, and the financial prospects of high fashion. The scene is very far from Suzuki's Zen, and so is the monk himself. Though he tries to continue answering questions, "He finished the prayer frantically scratching his head." And as he exits, he can only shout his wisdom "to the distracted crowd."[14]

We could read such a scene as suggesting that the pure philosophy of Buddhism is lost on the distracted crowd, or as a zany and empty gesture meant to drive us into ever deeper paroxysms of paradox and supposed enlightenment. But there is another possibility: that this scene is a demonstration of the embedding of Buddhism in the modern West. Sarduy does not directly praise Zen so much as show the complex and distracted way its ideas have been transmitted. Indeed, *Cobra* is hardly "Zen" in the stereotypical sense at all, unless one *presupposes* that what Sarduy seeks is some vague mystical union with the oneness of the universe. Rather than writing a "Zen" text, he is, if unwittingly, *exposing* this desire for Buddhism to help "us" overcome modern alienation. However that alienation is still drowning out the very message that might help. This is not a "refusal of worldly coherence," as one critic has written;[15] it is simply and unfortunately an incoherent world. There are better and worse ways for ideas to embed themselves in society—and there are better and worse societies for them to be embedded in.

Sarduy continues to explore this by setting part of the second half of the novel in what appears to be Dharamsala, or some other site for the Tibetans in exile throughout India. With quotes from the *Bardo Thödol* (commonly known as the *Tibetan Book of the Dead*[16]), a somewhat literal search for liberation and enlightenment, and variations on Tantric rituals, Sarduy creates a generic scene of Tibetan Buddhism as understood in the West. But the narrative goes on to raise some questions about this situation. Consider, for example, when Sarduy writes: "Death—the pause that refreshes—is part of life."[17] "The pause that refreshes" (and its Spanish equivalent, "la pausa que refresca") is a famous phrase from a Coca-Cola ad from the 1930s and after. The sentence, an otherwise straightforward thought on reincarnation, becomes tied up in more than generic thoughts on Tibetan Buddhism. This also occurs closer to the beginning of part 2, in "The Initiation," where, it seems, Cobra is being initiated into the motorcycle gang—although the scene is ambivalent about the sexual violence that may be enacted in this process. As "the initiation" comes to an end, the scene is narrated: "It wasn't Indian music. It was the Beatles. It was Ravi Shankar. The tabla served as background for a Shell commercial."[18] If the violence in the scene is real, then this is a very stark comment on the commercialization of religion as a distraction from injustice.

This apparent critique becomes most explicit toward the end of *Cobra* when the "Grand Lama" states, "Yes, white shaggy monks, I am fulfilling my karma in this suburban hovel, selling the ancient tankas [a kind of painting traditionally used for religious practices] of the Order and trafficking in copper scepters, now rusted green, in order to support the last lamas of the Yellow Hat."[19] Tibetan Buddhism is embedded here in a "suburban hovel," rusting and relying on the tourist trade to stay alive. Sarduy is not seeking an abstract knowledge of Buddhism in these lines; he is condemning colonization and the exile of the Tibetan people without falling into the "baby seal" trap that imagines a faultless precolonial Tibet. What is mocked here is precisely the desire for Buddhism to be something *for us*—for Tibet to fulfill dreams of commodifiable spirituality. The tourist buying the lama's *thangkas* is buying into that dream, whereas the lama is simply trying to keep himself and his teaching alive.

Further evidence of this complicated relation is given by the appearance of the Columbus-inspired "Indian Journal" section that closes the book. Unlike the Romantics, Columbus was looking for India not as the mythic origin of humankind, but as part of the origins of Europe's systematic colonization of the world. In a passage of his journal parodied by Sarduy, an Edenic landscape of natural beauty and riches is described, followed by the ominous closing line: "A most tame people."[20] That is to say, an easily dominated one. The search for India did not lead to the universal openness promised by capitalist cosmopolitans. It introduced centuries of genocide, slavery, and colonization. Sarduy suggests a parallel here between Columbus and the Chinese, who came with promises to "liberate" Tibet from tradition, just as the colonizers "liberated" the natives from savagery. We can see throughout the last few pages of *Cobra* the frustration at the fate of the exiles and Buddhism in general: "A neon tube lights golden Gautama whose lips are stretched in a rictus."[21]

But this tragic grimace of the ultramodern Buddha is not the end of Sarduy's story. The text moves after the rictus into a passage on the future (and here we can appreciate Jill Levine's remarkable translation): "At dawn we shall start out again, until upon the horizon, the peaceful and twilight-hoarding deities show their orange fingers."[22] The image of the dawn recalls the end of Edwin Arnold's classic Orientalist text, the *Light of Asia*, which closes with the stanza, "The Dew is on the Lotus!—Rise, Great Sun! / And lift my leaf and mix me with the wave. / Om mani padme hum, the Sunrise comes! The Dewdrop slips into the shining Sea!"[23] After repeating this motif of the rising sun, Sarduy concludes his own novel with a version of the mantra: "In the echo left by a cymbal, the deepest [*la más grave*] of the four voices will pronounce the syllables: May the Diamond come to the lotus flower [*Que a la flor de loto el Diamante advenga*]."[24]

However, although the passage seems to cite Arnold's poem, it does so with a significant variation. First, Arnold's interest is in the beautiful philosophy of the Buddha; he has no overt interest in politics. His concern is with the transmission of this way of life to Europe. Second, it is safe to assume that Arnold, following the scholarship of his day, believed that the saying *Om mani padme hum* meant something like, "Hail the Jewel in the Lotus," a common translation at the time. (A typical Spanish rendering would be "¡Om, la joya en el loto!") The poem closes with his salute to the Buddha and his vision of the transmission of Buddhism to the West.

Sarduy's ending is different. He does not find the Buddha in the written text transmitted unblemished through scholarship, but rather in "the echo left by a cymbal,"—in the fading sound that remains as a trace for the future, like the monk shouting his wisdom to the distracted crowd. Attending to the echo left by a cymbal suggests that there may be a future of more meaningful embeddedness ahead for Buddhism. This is a sounding to which the future must attend. Levine translates "la más grave" correctly as "the deepest," but it can also mean "the most grave," in the sense of somber or heavy. This is another meaning of reincarnation: the demand of the past to never remain settled with the conditions in which we find our worlds. We are to attempt to transform ours just as those in the past attempted to transform theirs. And we know full well, from their mistakes, that there is a frequent errancy in the process of embedding. But if we do learn from them, then reincarnation, rather than a form of condemnation, marks the path to liberation.

The intertwined warning and demand are also apparent in the novel's last line. *Cobra* closes with the hope that the diamond will come [*advenga*] to the lotus flower. The Spanish *advenir* signifies an event to come and can be messianic. And there is also Sarduy's intersexual/intertextual play here, since "the diamond" has appeared earlier as a diagram to demonstrate the process by which Cobra and Pup will experience the torture of their transition. The diamond is equally, of course, an object stolen from colonial mines. And it is also one of the most famous Buddhist texts today—*The Diamond Sutra*. Finally, it is the jewel (*mani*) of *om mani padme hum*.

Sarduy thus invokes an ambiguous set of possibilities— including even the colonial return to the mines he otherwise seeks to dispel. The choice of the verb *advenir* signals a future that is not guaranteed any more than any previous embedding of Buddhist ideals. It is a prayer—a hope for the future that must be worked through if it is to come to be. Sarduy in his closing lines is not hailing an abstract Buddhism; he is hoping for a future of knowledge capable of showing both wisdom and compassion, while knowing full well the limits of liberation in a world of such great oppression. This is not the mystical oneness of the universe; this is the revolutionary demand for change in both thought and being, the ultimate products of which the author cannot foresee.

Although this indeterminacy can be dangerous, it also is the mark of potential for change. Here the plot's focus on sexuality and danger dovetails with its probing of the role of Buddhism in the modern world. To appreciate this overlap, we can begin by noting an irony about the final line: *om mani padme hum* is actually an incorrect transliteration by the first generation of European Sanskrit scholars. The missionaries before them, who did not know the language but lived with the Tibetans, seemed to have known the truth: *Manipadme* is in fact one word, and it most likely refers to Avalokiteśvara, literally "The Lord Who Looks Down [in Empathy]."[25] So the "correct" translation is something like "Hail the Lotus-Jewel One," and the correct meaning is praise for Avalokiteśvara.[26] But this translation still does not explain why *padme* is feminine, since Avalokiteśvara is generally male in Tibet. This uncertainty of gender also led to a history of speculation that the "jewel in the lotus" had an implicit sexual meaning, though that too is debated.[27] Donald Lopez points to the scholarship of June Campbell, who has argued that there is a pre-Buddhist feminine deity who was covered over by the "zealous missionaries of Indian Buddhism."[28] Whether or not Sarduy was aware of this history, the final invocation of an inversion that can recover a feminized male Buddha fits rather nicely with Cobra's journey.

It is thus not insignificant that Cobra's sex transformation earlier in the book is rendered as a form of reincarnation: "If in the intermediate state the knowledge factor of the subject vanishes it is possible that he may founder in that limbo, or that, when coming to, he might not recognize himself in his restructured body."[29] Reincarnation, as I suggested in the previous chapter, can be a way to think through the multiplicity of identities that we have all inherited—to think that we have all been, quite literally, one another. This invites the possibility that a single sex cannot define us. But Sarduy is not sentimental about this fact, or about the pain we are still willing to inflict on each other as we process our varied identities.

Thus, Cobra's achievement of transformation is rendered as a scene of remarkable and often parodic torture for both her and Pup. Sarduy argues in his essay *Written on a Body* that "transvestism" signifies beyond the act itself toward a fundamental gesture of inversion on the textual body.[30] For Sarduy, the "planes of intersexuality are analogous to the planes of intertextuality that constitute the literary object."[31] In other words, we are all made up of texts and sexes that exceed what appears on the surface. Sarduy's trans subject is not "inherently" a different sex.

They are composed of many voices and possibilities for being, and they select a certain combination of those ways of being in order to make the sentence, or story, of their sexuality. They thus "invert" their sex by rewriting the sentence on their body. This is not free play and *jouissance*; it is, rather, the burden of reincarnation, of history, of the disjointedness of always being out of one's time and place yet still having to make an existence in the place and time where one's sentence appears. The desire for sexual liberation, or textual liberation, or political liberation, and the frustration or failure of that desire are what make the constant inversions of our joy and suffering. The liberating act of rewriting one's sex here provides not a guarantee for overcoming suffering as such, but a means of inverting a particular kind of suffering and embarking on a new story.[32]

As Janet Gyatso has shown in a fascinating essay on the concepts of sex and gender in Tibetan Buddhism, Sarduy's thinking through the relation of sex and liberation is not unprecedented. Gyatso shows that in both Ayurvedic and Tibetan medicine, there was a somewhat standard assumption of three sexes.[33] This did not automatically lead to generosity toward all those sexes, however. Gyatso notes that, against all other doctrinal assumptions about universal capacity for growth on the Buddhist path, there is a claim in some texts that "third sex" people should not even be taught Buddhism: "the third sex is incapable of any salvific activity whatsoever."[34] Later traditions broke with these prejudices and even suggested that nonbinary people were uniquely capable of becoming bodhisattvas. A fascinating document anticipates the Oedipus complex, arguing that most children will lust after the parent of the opposite sex and hate the same-sex parent. However, nonbinary people are said to be uniquely capable of evading this impasse and loving both parents equally with desire not for their bodies, but for their

liberation.[35] There is a further twist, though: "The salvific potential of Buddhist logic notwithstanding, we cannot help but
notice that the actual conditions of people, alas, do not necessarily improve in the wake of theoretical advancements. Even to
argue, as some Buddhist texts actually did do, that all sexual
identity is a construct and an illusion, did not historically erase
all sex discrimination in Buddhism—far from it."[36] Nonbinary
people came to stand for a general principle of nonduality and
being in the Middle Way, rather than actually being *"people,"* as
Gyatso puts it.[37] This is the problem of the two truths: understanding ultimate reality does not necessarily tell us what to do
about conventional reality. It may slacken the intensity of our
identifications and open us up to change, but there is no guarantee. So yet again we see that the best ideas can become disjointed
in their embeddedness—at least if and when their practice is not
cared for or is frustrated by countervailing forces. Liberation is
an ongoing struggle, not a singular achievement.

Rereading the novel in light of this history, I came to think
that the density of Sarduy's writing is perhaps less hopeful than
I suggested in an earlier version of this chapter.[38] The twilight-
hoarding deities may yet return to stake their claim. This is the
pain of inversion, the risk of history—it may liberate or incar-
cerate, and it may tomorrow undo whatever gains it made today.
As Sarduy would have it, liberation is made possible by the fact
that we have no essence and therefore are always capable of
change. But that lack of essence also means we suffer under the
constancy of change and have no secure destiny. Buddhism, of
course, seeks to secure liberation through the acknowledgment
and acceptance of this condition. What *Cobra* suggests, on my
reading, is that liberation on a personal level is possible through
an acceptance more of inversion than impermanence; that is, of
changes of state more than the ultimate emptiness of those

states. The parodic zaniness of this text is thus not folly but about developing the kind of subjectivity that can successfully live in such a world. This may translate to the political level, where the ability to persevere in conditions of cruel irony—such as the lama selling spirituality to maintain his material existence—is necessary for survival. We may not like the conditions in which we are embedded, but we have no choice but to work through them.

REWRITING THE SUFFERING SOUL

The reimagining of what constitutes and enables liberation is also central to Bessie Head's *A Question of Power* (1973), in which the possibility of entering enlightenment through what it once seemed to oppose—family life—becomes central. The novel resituates these questions of liberation between personal and political levels by adding a new dimension to our discussion: the analysis of patriarchy. What happens when Buddhism gets embedded into such a space? Reimagining the founding myths of all religions, including Buddhism, Head's narrative questions whether there can be any liberation if it is not for everyone and from all conditions of oppression.

A Question of Power is the story of a young, mixed-race South African woman, Elizabeth, and her son, Shorty, who self-exile from the apartheid state to Botswana. The story is driven by Elizabeth's struggles with insanity. Her nights are tormented by hallucinatory visions of Dan and Sello, two real men who live in her village but take on mythic and terrifying proportions in her mind. The visions are full of violence and sexual oppression. They also turn frequently on deceptive kindness that leads to even greater cruelty. These hallucinations cause her public breakdowns, job loss, and the inability to care for her son. Elizabeth experiences many worlds within this one. Slowly, through the kindness of several people in the village, coupled with a realization of her historical role in the founding of a new religion of "Man," she manages to overcome her visions and take her part in rural community life.[39]

The novel is at once a political tract about how ideologies of race and gender exacerbate latent psychic tensions and a philosophical journey through Elizabeth's struggle with the concepts of good and evil. The political and the philosophical are united in the book through its titular "question of power," which I take to be encapsulated in this passage from early in the novel: "no one had come to terms with their own powers and at the same time made allowance for the powers of others."[40] The question is how to make this coexistence possible. The concern, as the hallucinated Sello puts it near the novel's close, is: "If the things of the soul are really a question of power, then anyone in possession of power of the spirit could be Lucifer."[41] Elizabeth herself is especially concerned with those who have explored their own powers at the expense of others, whether in the realm of white supremacy, patriarchy, or, as is less frequently considered, spiritual exploration.

While the book engages with the breadth of the world's religions, Buddhism takes a paramount role, and Sello is presented as an African manifestation of the Indian Buddha. Head seems to share a sense with Gleig, hooks, and others that some of the primary themes of modern Buddhism—the dignity and capacity of all for enlightenment, the spiritual plentitude of the universe, the necessity to seek inner peace in order to calm the world, and such philosophical themes as nonduality and interdependence—can be used for good as much as for evil. She explores, for example, how interdependence can be perilously close to dependence and how a philosophy of harmony can mask existing oppressions and terrors. At the same time, she does not give up the desire to create an interdependent, harmonious world beyond such acts of domination.[42] The concern that emerges is how to develop a way of existence that acknowledges the potential dark sides of Buddhism without discounting the wealth of insight it has to offer.[43]

Part of where this begins for Head is with critiquing modernity's best-known origin story of Buddhism. The most common founding myth of Buddhism in modernism, after all, is the story of a prince who abandons his wife and child in order to liberate himself from the suffering of this world. Although he does eventually return to them in most versions of the myth, this is often rendered as the end of his personal spiritual journey, not as part of a communal undertaking.[44] (The actuality of women's role in Buddhism is in fact enormously complex and varied, both historically and today, and differs not only from country to country or sect to sect but also from monastery to monastery.)[45] *A Question of Power*, at one level, can be read as the mythic story of the mother and son who were abandoned. As the narrator tells us, Elizabeth married her husband in South Africa because "he was interested in Buddhism."[46] And when he goes on to explore his own pleasures with other women and does not care for her or their son, she abandons him and South Africa. From there, she begins a new story in which she (in her imagination) is integral to Sello's spiritual journey—in fact, the new enlightenment they will find is precisely one born of relation, with all its difficulties, not the intense singularity (and potential cruelty) of working solely for one's own salvation.

Elizabeth is not the first to reconsider the founding myth. As Miranda Shaw has shown in her study of Tantric Buddhism, there are texts that argue that the Buddha's departure from his family was only a story used to instruct "weak worldly beings" to overcome their dependence on sexuality.[47] The true path to enlightenment is in fact through sexual union. Shaw cites the following Tantric text: "Buddhahood is obtained from [sexual] bliss, and / Apart from women there will not be bliss."[48] And Liz Wilson, in the introduction to the volume *Family in Buddhism*, argues that "kinship making is a foundational form of practice in Buddhism."[49] She cites evidence from Buddhist scholarship across centuries and regions to show a continuing concern with various forms of family—both those one is born into and those whom one joins as a member of a monastic community.

John Strong has also noted that biographies of the Buddha in the West are much more standardized than the many narratives in the canonical and postcanonical texts. Indeed, I did not know until reading Strong that the frequently told story of the Buddha skipping out in the night, refusing to wake his wife, Yasodhara, and vowing to return for his son, Rahula, after his enlightenment is in fact postcanonical. The standard version speaks only of his weeping mother and father. Strong also points out that there is even another narrative in which Siddhartha, rather than fleeing his wife, makes love with her, and Rahula is conceived the very night he sets out on his quest. The rest of the text, the *Sanghabhedavastu*, concerns itself not so much with Siddhartha as with the connection between husband and wife. Strong writes: "In this tradition the Buddha is not alone in his quest for enlightenment. Instead . . . both he and Yasodhara, each in their own way, embark on their quest together, and the symbol of that quest is their son Rahula."[50]

A Question of Power takes place along these lines, though in a much darker setting. In the *Sanghabhedavastu*, Siddartha and Yasodhara practice parallel ascetic acts as he approaches enlightenment and she gestates the child (for six years!). In Head's narrative, Sello sits calmly as a reposing monk while Elizabeth undergoes three years of torture. We are told from the beginning that Elizabeth's development "paralleled his inner development," but also that we are witnessing an "insane pursuit" in which evil is "personified . . . in vivid detail, within themselves."[51] Indeed, *A Question of Power* dramatizes a mythic, religious struggle that goes far beyond the temptation of Christ or the Buddha's confrontation with Mara. A tremendous danger appears not outside the spiritual quest to challenge it but rather at the heart of the journey to enlightenment itself. The trouble with those other stories is that they represent the solitary man's struggle in which he breaks with family and friends and all worldly goods in pursuit of the truth. In so doing, he can seem to turn away from the world that he is claiming to save.

This, at one level (there are many) is the drama that will unfold in *A Question of Power*. When Elizabeth "meets" the historical Buddha late in the narrative, she describes him as moving slowly, with eyelids covering his eyes. "His whole life had been turned inwards. . . . He heard nothing. He cared about nothing. He had become nothing but his inward simplicity. To face that and at the same time face African destiny, African circumstances, was like signing my own death-warrant in advance."[52] Buddhism—at least this rather ahistorical portrait of it—is presented as incompatible with the needs of an "African" present that demands confronting the ravages of historical oppression and malfeasance. And yet, and this is one of Head's points from the very beginning of the novel, Africans are also specifically well suited to hear the message of the Buddha about the power of the humble and the ordinary. Sello, as noted above, is presented as a kind of African Buddha. The novel begins: "It seemed almost incidental that he was African. So vast had his inner perceptions grown over the years that he preferred an identification with mankind to an identification with a particular environment. And yet, as an African, he seemed to have made one of the most perfect statements: 'I am just anyone.'"[53] Ultimately, this Sello represents everyone's capacity to achieve enlightenment. But conventionally, he is capable of recognizing this because he is part of a people (a conventionally arisen designation, "African") who believe profoundly in humility as a way out of suffering. Indeed, in Elizabeth's soteriology, power is as much responsible for the world's problems as the classical Buddhist problem, desire: "half the source of human suffering was God itself, personalities in possession of powers or energies of the soul. Ordinary people never mucked up the universe. They don't have that kind of power."[54] Of course, ordinary people, joined together, do have that kind of power. The trick is that such humility is a double-edged sword that can equally keep one from being an oppressor and stop one from effectively fighting against oppression. What is needed, Elizabeth believes, is to develop a new kind of humility that is capable of fighting for itself.

This requires that Sello be pulled out of his inner sanctum. And it seems here that Elizabeth is part of a broader plot, hatched by an unidentified "tall, thin Asian man who looked like Sello."[55] This man is concerned about the Buddha's enlightenment and his refusal to live again. He says that he had to "use evil to draw him back to life again" and had to use Elizabeth and the Buddha's wife in order to do so.[56] This act of evil breaks the inner sanctum of the Buddha, where he carries out "his withdrawn meditations on oblivion and eternity," at the same time that it puts Elizabeth through unnarratable tortures.[57] In the end, however, it appears to have worked:

> The wife of Buddha emerged from Elizabeth's person and walked towards Sello. She quietly settled herself at his feet. She

was a queen of heaven who was a housekeeper. She'd travelled a journey with a man who had always deserted her in a pursuit after the things of the soul. He'd achieved his Nirvana and she'd toppled him out of it, she'd stained his hands with blood. Maybe the world would be a little saner, after the strains of the past were over and women were both goddesses and housekeepers and there was a time for loving. . . . She and Sello . . . had perfected together the ideal of sharing everything and then perfectly shared everything with all mankind.[58]

As a rewriting of the Buddhist tradition, Head's novel makes an extraordinary set of claims: that Elizabeth has found a path to serenity that is not about the grandeur of a single founding figure; that this path is about the ordinary person with no great power but at the same time, this ordinary path is greater than the religious path; and that she is an ordinary person with no great power who has overcome the founding figures. In short, she is not just "retracing the pathway to the achievement of Buddha"; her experience with evil has "blasted her to a height far above Buddha."[59]

The claim is tremendous: that in the psychic divisions of her soul, Elizabeth has overcome the prison of solitary religious grandeur and enshrined a new mode of being in the world that solves the problem of the book's opening chapter: how to both have and share power. This is nothing less than the founding of a new religion, based on the destruction of the cult of power and the newfound sanctity of the ordinary. "There is only one God and his name is Man. And Elizabeth is his prophet."[60]

The excess of Elizabeth's claims aside, the novel rightly exposes the way practices of liberation—even liberation from desire—are often predicated on the exclusive solitude necessary for the extended temporality of such practices. In joining

Tantric and other traditions to reimagine how liberation might occur *through* shared desire, *A Question of Power* calls on us to grapple with the interpersonal complexities of claims to liberation. And it sets those complexities within the even starker situation of socially inscribed patriarchy and colonial racism. Elizabeth ultimately finds Buddhism wanting. For this reason, she must end the Buddha's nirvana, "topple" him out of it, and force him to work through their enlightenment together. She is not, in other words, opposed to otherworldly liberation, but she is insistent that it only be achieved on the basis of equal conditions on this earth.

One name for such generalized equality is "universality." Head's aim is indeed to create a kind of universal "religion of Man" from Elizabeth's particular experience.[61] And the concept of the universal continues to unfurl the driving question of the novel: how to both have and share power. Head's universality here is a critique of another historical kind of universality: that of hierarchical revelations only available to some. She challenges the version of Buddhism that she has been taught, not because she does not believe in its principles—she pursues Buddhism precisely because of her interest in it—but rather because it presents those principles as the hidden province of an elite few. Head perceptively unpacks this false universality that at once proclaims its truth for all and denies the achievability of that truth to others.

But Head's story has its own troubled universality. One of the limits of finding such universal truths through Head's narrator is her struggle to appreciate and recognize queer men, whom she originally suggests are weak and effeminate because of colonialism.[62] She never moves past the assumption that they are some kind of perversion, but in a telling moment reveals the source of her rather classic homophobia—fear of the same. She asks another character how he feels about gay men, then quickly follows with the question: "What would you do if you were both God and Satan at the same time?"[63] What seems to scare her about men who sleep with men is a false analogy with the fear that drives her tortures: that they combine into one what she wishes would remain separate. The narrator comes to realize that she must admit this sameness, this proximity of good and evil within all of us and within all of our ideas and institutions. Nevertheless, in terms of sexuality, it troubles her in a way that the narrative never seems to come to terms with. Elizabeth and Sello turn out to be reincarnations of Siddhartha and Yasodhara, but, unlike what we might find in Sarduy, they also reincarnate a prejudice about what a spiritual couple looks like. Becoming liberated in one sphere does not mean that becoming liberated in all spheres. There is always more in our embedded conditions to work through.

REWRITING THE SUFFERING WORLD

"Oxherding Tale" is an alternative translation of "The Ten Cow-Herding Pictures," a visual representation of the path to enlightenment, and also the title of the final essay of D. T. Suzuki's first major international work, *Essays in Zen Buddhism* (1927). It is about a series of pictures by the twelfth-century Rinzai Zen monk Kakuan[64] depicting the spiritual progress of a young man. It is often argued that the ox represents our untutored mind before we embark on the Buddhist path.[65] We must find the ox, tame it, and then transcend it, since it is only a nominal (or pictorial) designation for what is in fact beyond words. Suzuki notes that Kakuan's paintings are an innovation on an earlier version that ended with an empty circle, representing the transcendence of the karmic cycle. This is only the first truth—the emptiness of ultimate reality. The second version ends with an image of a man returning to the world and bearing gifts. The lesson is that the point of spiritual practice is not transcendence but the bodhisattva path of returning to express one's understanding and help others on their way. This is the second truth—the meaningfulness of conventional reality.

Charles Johnson uses this story as the framework for his novel, *Oxherding Tale* (1982). As he notes in the introduction, he had "envisioned [the novel] as being a slave narrative that in its progress paralleled the 'Ten Oxherding Pictures' depicting a young man who *believes* he has lost his ox . . . searches for and finds it, then . . . the ox (self) disappears, leaving only the young man who returns to his village."[66] The question of the relation among this twelfth-century story, slavery, and Johnson's own historical present is thus crucial to understanding the novel. Johnson's work has received increased and deserved critical attention in the past few decades, including a handful of book-length studies.[67] His fiction is complex and takes place at the intersection of numerous concerns. Johnson is a teacher and practitioner of creative writing, a trained philosopher with an advanced degree in contemporary European philosophy, a practicing Buddhist and martial artist, a literary critic, and an omnivorous reader. All are on display in *Oxherding Tale*, which crosses narrative with philosophy and essay writing. Johnson is unique among the figures considered so far, because he is not only well-read in the textual history of Buddhism up to the present but also an avowed believer in its soteriological message.[68] Across the text we will see the weight of his philosophical desires run up against the difficulties of embeddedness in narrative and history.

The intensity of the pedigree we as readers must reckon with begins with the book's epigraphs, which are drawn from St. Augustine, the *Rig Veda*, a commentary on the *Ten Oxherding Pictures*, and Franz Kafka's short story "The Great Wall of China." The latter three quotes are all given in English. The first quote, from Augustine, is the only one to appear in the original language and runs as follows: *Noli foras ire, in te redi, in interiore homine habitat veritas.* Charles Taylor, the noted chronicler of Western thought, translates this line: "Do not go outward; return within yourself. In the inward man dwells truth."[69] For him, the quote signifies the rise of interiority in Western thought.[70] But Taylor, in calling this remark "formative of our entire Western culture," glosses over Augustine's own historical situation (in North Africa) and a global inheritance that Johnson seeks to recover in his narrative.[71] In a brief, essayistic chapter, "On the Nature of Slave Narratives," Johnson's narrator, Andrew Hawkins, gives this genealogy to the form he practices: "In point of fact, the movements in Slave Narrative from slavery (sin) to freedom (salvation) are identical to those of the Puritan narrative, and *both* these genuinely American forms are the offspring of that hoary confession by the first black philosophical writer: Saint Augustine."[72]

As we move on to understand this connection of spiritual narratives, black philosophical writing, and freedom, it is worth pausing to ask why the Augustine quote alone is left untranslated. Perhaps the answer is that this is not a citation of Augustine alone but also a citation of a citation of Augustine, the closing lines of Edmund Husserl's *Cartesian Meditations*, a classic work in phenomenology (Johnson's field of expertise): "I must lose the world by epoché [bracketing], in order to regain it by a universal self-examination. '*Noli foras ire,*' says Augustine, '*in te redi, in interiore homine habitat veritas.*'"[73] The meaning of this passage for Husserl is that in order to achieve knowledge of the world, I must first lose the world by going into myself. The truth within is not interiority, but only my capacity to understand the world better by first bracketing it. When I understand how my mind understands the world, then I will be able to understand the world. This wandering into thought and self in order to improve one's understanding is echoed in the next two epigraphs. From the *Vedas*: "I do not know what I am like here, I do not know in relation to what I can say, 'This I am.' Bewildered and lost in thought, I wander." And from the commentary on the oxherding pictures: "Desolate through forests and fearful in jungles, he is seeking an Ox he does not find." These are all images of the fact that on the path to insight and the liberation it promises, some amount of wandering, vagrancy, and mistakes will occur. These will not be the mistakes of the solitary subject alone but also those of the intersubjective world she inhabits—the world to which she will bring gifts.

This intersubjectivity is signaled explicitly by the final epigraph, from Kafka: "one can only deduce the existence of different subjects in the same human being." But, perhaps surprisingly, this was already implicit in the Augustine citation. Johnson is no doubt aware that this citation from Augustine is also used by Maurice Merleau-Ponty in his disagreement with Husserl about Augustine in the preface to his *Phenomenology of Perception*. Merleau-Ponty takes exception to one particular word in Augustine: *habitat*. And since the question of habitation, of where things belong and where they dwell, is, as we will see, central to the *Oxherding Tale*, it is worth repeating what Merleau-Ponty has to say about this: "Truth does not 'inhabit' only 'the inner man,' or more accurately, there is no inner man, man is in the world, and only in the world does he know himself."[74] We are always embedded in something, even when we are thinking. This is why truth cannot live in or "inhabit" the inner human alone, since what is most "inner" in the human subject is her relation to the world. Johnson's story is said to be told by a "first-person . . . universal" narrator who, rather than "falteringly interprets the world . . . *is* that world."[75] This is, almost verbatim, Merleau-Ponty's critique of Augustine. I do not think this series of citations within citations, of languages (Latin, German, French, English) inhabiting many voices, culminating with a critique of the idea of habitation, is merely an accidental preface to a novel whose first part is entitled "House and Field" and which begins precisely with a confusion about which space each character inhabits.

In the novel's opening sequence, the narrator's father, George Hawkins, is drinking late into the night with his master, Jonathan Polkinghorne. Afraid to go back to his wife in such a drunken state, Polkinghorne suggests that they swap beds for the night. Hawkins's protests eventually give way to a not entirely accidental scene of lovemaking with Anna Polkinghorne, who will, nine months later, give birth to Andrew Hawkins. The novel is told largely in the first person by Andrew. I say "largely" because in a philosophical aside within the narrative we are told about the Merleau-Ponty inspired "first-personal universal" narrator—Hawkins's "I" embodies the world. Thus, *Oxherding Tale* is not a novel about the prison house of subjectivity; it is about a house that extends into the world. But that imbrication of house and field is deeply troubling when the house in question is on a plantation.

That context means that we would be wrong to see Merleau-Ponty as the philosophical hero of the novel, which is less about a singular philosophy than about what Johnson in his introduction speaks of as "our inheritance," namely, "the effort of all men and women, East and West, to make sense of the world."[76]

One of the things absent from Merleau-Ponty's thought, and why Johnson needs a greater inheritance of thinkers in order to make sense of the world, is what Frantz Fanon called "epidermalization," or the way the truth of one's being is reduced to the color of one's skin.[77] This is Fanon's own critique of Merleau-Ponty: that he appreciates only the body schema and cannot come to terms with the "historical-racial schema."[78] Johnson cites Fanon almost verbatim, as he does Merleau-Ponty: "the wretchedness of being colonized was . . . the fact that men had epidermalized Being."[79] Still, Johnson is not merely replaying Fanon's critique; he is extending it out into the oxherding tale itself. This means that the ox we are looking for is not a generic self or the ego. It is the historical, corporeal, and racialized ego. And thus the adventures of Andrew Hawkins will require him to uncover his history, his body, and his skin. This attempt to overcome the racialized ego does not mean denying race or its importance or its embeddedness in history; it means suggesting, with Fanon, that what race means is evolving as much as any other thing in this world. The point, which Johnson sees in Fanon and Suzuki, is not to *accept* one's condition as binding but to take it up, assume it as a position from which to move into a new space. This is the spiritual progress of finding the ox, taming it, having it vanish, and then continuing on in the world.

Much of *Oxherding Tale*, however, is about not the linear progress of the character through these steps but rather his slow process of moving through the various "ways" that he finds offered to him, assuming them, then finding them not to be his own.[80] Our narrator is not going straight through on a path; he is wandering on a rocky road buffeted by various forms of discrimination. There are several major differences, in fact, between the traditional tale and Johnson's. First, the character in the original is depicted as a solitary meditator. Hawkins only achieves liberation through social means. Second, there are no impediments to the man's spiritual exploration in the original tale: the only thing that can stop his progress is his own ignorance or lack of will. As bell hooks has argued, Buddhism did not immediately appeal to African Americans of her generation because it was "communicated that the teachings were for the materially privileged and those preoccupied with their own comforts," and therefore meaningless if you did not have material comforts or the leisure time to do things like go on month-long retreats[81] *Oxherding Tale* thus probes what it would mean to achieve spiritual liberation while embedded in "epidermalization" and material deprivation.

To get to the heart of Johnson's story, we can skip over a number of interesting moments in the book and locate Hawkins as a runaway slave along with his companion, the mystic Reb. They are being chased by the "Soulcatcher," Horace Bannon. Reb and Andrew split up, and Horace pursues Reb. Andrew (now going by the name William Harris) has been made sick by the travails of escaping and ends up convalescing under the care of Dr. Undercliff (a "crypto-Schopenhauerean") and his daughter, Peggy, who bonds with Andrew over a love of Herman Melville.[82] (It is not coincidental that Andrew's final vision of liberation comes from touching the Soulcatcher's tattoos, which bear a resemblance to Queequeg's philosophical tattoos in *Moby Dick*.) Andrew takes up a post teaching, and he and Peggy plan to marry. It is at the wedding that Andrew (William) has his first enlightenment moment:

> "William," croaked Peggy, "this is *dumb!* It's the gaudiest thing since the carnival came to town. It's silly. And unnecessarily

noetic, and"—she hiccoughed; I gave her a hefty whack on her back—"wonderful!" . . . And me? I heard only the run, the gentle ribboning of his [the minister's] words. A longish dream, I thought . . . And, all at once, the guests weren't there. Only the Minister, the Woman, the Man. We stood, I felt, translated, lifted a few feet off the ground . . . [in] a realm of changeless meaning for which the only portal was surrender. After the ceremony this nearly mystical feeling of transport faded.[83]

There are a number of motifs here taken directly from Suzuki's description of the experience of enlightenment: that the experience is "noetic" (a term Suzuki borrowed from William James's writings on mysticism), that it is like everyday life but "a few feet off the ground," that the resistance to it is broken by a whack (as with the *keisaku*—a flat wooden stick used to hit sleeping meditators), that this puts the characters in a realm beyond normal meaning where everything becomes one, and finally, that this is a "transport," a movement of enlightenment, which eventually yields and returns us to the world.[84]

There is still much more to happen before the book's close. As in Head's narrative, it is not within the marriage plot that liberation is secured because the couple requires a broader world of which they are a part. This moment of *satori*, as in the second set of oxherding pictures, is not the end, since enlightenment in modernity *is itself a process of learning how to be in the world.*[85] Thus, it is after this moment that Andrew, after seeing so many different ways of life, begins to get a sense of his own path: "I discovered that my dharma, such as it was, was that of the householder. I wanted, though good fortune made me feel guilty, nothing more than forty years of crawling home from the classroom."[86] But his feeling of guilt because of the state of the world around him means that, as in the ninth of the oxherding images, this return to his own source is not the story's completion. Johnson has set us up for this since the book's first epigraph stating that the meaning of habitation, of householding, is that there is no such thing as an inner space removed from the world. Andrew's spiritual liberation, like that of the original oxherder, will not be complete until he returns to the village bearing gifts.[87]

The way that this occurs in *Oxherding Tale* is that Hawkins receives a "wedding gift" of Reb's ring from the Soulcatcher. Thinking that this means his friend Reb has been caught and he must confront Bannon, he rides into town searching for him. It turns out, to Hawkins's happy surprise, that Reb had lost his ring not when Bannon tracked him down, but when he sold it so as to lose the last trace of personal identity. Bannon's method of catching slaves was to enter their psyche and catch them through their own desires. But Reb, a man of infinite resignation, had no desire: "Yo friend didn't want *nothin*.' How the hell you gonna catch a Negro like that? He can't be caught, he's *already* free. Not legally, but you know what Ah'm sayin.'"[88] Bannon continues that he tried to locate Reb anyway but "He wasn't *positioned* nowhere . . . He had no home. No permanent home."[89] His home was the world. Having sworn that if he failed to catch a slave he would quit, Bannon has come only to ask Hawkins for thirty dollars that he "owes" him so that he can start a new life. This moment continues Hawkins's realization that, ultimately if not conventionally, there is no difference between self, home, and world.

Perhaps this is why the final moment of Hawkins's enlightenment, the one that brings him to his final realization of the symbiosis of self and world, occurs through Bannon himself. On Bannon's chest are the forms of all the beings he has killed in an intricate tapestry. By touching these forms, Hawkins has his final insight into interdependent selfhood: "the profound mystery of the One and the Many gave me back my father again and again, his love, in every being . . . for these too were my father, and, in the final face I saw . . . I was my father's father, and he my child."[90] Again, there is no inner man who struggles and achieves the truth of the situation: there is only the narrator who is the world, who is the transmitter and inheritor of a global wisdom shared by all, though unequally and unjustly distributed.[91] Andrew receives his final lesson: that his dharma as a householder is inseparable from his dharma as an activist subject. He no longer has "business" with the Soulcatcher, but something far greater: "After the [civil] war, Fruity and I turned to the business of rebuilding, with our daughter Anna (all is conserved; all), the world. This is my tale."[92]

Conventionally real identities (and epidermalizations) cannot trump ultimate liberation, but they can put impediments in its way. Political liberation and spiritual liberation are thus not the same. Rather, as in some canonical versions of Buddhism, politics enables the conditions in which we may better seek our salvation. As Matthew Moore puts it in his writing on Buddhism and politics, "legitimacy is . . . about creating conditions to allow human beings to make spiritual progress."[93] At the same time, of course, there is the question of how to go about that progress in the midst of domination. *Oxherding Tale* seems to offer a vision of how, when politics fails, spiritual pursuits may create in us the capacities to make political change.

I take this vision of Johnson's seriously, and would not go so far as some other critics as to see in it the evacuation of "actual politics," since well-being and mental health are themselves fundamental political concerns.[94] But *Oxherding Tale*, in spite of its claims to upending the distinction between self and world, may in the end rely too much on the capacity of an enlightened self to make a difference. The difficult questions of *how* to rebuild a world—of institutions, of labor, of conflicting passions, the very kinds of things that damage the characters throughout the narrative—are perhaps too quickly removed at the close through the claim of insight. ("He can't be caught, he's *already* free. Not legally, but you know what Ah'm sayin.") The weight of the narrative, seemingly erased in the utopic ending, manifests the possibilities for failure that in fact carry into the future. After all, the final words of the novel look ahead to the significant period of Reconstruction and its promises. In that time, in spite of the earnest effort of men like Hawkins to remake the U.S. republic without racism, the result was tragedy and betrayal.

I have experienced some element of each of the visions of Buddhism discussed in this chapter. I have felt Johnson's hope for it as a path to pure liberation. I have experienced Head's disillusionment and desire to find (or in her case, found) something new. And I was deeply impacted by my experience with Tibetans in exile, similar to what Sarduy's novel depicts. But, of course, I also have not experienced many of the elements in these narratives, especially the oppressions of colonization, patriarchy, transphobia, homophobia, and racism. In times of great injustice, an interest in Buddhism can feel to me like a distraction from the political matters at hand. But this feeling ignores the meaningful and ongoing histories of Buddhist diversity and the ways struggles for justice can rely on Buddhism as a philosophical and spiritual source for power. That does not mean that it is a perfect source of justice; it too must be continually engaged and uplifted and transformed by communities clamoring for justice. Each of these novels shows us both the depths and the limits of modern Buddhism's capacity to confront terror. It can be a progressive force, a patriarchal force, a site of tragedy, and an archive of sources to enable reinvention. If one overarching theme does emerge, it is that Buddhist liberation in global modernity is not a solipsistic act but a continual struggle for both social and personal transformation.

4

AUTHENTICITY

If there remains an indissoluble tension between who we are and how we can act in a divisive social world, what does that mean for authenticity—the idea that there is a direct connection between our beliefs and actions? The desire to overcome this tension has been central to the formation of the modern self, and it is something I have felt very intensely in my life. Perhaps there was nothing that I wanted more from Buddhism than for it to make me an authentic person. When I arrived in Dharamsala, authenticity for me meant being someone who had no separation from the world around him. A line that I had read in high school Spanish class, where Gabriel García Márquez describes one of his characters, named this for me: "his movements had that suave efficacy of people accustomed to reality."[1] To be authentic, I believed, was to appear in the world smoothly, effectively, and elegantly, even in difficult moments (to have a manner of stumbling with grace). I saw it in some others around me—the way that they seemed to fit into a world that I found unbearably alienating. I knew I would never be like them, but thought that if I could get out of my head, I could at least *be like me.*

The idea of authenticity permeates modern culture. It drives our sense of being principled: to be authentic is have your beliefs and your practices align. To do so, you must be of your moment. A person is authentic to the extent that they do not simply follow the crowd but also do not imagine that they can escape the limits of their time and place. To once again paraphrase Marx: the authentic person makes their own life, but not in conditions of their own choosing.[2] The French apostle of authenticity, Jean-Paul Sartre, defined it in relation to a given "situation": "For us, man is defined first of all as a being 'in a situation.' That means that he forms a synthetic whole with his situation—biological, economic, political, cultural, etc. He cannot be distinguished from his situation, for it forms him and decides his possibilities; but inversely, it is he who gives it meaning by making his choices within it and by it."[3] Authenticity is not to be found by escaping the situation, but by recognizing it and living up to its demands.

Some critics have suggested that authenticity in this sense is *only* a modern problem, and that people in earlier ages were "more authentic" simply because they had fewer choices. In other words, because they lived automatically within their immediate culture and did not seek other possibilities, authenticity did not even present itself as a problem. Charles Taylor, for example, has suggested that authenticity is born of an era of individualism (sundering us from our authentic base in the community), instrumental reason (sundering us from the non-calculative aspects of our soul), and the effects these have on our political lives (living alienated from impersonal bureaucracies that dictate our forms of life).[4] But although modern conditions may have exacerbated the issue, it's important to remember that this feeling of being sundered from the authentic or true has appeared in other places and times. It was, for example, felt already by the prophet Isaiah nearly three thousand years ago: "These people draw near with their mouths and honor me with their lips, while their hearts are far from me, and their worship of me is a human commandment learned by rote."[5] And as Robert Sharf has noted, this kind of critique recurs throughout Buddhist history as well: "The rhetoric of reform—of returning to an earlier, more pristine monasticism oriented toward lofty soteriological goals—has been a ubiquitous if not beguiling trope throughout Buddhist history."[6] Buddhists, in spite of my hopes, have themselves wanted to be more authentic. The term may be new, and it certainly speaks to different conditions at different times, but the basic problem cannot be confined to the alienating effects of modernity without falling into somewhat trite visions of the human past.

Perhaps this is why Martin Heidegger—great philosopher, terrible human—proposed authenticity and inauthenticity as transhistorical and transcultural problems. While what authenticity *felt like* might be different in Freetown, Sierra Leone, than in Freiburg, Germany, the *possibility* of being authentic or inauthentic remained in each.[7] Each culture generates its own version of being authentic. Becoming authentic was a complex process for Heidegger, and I will discuss this more below in connection with J. D. Salinger. But the basic idea is that through confronting the possibility of our own death—the thing that makes us unique—we can realize the singularity of who we are. This does not mean that we fall out of our culture, but rather that we become the specific individual that our moment in time and place makes possible.[8]

Of course, such a concept is dependent on a rather narrow vision of culture and its relation to place. Heidegger was not exactly a great thinker of the real world, to put it unduly mildly. He could not envision in his philosophical system what it might mean to be authentic for someone like the young W. E. B. Du Bois, who famously described his "double consciousness" of living not only between African and American cultures but also through the oppression by the latter of the former.[9] Although Du Bois did not, so far as I know, write much about the term "authenticity," we can assume that for him there could be no possibility of an authentic life so specifically cultural that did not take up the heterogeneity of identity and the problem of oppression.

Thus, another question arises: To what is one being authentic? Does authenticity require us to have a substantivist and self-enclosed view of selves, cultures, or religions to which we can adhere? And wouldn't that promote aggressive forms of self-assertion, purist claims about nationalism, and even (in the cases of Heidegger's Nazi affiliations and the ethnic cleansing by Buddhists of Muslims in Myanmar) genocidal tendencies? Such questions have led philosophers of culture like Lewis Gordon to reject certain forms of the authenticity discourse entirely. The trouble, Gordon writes, is that "the search for the genuinely authentic tends to be one for the unadulterated, for what is not polluted by the impact of *outsiders*."[10] This leads of course to problematic forms of denying relations to both immediate and foreign others. But since those relations are always present and real, claims to authenticity result in "a paradox: The failure to be authentic is perhaps the most authentic human condition."[11]

But, as Gordon noted also in his other writings, authenticity has never only implied fidelity to an enclosed totality.[12] It has also meant having the ability to live with and recognize others in their full and diverse humanity (Gordon), the ability to find one's self within a communal horizon of meaning (Taylor), an "exigent" demand to link what one says one is and what one actually does in the world (Lionel Trilling), and the ability to come to terms with who one is in relation to a concrete situation (Sartre).[13]

My idea that Buddhism could help me become authentic in *all* of these ways—present and caring to others, ingrained in the world but not buffeted by it, genuine in everything said and done, and definitively of my moment—was not accidental. As I discussed in the introduction, modern Buddhists took up and transformed the modern idea of authenticity. Writers like D. T. Suzuki and Alan Watts promised that we could become authentic by overcoming our ego and embracing our transparency to all beings. As Watts put it, we would be "much more at home in the world, floating much more easily upon the ocean of transience and insecurity."[14] "Being Zen" was a new way to be authentic. The secret, Watts taught, was to embrace the flux of life. Authenticity wasn't a code or principle but an acceptance of the chaotic play of reality. By clearing out our mind, getting in touch with our body, and purging ourselves of subject-object dualisms, modern Zen offered a path to a life shorn of the desire for the world to be other than it is. And if to be authentic is to be meaningfully aligned with reality while remaining open to its flux of difference, it is hard to imagine a more authentic position than that of the Zen master.

Yet here more questions of authenticity arise. If reality is so complex and multifaceted, can the modern Zen master really be attuned to all of it—to the monastery as much as to the laity, to the politics of confronting fascism as much as to the tranquility of the mountain? After the end of World War II, for example, Suzuki was forced to conclude: "In *satori* [the experience of enlightened insight] there is a world of *satori*. However, by itself *satori* is unable to judge the right and wrong of war. With regard to disputes in the ordinary world, it is necessary to employ

intellectual discrimination."[15] We might say with Zen's supporters that Suzuki shows his authenticity here, admitting to
the limits of his philosophy. But we might equally say with his
detractors that a more authentic philosophy would have recognized this *before* the war.[16]

This has led some critics to question the value of both Buddhism and the quest for authenticity. Perhaps the best known is
the popular philosopher of culture Slavoj Žižek. Žižek's criticisms of Buddhism go back nearly two decades, as do critical
responses to his claims, so I won't go into the problems with his
writing on Buddhism in general.[17] On the topic of authenticity,
however, Žižek has something very interesting to say: "The difficult thing to accept is that one can be totally authentic in overcoming one's false Self and yet still commit horrible crimes—
and vice versa, of course: one can be a caring subject, morally
committed to the full, while existing in an inauthentic world of
illusion with regard to oneself."[18] This is an essential realization—
that the moment of realization itself is not sufficient; it must be
coupled with values and struggle. This understanding was at the
heart of my own early disenchantment with Buddhist studies.
But to rest here is to ignore that there are several schools of
contemporary Buddhism—the most prominent perhaps being
"Critical Buddhism"—that are similarly concerned with an
excessive emphasis on topics like "harmony" that may mask the
violence that creates such a stable social order.[19]

And Žižek's conclusion goes too quickly to a resolution in
the opposite extreme: "In order to be fully engaged ethico-
politically," he writes, "it is necessary to exit the 'inner peace' of
one's subjective authenticity."[20] But it is unclear why we should
draw this conclusion. Just because there is no necessary relation
between caring for one's self and being an engaged ethical subject, it does not follow that the opposite is true: that it is

necessary to give up on inner peace in order to become politically engaged. Žižek effectively dismantles a false connection only to reconstruct it at the other extreme. Certainly the struggle for inner peace can be correlated to political struggle. And given that many revolutionary movements fail because of infighting, or fail after they succeed by replicating the very structures they overthrew, some kind of work on the self may be absolutely necessary. This is something that modern Buddhism has stressed again and again, even if, at times, it has fallen too far on the inner peace side of the spectrum.

In the rest of this final chapter, I will consider two novels that take up the relation between "being Zen" and being authentic in the context of these broad philosophical concerns. In the first, J. D. Salinger's *Franny and Zooey* (1955/1957/1961), the characters' attempts to live out authentic Zen lives amid postwar American affluence are nearly undone by the social world that surrounds them. In the second, Zadie Smith's *The Autograph Man* (2002), the main character accidentally becomes authentic through a very inauthentic form of Zen. My argument across the texts will be that authenticity—in any of its forms—is not to be entirely rejected or absolutely affirmed, but rather contingently embodied as part of an evolving, plural self. The point is to find a means of ordering one's doctrine and practice while acknowledging that it is but one possible ordering. Sometimes in life we need to be suave and efficacious, graceful in all our movements and witty in our responses. But sometimes being like this runs the risk of becoming over-aligned with malignant times and too "in the flow" to put up sufficient resistance. To admit this is not to give up on authenticity but to recognize its specific uses, and that what we have at best are authentic moments alongside embarrassingly—and necessarily—inauthentic ones.

AUTHENTICITY BY FAILURE AND
THE FAILURE OF AUTHENTICITY

In spite of all the famous cursing by Holden Caulfield, J. D. Salinger's most famous character, the worst insult he gives in *Catcher in the Rye* (1951) is to call somebody a "phony." The word appears about three dozen times in the narrative, and it covers just about everyone. Caulfield, in a climactic moment, even wonders if he himself might become a phony. He is thinking about lawyers. He considers that there might be some good to being a lawyer, but he doubts that even if he really were committed to saving the innocent, he could ever know if it was in fact for the moral good or because he wanted everyone to think so. "How would you know you weren't being a phony? The trouble is, you *wouldn't*."[21]

In this context, Caulfield imagines another scene of what he would really like to be, a scene in which nonphoniness (his authenticity) would be secured. It is a poignant vision from which the novel draws its title. He recalls (incorrectly, his interlocutor tells him) a line from a Robert Burns poem: "If a body catch a body coming through the rye." (The correct line, it turns out, is "meet a body," but Caulfield continues.) What he'd like to be is someone out on the edge of a field of rye where all these kids are playing. The field is perilously close to a cliff edge. There is no grown-up there besides himself, and his task is to catch the kids as they exit the field, before they fall over the edge. One after another, and forever, it seems.

In this dream, Holden seeks an authentic position in the world, and he recognizes it as an endless sacrificial job with no chance of recognition. There is no possibility of being a phony because there is no possibility of *amour-propre*, yet at the same time there is the necessary community—the children—to

ensure the genuine purpose of the task. Ironically, the achievement of personal authenticity is based on an inauthentic rendering of the text ("catch a body" instead of "meet a body"). One
could certainly argue that Caulfield's problem is that he just
wants to catch and release, rather than actually connect and
meet. But one could equally claim that part of what makes his
vision so authentic, so opposed to phoniness, is that it has such
an original (inauthentic) relation to the original text.

The key connection for our purposes is between textual
authenticity and personal authenticity. It is a theme that pre-
dominates in Salinger's fiction, and, I will argue, is fundamental to his engagement with Zen Buddhism, especially as he
learned it from the writings of D. T. Suzuki. (There are even
rumors that Salinger attended Suzuki's lectures in New York.[22])
Although Salinger was unlikely to be aware of criticisms of
Suzuki's presentation of Zen as "Westernized" and "inauthentic," he certainly had reasons to doubt that Zen itself was being
authentically practiced in the United States. In *Seymour—An
Introduction*, for example, the narrator, Buddy, remarks that
"Zen is rapidly becoming a rather smutty, cultish word to the
discriminating ear, and with great, if superficial justification. (I
say superficial because pure Zen will surely survive its Western
champions . . . Pure Zen . . . will be here even after the snobs
like me have departed.)"[23] "Western Zen" is not an authentic
version of Zen, and thus the critique of it being promulgated in
contemporary America is itself inauthentic; it critiques a bad
copy as if it were the thing itself. The ironic layer here, again
one that I doubt Salinger would have been aware of, is that what
is called "pure Zen" is itself a modern construction by Suzuki
and others.

This in turn raises another question, one generally over-
looked by Salinger's critics, although it seems to me to be at the

heart of Salinger's later fiction: Can one live an authentic Zen life in modern America? Is Zen a path to overcoming phony-ism, or does it inevitably lead to the pious vacuity for which Buddy says it is rightly rebuked? Although recent critical appraisals of Salinger by critics like Amy Hungerford and Ross Posnock have helpfully turned attention to the religious themes in his work, both have also missed the central contestation about the plausibility of Zen that his characters enact.[24] Hungerford, in attempting to articulate the nondoctrinal heart of "postmodern belief," erases the specificity of Zen. Posnock, at the opposite extreme, finds everything that Salinger says to be entirely "Zen," smoothing out the real dilemmas that Salinger's fiction poses. Focusing on the same text they do—*Franny and Zooey*—I will suggest that the specificity of Zen matters very much to the characters, in large part because they find them-selves incapable of living fully in accord with its demands. To be authentic, they will need not to become Zen but to achieve a spectral illumination about its meaning for their lives.

The narrative action of *Franny and Zooey* takes place as Franny has come home from university in the midst of a ner-vous breakdown, precipitated by her attempt to "learn the Jesus prayer." The prayer is a technique passed down by her older brothers, Seymour and Buddy, through their copy of *The Way of the Pilgrim*. This religious text calls on its readers to learn how to pray without cessation through the act of repeating the prayer, "Lord Jesus Christ, have mercy on me" until "the prayer becomes self-active."[25] Franny tries to explain this to her boy-friend, who in turn attempts to psychologize her desire for "reli-gious experience," and then she passes out.[26] She revives, but the damage seems to have been done, and when we find her next, it's at her family home, lying on the couch, crying for hours on end.

As the story unfolds, we learn that *The Way of the Pilgrim* is one of several mystical religious texts that Franny and her brother Zooey were taught by Buddy and Seymour as part of their homeschooling. Buddy reveals his pedagogic intentions in a letter to Zooey some years after the fact: "[We began your education] not with a quest for knowledge at all but with a quest, as Zen would put it, for no-knowledge. Dr. Suzuki says somewhere that to be in a state of pure consciousness— *satori*—is to be with God before he said, Let there be light."[27] Buddy continues, with a hint of melancholy: "That, anyway, was the big idea."[28] The failure of the big idea is signaled first by the fact of Seymour's suicide, and then by the ongoing struggles that both Franny and Zooey have with this education. The question now is whether or not the spiritual quest bequeathed to them can be realized in their bourgeois, materialist conditions.

The specificity of "Dr. Suzuki" is important for understanding this situation. In the mid-twentieth century, Zen exploded onto the international scene, especially in the United States. The man behind the boom was Suzuki (who did not in fact have a doctorate). He was a soft-spoken Japanese man who had lived, studied, and lectured extensively in Europe and America throughout his life. In the 1950s, he graced the pages of *Time, Newsweek*, and *The New Yorker*. When he lectured at Columbia in the same decade, people on the New York art and intellectual scene, including possibly Salinger, flocked uptown to follow his courses.[29] His writings had a remarkable global and interdisciplinary reach. A still minimal list of those who cited him as an influence would include Jorge Luis Borges, Octavio Paz, Roland Barthes, Michel Foucault, Martin Heidegger, C. G. Jung, Agnes Martin, John Cage, Jack Kerouac, Yoko Ono, bell hooks, and Salinger.[30]

The centerpiece of Suzuki's Zen was his interpretation of *satori*, which he often translated as "awakening," "enlightenment," or "enlightenment-experience." "To understand Zen," he wrote, "it is essential to have an experience known as *satori*, for without this one can have no insight into the truth of Zen."[31] Satori for Suzuki is when we experience the universe exactly as it is—not without any thinking, but with a kind of thinking that is absolutely aligned with what is. Suzuki calls this being "transparent" to the universe. "For here is no negation, no affirmation, but a plain fact, a pure experience, the very foundation of our being and thought. All the quietness and emptiness one might desire in the midst of the most active mentation lies therein."[32] There is at once activity and quietness.

The relationship to authenticity is to be found here too. If part of what makes modern life feel so inauthentic is the falsity of advertising language, the flood of information that cannot be comprehended, and the self-conscious knowledge of one's place in history, Zen promises to level all of these in a stroke—or better, in silence. It is not in grasping the world that one finds authentic being, and it is not in some mythic Romantic self. Rather, it is in undoing the very idea of self, in the recognition that the universe is nothing more—and nothing less—than a vital emptiness that grows into forms that inevitably transform and return to emptiness. It doesn't matter if one catches another body or meets another body in the end; that's just a linguistic problem, and authenticity is beyond language. Abandoning language and the idea that truth was ever available in it, we find that we are all equally nothing and everything.

But Suzuki also offered authenticity in concrete ways: he *embodied* it in his simple demeanor and carefully crafted image, and he *culturalized* it, suggesting that Japan as a nation showed the possibility of being Zen (even if that cultural essence had gone horribly awry in the war).[33] To a generation adrift in post-war trauma, affluence, and contradiction, Suzuki showed that it was possible to be otherwise. And, by appearing as an "other" himself who was nevertheless perfectly comfortable in American culture, Suzuki suggested that one could achieve enlightenment and still act with "suave efficacy" in the world. John Cage and Alan Watts (like Charles Johnson) cite Suzuki as saying that life after satori is like everyday experience, but a few feet off the ground.[34] You are in this world, but at the same time, you experience it in a new way, full of quiet, calm, wonder, and perspicacity.

One might wonder whether such a marvelous experience is possible, or even desirable. The debate continues, but decades of scholarship in Europe, Japan, and the United States have responded to this question with a resounding no. Hakugen Ichikawa, for example, contended that satori should signify not only this moment of calm but also a simultaneous experience of understanding the social world.[35] Hakamaya Noriaki has argued that satori is in fact a meaningless aim, since it is only being awakened as from sleep, not gaining enlightened insight into the true structure of reality.[36] Robert Sharf and others have even suggested that satori—as a mental state that is beyond discrimination and judgment—can be used to create pliant subjects, and thus was part of the ideological framework of Japanese fascism.[37] And even those within Buddhist studies who defend Suzuki, such as Victor Hori, believe that the idea of "pure consciousness" goes too far and disables Zen acolytes from understanding how it is that Zen relates to everyday, impure experience. "There is no Zen enlightenment beyond thought and language in a realm of pure consciousness," Hori states unequivocally.[38] I have argued elsewhere that this scholarship misses some of what is important in Suzuki's thought, but the point here is simply that Suzuki's ideas are contested in Buddhist studies scholarship, while left largely unquestioned in literary studies.[39] This is especially important because they are contested in the fictional accounts themselves.

The debate over the plausibility of enacting Suzuki's ideas is central to Salinger's *Franny and Zooey*. Posnock notes that the story "insists on the distance between the spiritual ideals the main characters articulate and the pettiness of their behavior,"[40] but he goes on to conclude that the distance *can* be overcome "via the radical critique of instrumentality or attachment found in Eastern and Christian mysticism."[41] In other words, by overcoming our desire to grasp and manipulate the world, we can be freed from the mental habits that block our path to enlightenment. Posnock's book is an intriguing model of a wandering literary criticism that takes renunciation and its potential for creativity very seriously. But it runs a genuine risk in statements like this, which tend to level all modes of renunciation into general themes. He is thus mostly unconcerned with whether he is quoting Suzuki or the *Tao te Ching*, or a generalization of both in the late work of Roland Barthes. This allows Posnock some rather lovely riffs on Zen, such as the possibility of being "in tune with the Zen edict that abolishes closure and hierarchy for receptivity to the ubiquity of the divine in the things of this world" (a rather idiosyncratic but not implausible modern Zen gloss on the idea of buddha nature).[42] But by ignoring the actuality of Buddhism, Posnock eventually turns away from the rather bedeviling question he points to in *Franny and Zooey*: What *are* we to make of that troubling gap between the textual inscription of such a possible life and the embodied possibility of actually living it? This is the problem at the heart of Sharf's critique of modern Buddhism: "scholars read ideological prescription as phenomenological description."[43] In other words, they think that because there is an ideal in Zen, it necessarily follows that that ideal is perfectly embedded in the culture. But this is rarely, if ever the case. And that matters here because it is also what is at stake in the novel.

This problem is similarly glossed over in Hungerford's reading. For her, *Franny and Zooey* is a perfect embodiment of mid-century American religion, which strove to unite religious belief with pluralism.[44] How does one hold on to faith without assuming that one's faith is more correct than everyone else's? Hungerford suggests that this requires a balance between specificity and transcendent truth that the characters propagate through the idea of acting: Zooey "solves the tension between syncretism and specificity, between wisdom and no-knowledge, by transforming a theory of religion into a theory of acting."[45] This is because in acting one may embody specific role after specific role, but then always return to a kind of primordial silence from which the acting draws its power. Curiously, Hungerford only concerns herself with the specificity of Christianity as enactment in her brief reading of the novel, in spite of the fact that the idea of the primordial silence, of "no-knowledge," comes from Suzuki. When citing the passage about Buddy and Seymour's teaching of satori, she literally erases Suzuki's name by ellipses.[46] And when she gives a list of religious figures who have inspired the brothers, she doesn't pause to note the one exception, "Mu-Mon-Kwan," which is not a person but a collection of kōan.[47] These details suggest that Zen, and especially Suzuki's presentation of it, is being singled out, and perhaps precisely for the reasons Buddy gives in *Seymour*: because its promised ability to deliver authenticity just does not seem to be working in modern America.

Suzuki's Zen promised something very specific: that there was an experience of purity available in this world that could change the entire nature of everyday life, making us the authentic creatures we all seek to be. This was not Zen wisdom from time everlasting. This was a spiritual doctrine carefully updated for the modern world. When we focus on Suzuki's place in the novel, we discover that Salinger's characters are struggling to discover whether or not the experience he offered is possible. And what the narrative ultimately suggests is much closer to Suzuki's critics. Franny and Zooey find that Suzuki's Zen fails to offer them a new mode of being in the world. Instead, it leaves them stuck between the imagined ideal of their brothers and the sordid realities of commercialist America.

We can see this beginning in Zooey's discussion of his sister's situation with their mother. He pins the blame squarely on the older brothers' failed education: "We're *freaks*, the two of us, Franny and I . . . I swear to you, I could murder them both [Buddy and Seymour] . . . The great teachers. The great emancipators. My God. I can't even sit down to lunch with a man any more and hold up my end of a decent conversation."[48] Zooey is too obsessed with the spiritual ideals of his brothers to be able to function in the daily world. His brothers never actually gave him spiritual emancipation, and unfortunately the "social liberation" they offered was only from the ability to be a good friend! He repeats the same lament to Franny herself later: "We're freaks . . . with freakish standards. We're the Tattooed Lady, and we're never going to have a minute's peace, the rest of our lives, until everybody else is tattooed, too."[49] They were brought up with a spiritual value system that is completely unrecognizable to the rest of the world, so they constantly crash up against the values of that world. They are always seeking the before-the-world, the authentic moment of satori that is the unconditioned beginning of the universe, and instead finding themselves in the materialist conditions of this world.

Material things are everywhere in the story. The clash between things and the conditions that enable enlightenment (becoming unconditioned, in classical descriptions of nirvana) comes across particularly nicely in a classic pun from German Romanticism. In a fragment from *Miscellaneous Remarks*, Novalis wrote, "We seek everywhere the unconditioned (*das Unbedingte*), and we find only things (*Dinge*)."[50] *Franny and Zooey* at times reads like an updated version of this claim within the conditions of modern-day American materialism. Indeed, as the characters seek enlightenment, they keep finding only things. Their apartment may not be "impressively large," but it does have "accumulated furnishings [that] might have lent a snug appearance to a banquet hall in Valhalla."[51] A description of just one bathroom's medicine cabinet lists forty items (not including duplicates), and "inconceivably or no, quite a good deal more."[52] Franny and Zooey are spiritual freaks in this materialist world, and they can never quite fully separate the two. Thus Franny states: "Just because I'm choosy about what I want—in this case, en*light*enment, or peace, instead of money or pres*tige* or *fame* or any of those things—doesn't mean I'm not as egotistical and self-seeking as everybody else."[53] She seeks the unconditioned but suddenly finds that it too is a thing, a social commodity. Of course, Buddhism always had a relation to economy.[54] But a general relation to economy is not as undermining as the specific modern power of money, which, as Lionel Trilling notes in his book on authenticity, is "in short . . . the principle of the inauthentic in human existence" since it has the power to transform anything into its opposite simply by paying for it.[55]

Franny and Zooey's education not only put them at odds with the vanities of the world but also failed to actually help them transcend that world. This is, again, the double pain invoked when Zooey calls Buddy and Seymour "the great emancipators": they did not emancipate their siblings from the world or from its vanities. Modernized Buddhist wisdom simply cannot perform its task of rendering Franny and Zooey authentic because they do not find the right conditions for its enactment. Whether or not they have really lost the object—the other world—they eventually decide that they must learn to act as if they have. This is their final lesson to each other.

In the novel's closing sequence, Zooey attempts one last time to overcome Franny's spiritual malaise—and, by extension, his own—by impersonating Buddy on a phone call to her. The jig is quickly up, but Franny agrees to hear Zooey out through his long-winded advice:

> "If you've had a freakish education, at least *use* it, *use* it. You can [seek enlightenment] from now till doomsday, but if you don't realize that the only thing that counts in the religious life is de*tach*ment, I don't see how you'll ever even move an *inch* . . . It's this business of desi*r*ing, if you want to know the goddam truth, that makes an actor in the first place . . . Somewhere along the line—in one damn incarnation or another, if you like—you not only had a hankering to be an . . . actress but to be a *good* one. . . . The only thing you can do now, the only *religious* thing you can do, is *act*. . . . You'd better get busy, though, buddy . . . You're lucky if you get time to sneeze in this goddam *phenomenal* [my emphasis] world . . . I used to worry about that. I don't worry about it very much any more. At least I'm still in love with Yorick's skull . . . I *hanker* after an honorable goddam skull like Yorick's. And so do *you* . . . You had the exact same goddam freakish upbringing I did, and if you don't know by this time what kind of *skull* you want . . . then what's the use of talking?"[56]

The question for Franny and Zooey is what to do with the fact that they are spiritual freaks, brought up to believe in a world that no longer seems available to them. They cannot live the religious life, with its call for detachment. They simply cannot get back to that Suzukian moment before. They live in the after, in the light of creation, so they must learn how to create. "The only thing that counts in the religious life is detachment," *but* "It's this business of des*i*ring, if you want to know the goddam truth, that makes an actor in the first place." To turn to acting is to turn against the renunciation of desire that their religious upbringing demands.[57] It is also to learn that one has to lie a little, assume the death of the other world, in order to end the in-betweenness. For Franny and Zooey this means that rather than become one with everything, they must become radically singular and find their own, individual paths.[58] Like Yorick, the famous jester whose skull is eulogized by Hamlet, they must be so deeply themselves that their whole personalities will be encased in their skulls.

This is a philosophical orientation that clearly departs from Suzuki's selfless Zen. Suzuki, or at least Buddy's Suzuki, recommends overcoming the self via proximity to the planet's original birth, but what we find here is advice about becoming individualized through one's own death. Buddy says that this citation about satori is "somewhere" in Suzuki. Suzuki in fact says it in many places. One possible source for Salinger would have been the popular 1956 collection of Suzuki's selected writings, edited by William Barrett.[59] Barrett, then a professor of philosophy at New York University, was also a mainstream conduit of existentialism into the United States. There is an apocryphal story, recorded in Barrett, that Heidegger said when reading Suzuki: "If I understand this man correctly ... this is what I have been trying to say in all my writings." But Barrett marked also their differences: "there is much in [Heidegger] that is not in Zen, but also very much in Zen that is not in Heidegger."[60] One of the key distinctions, at least with the Heidegger of *Being and Time*, is the focus on death. For Suzuki, selflessness ultimately means that there is no singular subject who dies. For Heidegger, it is through the singularity of our own death that we achieve individuation.[61]

Thus the concept of finding one's own unique project in "this phenomenal world" (as Zooey says) through a relation to death is in fact much closer to Heidegger's "existentialism" than Suzuki's Zen, which is associated in the novel with not death, but the birth of the universe itself.[62] Franny and Zooey appear to have abandoned Suzuki's universal authenticity for Heidegger's individual form. Indeed, there is an uncanny resemblance between Zooey's advice and the extremely popular summary of Heidegger's thought in Barrett's *What Is Existentialism?*, published by the *Partisan Review* in 1947. There Barrett gives a general overview of Heidegger's ideas about being-toward-death, which he would present in slightly more poetic language a few years later:

> Only by taking my death into myself, according to Heidegger, does an *authentic* existence become possible for me. Touched by this interior angel of death, I cease to be the impersonal and social One among many . . . and I am free to become myself. Though terrifying, the taking of death into ourselves is also liberating: *It frees us from servitude to the petty cares that threaten to engulf our daily life* and thereby opens us to the *essential projects* by which we can make our lives personally and significantly our own. Heidegger calls this the condition of "freedom-toward-death" or "resoluteness."[63]

A resolute actor of her own life is precisely what Franny now becomes. Confronting her singularity as an actor (which is to say, her singularity as someone who takes on a project from within the possibilities of her social world), she feels—at least momentarily—freed from the petty cares of bourgeois life.

After Zooey hangs up, Franny listens to the dial tone. "She *appeared* to find it extraordinarily beautiful to listen to . . . But she *seemed* to know, too, when to stop listening to it, *as if* all of what little or much wisdom there is in the world were suddenly hers . . . She *seemed* to know just what to do next, too." She lies down to go to sleep, but before she does, "she just lay quiet, smiling at the ceiling."[64] Her sudden resoluteness is that of an actor in a "phenomenal world"; thus everything she does is written about in the language of appearances. In deciding that she is but a finite, phenomenal subject, she recovers acting as her "essential project" and abandons her quest for something greater than being who she is. She cannot experience the ultimate light of all things, but she can embody her singularity as an actress on the world's stage. That does not mean she is fake, or "phony," in Salinger's famous word. In the world of this novel, a phony is someone who tries to live purely in an impure world, who tries to give up desire in a world saturated by it, who seeks another world rather than this one.

And yet, it would be equally phony to presume that there is no Suzuki-like insight in this moment. Heidegger's authentic subjects (at least in his early writings) do not have blissful calm as their end goal, but this is what Franny claims as she lies smiling at the ceiling. She appears to have achieved a Suzukian calm via a Heideggerian method. In this sense, an analysis like Posnock's speaks to something significant in this fiction. There is a veritable peace here, one that matters, even if Franny holds on to it for just an instant. After all, that instant will continue to reverberate throughout her life, as anyone who has experienced a moment of pure bliss can attest. To ignore the power of this moment, then, is just as phony as to presume that one can live one's whole life in such blinding insight. This is the cause of Kurtz's mania, Marlow's resignation, and Seymour's depression. We must accept that even after such a moment of clearing, we inevitably find ourselves back in the world. To repeat Suzuki's postwar claim: "In *satori* there is a world of *satori*. However, by itself *satori* is unable to judge the right and wrong of war. With regard to disputes in the ordinary world, it is necessary to employ intellectual discrimination." The trick is to learn both sides of this problem, to both experience the miraculous feeling of nonverbal transcendence and remember that that moment is just one among many in the complex force field of being alive. Perhaps, if Franny learns something at the end of the novel, it is that she can keep striving for those moments of unmediated happiness, but she will also need to learn to live as a singular individual—a conventional truth—in this mediated world.

Why should we not experience the world as a shifting space of possible relations to authenticity? Why should we not have available to us kitsch Zen and pure Zen and many other Zens, and Heideggerian and Sartrean authenticity too, so long as we are aware of the implications of each? Each offers a spectral illumination of our existence. We may find that one situation calls us to be resolute subjects with some tragic mastery while another forces a comic consolation and still another opens onto the exquisite feeling of no-knowledge. To suggest that one or any of these conditions trumps all the others is, as Mishima would say, to fail to recognize the fundamental diversity of life. Any individual may find that their personal radar tends to a particular mode, but they will likely also find that other modes speak to hidden dispositions in their soul. This openness is not an evasion of choice but a claim that the demands of choice are multiple and ongoing.

Thus, although Salinger's characters bend toward Heidegger's version of authenticity, I do not think they abandon the Suzukian ideal of selfless meditative calm. They only seem to suggest that, in the midst of midcentury American affluence, trying to *always* live as Suzuki recommended was more likely to drive one to madness or suicide than to produce authentic insight. I think it was on these grounds that so many of Suzuki's followers turned toward the partial illuminations he offered rather than the grand discovery of arriving at the world before God said, "Let there be light." Those who were too disappointed to accept this—like myself at a certain age—foolishly abandoned his work altogether.[65] *Franny and Zooey* offers another option: less a dismantling of Suzuki than a Conrad-like critique of taking his advice too far. Being fully authentic in Suzuki's sense in a time and place as inauthentic as consumerist America meant falling out of the social world altogether—something that Buddy suffers and Franny briefly experiences. It is also something that goes slightly awry in *Cobra* and *Oxherding Tale*. But that does not mean we should lose the power of Suzuki's voice altogether. Salinger gives us a melodramatic narrative to show this. But sometimes to arrive at the insight of how to embed Zen in this world—or a similar one—we might need a more lighthearted approach.

AUTHENTICITY BY ACCIDENT

Lama Zopa Rinpoche, a popular Nepali-Tibetan monk who works extensively in the United States, claims that his Animal Liberation Fund has released more than 200,000,000 animals ("and counting") from samsara.[66] Part of the work is actually releasing the animals from captivity. But the full samsara release has to do with reciting some mantras before they are let go. This is what liberates them not only from cages but also from the cycle of reincarnation. So far as I can tell, the text on which his practice is based is a sutra that he has discussed in various lectures. In the story, a being becomes enlightened extremely quickly. It is revealed that his enlightenment is actually the result of an accident that happened in a past life when he was a fly. Sighting some cow dung floating on the water, the fly landed on it. The current in the water caused the fly to circumambulate a stupa, and the power of this ritual earned him the tremendous merit that later led to his enlightenment. Even though, Lama Zopa explains, the fly "was acting totally out of attachment to the smell of the cow dung" and had no virtue, the power of the pilgrimage still mattered.[67] In this story, then, the pursuit of the smell of shit leads to accidental enlightenment.

I do not think that Zadie Smith is aware of this story, for if she were, I have little doubt that it would have appeared in *The Autograph Man*. Indeed, the novel might as well have been called *The Accident Man*. It is the story of Alex-Li Tandem, a Jewish-Chinese-British philographer, or autograph man. Philographer itself is a word and a profession that he learns by accident when his seat at a wrestling match turns out to be next to that of Joseph Klein, an amateur autograph collector who becomes one of Alex's best friends. An accident of human cells—a tumor—kills Alex's kindhearted father, Li-Jin, at the same event. The story then jumps ahead to the older Alex (and friends Joseph, Adam, and Mark), the night after Alex has had a car accident after a bad drug trip. The first physical description of the older Alex is that he has "Accidental eyes ([Mark]

Rubinfine's term: halfway between Oriental and Occidental)."[68] The story proceeds with one accident after another propelling Alex's life, or, as the narrator later puts it, "the accident we call our lives."[69]

The series of accidents that have created Alex have not turned out so badly. He has a beautiful and caring girlfriend, Esther, whom he treats terribly; three close and intelligent childhood friends, who stick with him throughout his idiotic escapades; and a relatively lucrative job in the autograph trade. His white whale of an autograph is Kitty Alexander, a onetime movie star who signed very little and quickly faded from the limelight. He writes her constant letters, which it turns out her overprotective manager, Max, has been hiding, until through a series of accidents, of course, she goes to his apartment and finds the letters. Taken with them, she at last sends Alex an autograph, which he opens, in private and on drugs, the evening before his car accident. The authenticity of the signature is thus universally doubted. But, as it so happens, he is about to fly to New York for an autograph convention. He meets Kitty, rescues her from Max by taking her to London, and makes her a small fortune by selling her autographs. Max helps out by declaring her dead in his paranoia, greatly increasing the value of her items. At the novel's close, Alex's friends finally rope him into saying Kaddish for his deceased father.

The novel is structured in two parts: "The Kabbalah of Alex-Li Tandem" and "The Zen of Alex-Li Tandem." Each uses a classic trope of Kabbalah or Zen based on the number 10 (a mere accident that it appears in both religions?): the ten *sefirot* (emanations of the infinite in our world) and the ten oxherding pictures (the series of paintings depicting the path to enlightenment I discussed in the section about Charles Johnson). Critics of the novel are divided on what to make of these religious framings: reject them as a ruse or find in them the key to the novel's meaning?[70] Many texts support diametrically opposed readings, but there is something specific about Smith's use of Zen that invites this dual possibility. Indeed, in a sense, they are two equally plausible answers to the question that plays out across the narrative: Can our artificial, image-obsessed, detached modern life produce anything like the feeling of holy illumination? It is no coincidence, for example, that the two philosophers who have starring roles in the book—Walter Benjamin and Ludwig Wittgenstein—were both Jews who reflected on such a possibility. The fact that any modern religious feeling will be bound up with image culture comes through the homonymic overlap of enlightenment and entertainment. Alex, for example, "was certainly suspicious of enlightenment. Above all he liked to be entertained." And later: "I'm just here for the— 'Enlightenment.' Actually, I was going to say entertainment."[71] Throughout, Zen itself is a form more of entertainment than of enlightenment. When it's invoked, it's almost always as a cliché: for example, when a sleazy autograph man says, "That's why we don't bid. We rise above. We are Zen." Or another: "Whatever . . . Me and the Doveman, here: we're Zen, we're down for whatever. Wax on, wax off."[72] The last line, as many will recognize, comes straight from Hollywood Zen (*The Karate Kid*).

When Salinger wrote, Zen, at least in its modernized forms, was already beginning to be associated with inauthenticity. By the time that Smith writes, it seems almost entirely subsumed into pop-cultural meaninglessness. Is there really nothing left, then, of the search for enlightenment? Is the Zen quest itself a wild-goose chase? Or is it possible that, even if only by accident, we might still arrive at some insight? The novel, I believe, is less about answering the question of whether we can be authentically Zen and more about probing the accidental conditions that might give us moments of authenticity.

"Accidents" and "authenticity" seem like opposing terms. Authenticity is an achievement, while an accidental fortune is just good luck. And we are also back here on the grounds of the sudden versus gradual debate: does enlightenment require eons of practice, or can we achieve it just by the accident of floating on the right pile of cow dung? But there is also a logic for understanding accident and authenticity as related. After all, if, in Sartre's sense, authenticity has to do with coming to terms with our situation, then it is hard to see how authenticity could begin with anything other than a recognition of the accidental history by which we were born as we were.

For Alex-Li Tandem, however, even this basic recognition hardly seems possible. He just can't get his life together. In the story's most wretched example, when he gets into his drug-induced car accident at the novel's beginning, Esther is in the car. Rather than ask her if she is okay, the first thing Alex does is to make sure that his newly arrived Kitty Alexander autograph has not been damaged. He is always groping at the wrong element. Whether or not being mindful would be a solution to Alex's problems is somewhat moot, since he is not exactly the type to start meditating in the first place. By the book's end, try as he might, he seems barely closer to being enlightened—to completing the oxherding tale—than he was at the beginning. In a poignant scene, he confesses to Adam that all the good he has tried to do—being more honest with Esther, helping Kitty, agreeing to go to his father's Kaddish—has not made him *feel* any better. Adam replies, "It *is* better, even if you can't feel it." Alex responds by laughing and chewing on his nail while he says, "There's no other good but *feeling* good . . . that's what good *is* . . . It's not a symbol of something else. Good has to be felt. That's good *in the world*."[73] But what Alex presents as his world-liness against Adam's religious interpretation is philosophically untenable. That Alex cannot feel good of course does not mean that good has not been done, or that others have not felt good. Alex is not depressed so much as repressed. And his repression is not the classical form of self-censorship. He is buttressing his ego in order to repress his capacity to feel what's good for others.

When Adam does not respond immediately, Alex asks if he wants to get high before the Kaddish. Adam waves this off: "I think we need to be present today, fully present."[74] And now, at last, for no immediately clear reason, Alex responds in a sur-prisingly authentic manner. He does not speak but rather makes a gesture. Hanging on Adam's wall are a series of autographs that he has bought from Alex over the years and compiled into a diagram of the ten sefirot. The last two points before the crown are Ludwig Wittgenstein (understanding) on the left and Virginia Woolf (wisdom) on the right. The top, the crown, represents nothingness, and so was left empty. Alex places his own father's autograph there. Nothingness as void has suddenly been replaced by nothingness as the selflessness of a parent's care. He finally stops repressing the connection. Whether or not this makes Alex feel good, it is clear that he has done some good in this moment.

I of course do not know Smith's intention in choosing Woolf and Wittgenstein, but they call up certain (accidental) associa-tions for me. In *Moments of Being*, Woolf attempts to articulate what makes a "scene" in a literary work. "A scene always *comes to the top*; arranged; representative. This confirms me in my instinc-tive notion—it is irrational; it will not stand argument—that we are sealed vessels afloat upon what it is convenient to call reality; at some moments, without a reason, without an effort, the sealing matter cracks; in floods reality; that is a scene."⁷⁵ A scene represents the moment when someone who has not been able to feel the good of the world, the reality of that goodness, suddenly opens to it. If this moment of Alex hanging his father's signature works as a scene, and I think it does, it may be because it shows us what it's like for a character to experience a scene—to watch them suddenly stop repressing and let reality flood in.

Again, I do not know if this is the passage that Smith alludes to in Woolf, but it, or something like it, provides a certain logic to me for the Wittgenstein pairing. In a lovely essay on David Foster Wallace, Smith engages with so many themes from *The Autograph Man* that the essay almost feels like autocriticism at times. At one point, she discusses Wallace's reading of Wittgenstein. According to Wallace, Wittgenstein accepts the schism between human language and reality. This leaves us with two options: either to feel forever sundered from others in our own language, or to realize "that for language even to be possible, it must always be a *function of relationships between persons*."⁷⁶ Language is not what separates us from the real world, if indeed we are separated, but rather what makes possible a connection to other humans. As Wittgenstein famously if cryptically put it, "to imagine a language means to imagine a form of life."⁷⁷ In other words, to understand what words mean, what they do, how they signify, and what they relate to, I cannot imagine them just in relation to a chain of other words (as in structural linguistics) but rather in relation to a whole way of making sense of the world.

But this only solves the problem so far as it goes, for the philosophical understanding of language is not the same as our actual recognition of others. We need both Wittgenstein and

Woolf: both the understanding of our connection and the (literary) scene that opens us to the connection itself. And even this may not be enough: we may also need Li-Jin, the selfless father who, even though he's annoyed by everything, still does his best to take his son to the wrestling match at the novel's opening, where the tumult and tumor end his life. Smith's analysis of Wallace continues: *"How do I recognize that other people are real, as I am?* And the strange, quasi-mystical answer was always the same, too. *You may have to give up your attachment to the 'self.'"* This is the "Zen" hope, the crossing of Alex's Jewishness and Chineseness, the logic of placing Li-Jin at the top of the sefirot, the place of "nothingness." He represents that selfless moment of abandoning the focus on one's own chaos to feel the chaos of others.

And yet, that still is too neat an answer. Smith continues: Wallace was no preacher of no-self. "On the contrary, he was a writer who placed himself 'in the hazard' of his own terms, undergoing them as real problems, both in life and on the page. . . . The struggle with ego, the struggle with the self, the struggle to allow other people to exist in their genuine 'otherness'—these were aspects of Wallace's own struggle." This is the struggle of anyone who must think through the relation between an ideal they hold and the way it may actually become embedded in their lives. It is, in other words, the struggle of modern Buddhism across its literary history. It appears here as Alex's struggle with selflessness, which, after all, may border on a classic modern Zen problem: indifference. How is losing one's self supposed to connect one with others, rather than disconnect one from the world entirely?

A possible solution is offered by Stanley Cavell, who reads Wittgenstein differently than Wallace. In a brilliant move, Cavell suggests that the two paths Wallace offers are, in a sense, the same: they both draw the wrong lesson from skepticism. The important truth of skepticism is not the claim that I cannot know the world exists. It is, rather, that *knowledge is not how I know the world exists*—whether by language or by immediate intuition. As Cavell puts it: "What skepticism suggests is that since we cannot know the world exists, its presentness to us cannot be a function of knowing. The world is to be *accepted*; as the presentness of other minds is not to be known, but acknowledged."[78] We don't need proof of the world. We *are* the proof of the world.

But even here the struggle of embeddedness remains. In another passage, Cavell says that what is being called for is "the tumbling of our ideas of the great and the important, as in conversion." He asks, "Who knows what will cause such a shift and tumbling? Sometimes satire works; sometimes shame does not. Sometimes the loss of old interest is so scary that one seeks to convert anything but oneself."[79] Throughout *The Autograph Man*, satire and shame have indeed not brought Alex the necessary realizations. Neither has the potential loss of Esther, the discovery of Kitty, the turn to trying to be good—at least not any of these on their own. If there is a conversion here to the reality of the social world, the only place where one can *feel* good, it may just come as an accidental result of Adam's desire not to get high in the climactic scene. But if part of what constitutes inauthenticity (according to Lewis Gordon) is the inability to recognize other humans, then the accidental moment of a scene, the slight jarring by an offhand remark that allows reality to fall in, may be one of the most important paths to authenticity.

This, I think, is the ultimate lesson of Smith's reading of Wallace's reflection on the problem of selflessness. "To Wallace, a gift truly was an accident; a chance, a fortuitous circumstance.

Born intelligent, born with perfect pitch, with mathematical ability, with a talent for tennis—in what sense are we ever the proprietors of these blessings? What rights accrue to us because of them? How could we ever claim to truly own them?" Because who we are is an accident, and because no matter what we do, no matter how well we design our lives, we may still fall prey to an accident, we must also be cognizant that we do not own anything, that we do not deserve anything, that we are responsible for our gifts but not owed anything because of them. Although "I" may not be the authentic one who deserves the credit or the reward, "I" am still responsible for the series of accidents that have accrued in making me what I am. Here again we have a plurality of authenticities: both ones that acknowledge accident and ones that take up that accident to design something better—perhaps a social system that recognizes the place of luck in our lives and redistributes awards accordingly. Pluralism in this sense is not a cop out. It's a claim that we waste a fair amount of time arguing over which is "more true," or at fundament true—what kind of authenticity or inauthenticity—when actually we should be learning to gain wisdom about what mode to rely on and when.

In this context, I would say that what the ten bulls represent in the novel is not the march toward enlightenment but the fact that one is always searching again for it, going through a process, unsure if one has found what matters. Nevertheless, there will be moments, glorious moments, when all the fragmented upheavals of our existence bind together in meaningful ways. Sometimes what we've been promised—even by an inauthentic version of something like Zen—changes our life, makes us more responsive to each other, more just with each other, more capable of hearing and responding to and challenging and being challenged by each other. At that moment, the authenticity of the thing that brought us there is merely accidental.

This was the lesson of my own experiences with modern Buddhism. I began by falling into an Orientalist trap of believing that "Asian wisdom" could overcome the doldrums of my modernity. In so doing, I ignored the lived reality—including the doldrums—of Buddhists themselves in modernity. Once I realized this on my trip to Dharamsala, I concluded that modern Buddhism was inauthentic and not worthy of further study. But this was equally foolish: that something has come about through accidents does not make it any less meaningful. Indeed, as Smith shows, much of what is meaningful in life is the product of chance as much as design.

It was lessons like these that I would eventually learn by studying modern Buddhism as it was embedded within literature. Following Buddhism through these narratives helped me see just how much modern Buddhism and literature had to teach about living well in a world where full enlightenment is impossible, where we keep reincarnating some of our worst mistakes in both our private and social lives, where our personal liberations often conflict with our political aspirations, and where our desire to be authentically ourselves proves an illusory goal. It teaches that though our issues will likely never be cleared away in a single enlightenment, we can work on ourselves and others to improve our shared conditions. It encourages us to learn the difficult work of interpreting spectral illuminations, seeing through the fog of lies and deception to find surprising truths about how to generate lives of meaning and compassion, capable of withstanding the inevitable dissatisfactions of our experiences. It reminds us that though we live embedded in an imperfect world, there are still moments of insight when chains of dependence are broken, when there are irruptions of liberatory practice and thinking, when these breakings and irruptions enable our multiple identities to flourish. In these moments, we can learn how to be authentic to this complex jumble of a world. That, at least, is what I have learned from modern literature and Buddhism.

CODA

In summer 2014 I was about to begin a two-year post at Rutgers University in New Jersey. I was living in Philadelphia at the time and, though I wanted to move back to New York, thought the rents were just too high on what my salary would be. A few days before I had to renew my Philly lease, I went to a friend's birthday party in New York. Another friend there received a text message, read it, and turned to his girlfriend: "We don't want to move to a rent-controlled sublet in the East Village for two years, do we?" She shook her head no. I jumped in: "Yes." Out of that accidental overhearing, my life would change dramatically. A few months later, I walked into a party in Lefferts Gardens, Brooklyn, hosted by new friends I had made because of my move to the city. Just as I was entering the living room, a person I did not know was walking away from a conversation. I looked at the spot they had just left and saw a woman now sitting by herself. I walked over to her and introduced myself. We talked till the party ended.

A few years later I was driving with the same woman (today we are married) through the Blue Mountains outside of Sydney, Australia, where she is from. The beauty of the mountains reminded her of being in Dharamsala as a young backpacker, and a meditation retreat she did there. I, perhaps jetlagged or annoyed about something or just because I was being annoying, responded by giving my usual litany of critiques of Western Dharma seekers. She, quite rightly, was offended. I hadn't asked about her experience or what she knew about this history or what it all meant to her. I had just gone on a diatribe about the inauthenticity of modern Buddhism. It was something I had been doing since my own trip to Dharamsala a decade earlier. I retrenched into my anger about Western ignorance about Buddhism and the suffering that ignorance caused. She stood by her offense that I was yelling at the world and not listening to her.

The truth is, not only was I being a bad partner, I was wrong in what I was saying. It is true that the Buddhism we know today was largely invented in the twentieth century. It is true that many people who meditate today do not think about the actual living conditions of most Buddhists. And it is true that such ignorance can cause real problems, as Jamyang Norbu and others have pointed out. But it is no less true that the experiences and meanings of modern Buddhism circulate far beyond this critique. We should neither be so ignorant of the complexity of Buddhist history as my young self nor, once we learn more, be so smug about our knowledge that we reject the meaningfulness of modern Buddhism.

Indeed, my companion was not spouting any nonsense about Buddhism as a cure for all that ailed the world. She was just telling me how useful meditation had been in helping her deal with suffering and loss: in other words, that this modern Buddhist form had given her a spectral illumination about how to live with grief. She was, in a way, telling me the lesson of the very book I was writing at the time, and I was not smart enough or open enough to hear it. Perhaps I myself should have been meditating more! But I was not, and as we stayed in our locked positions, an uncomfortable silence consumed the car ride.

But then some minor shift occurred. Perhaps it was the calm induced by the beauty of the mountains, an insight beckoned by a ray of light passing through the windshield, or just a feeling of love when I looked over at her. Whatever accident of vision it may have been, the Woolf-like scene finally broke through. My sealed vessel of a self cracked and reality flooded in. I understood what she had been saying, and that it was in fact the same thing I had been trying to say in my writing: that modern Buddhism, although not authentic to some imagined original Buddhism, was not therefore to be ridiculed. It was replete with the authentic meaning that all the accidents of our life can have if we are willing and able to perceive them. I didn't say this, but I did put my hand on hers and apologize for not listening. She smiled. We continued on in a new kind of silence.

NOTES

INTRODUCTION

1. The most helpful (and nonjudgmental) overview to this general process that I know of is David McMahan, *The Making of Buddhist Modernism* (Oxford; New York: Oxford University Press, 2008). For other
overviews and some important studies of local histories see: Erik
Braun, *The Birth of Insight: Meditation, Modern Buddhism, and the Burmese Monk Ledi Sayadaw* (Chicago: University of Chicago Press,
2013); Joanna Cook, *Meditation in Modern Buddhism: Renunciation
and Change in Thai Monastic Life* (Cambridge; New York: Cambridge
University Press, 2010); Georges Dreyfus, "Are We Prisoners of
Shangrila? Orientalism, Nationalism, and the Study of Tibet," *Journal of the International Association of Tibetan Studies* 1, no. 1 (2005):
1–21; Richard M. Jaffe, "Seeking Sakyamuni: Travel and the Reconstruction of Japanese Buddhism," *The Journal of Japanese Studies* 30,
no. 1 (2004): 65–96; Richard M. Jaffe, "Introduction," in *Selected Works
of D. T. Suzuki, Volume I: Zen*, by Daisetsu Teitaro Suzuki (Berkeley:
University of California Press, 2014), xi–lvi; Jason Ananda Josephson,
The Invention of Religion in Japan (Chicago: University of Chicago
Press, 2012); Steven Kemper, *Rescued from the Nation: Anagarika
Dharmapala and the Buddhist World* (Chicago: University of Chicago
Press, 2015); Donald S. Lopez Jr., "Introduction," in *A Modern Bud-
dhist Bible: Essential Readings from East and West*, ed. Donald S.
Lopez Jr. (Boston: Beacon, 2004), vii–xli; Christopher S. Queen and

Sallie B. King, eds., *Engaged Buddhism: Buddhist Liberation Movements in Asia* (Albany: State University of New York Press, 1996). On the problem of using "modern Buddhism" as a rubric for understanding *all* forms of contemporary Buddhism, see Thomas Borchert, "Worry for the Dai Nation: Sipsongpannā, Chinese Modernity, and the Problems of Buddhist Modernism," *The Journal of Asian Studies* 67, no. 1 (February 2008): 107–42.

2. For classic critical accounts see: Robert Sharf, "Buddhist Modernism and the Rhetoric of Meditative Experience," *Numen* 42, no. 3 (1995): 228–83; Gananath Obeyesekere, "Buddhism and Conscience: An Exploratory Essay," *Daedelus* 120, no. 3 (1991): 219–39.

3. Donald S. Lopez Jr., "Introduction," in *Curators of the Buddha: The Study of Buddhism Under Colonialism*, ed. Donald S. Lopez Jr. (Chicago: University of Chicago Press, 1995), 1–30; Donald S. Lopez Jr., "Buddhism in Practice," in *Asian Religions in Practice: An Introduction*, ed. Donald S. Lopez Jr. (Princeton, NJ: Princeton University Press, 1999), 56–87. This is of course true of many religions and other world-views as they transform over time.

4. On the rise of these types of connections, see, for example, Jaffe, "Seeking Sakyamuni"; Kemper, *Rescued from the Nation*.

5. I understand the strangeness of speaking of "we" in a book that crosses so many different times and periods and that may encounter (if I am lucky) readers coming from many different positions. It sometimes refers to readers in positions like myself—academics in the global north—but I also use it as a writerly shorthand for welcoming any reader into the dialogue about these novels. I do not intend by it to assume any necessary shared identity or history with the reader—beyond that of the basic humanity we all share.

6. Samuel Beckett, *Endgame and Act Without Words* (New York: Grove, 2009), 61.

7. Samuel Beckett, *Nohow On: Company, Ill Seen Ill Said, and Worstward Ho* (New York: Grove, 2014), 89.

8. One recent exception here is Evan Thompson, a philosopher focused on cognition and phenomenology, who has engaged seriously with both the history and the philosophy of Buddhism. For reasons that I will explore in this book, I think that Thompson is ultimately too

critical and overlooks the rich possibilities of modern Buddhism. Evan Thompson, *Why I Am Not a Buddhist* (New Haven, CT: Yale University Press, 2020).

9. The strident criticisms of Buddhism by leading literary theorists Peter Hallward and Martin Hägglund, for example, are irresponsibly bad. The confidence with which they attempt to criticize all of Buddhist thought and its meaning based on very limited knowledge is disturbing to see in scholars who are otherwise so strenuous in their work. Peter Hallward, *Absolutely Postcolonial: Writing Between the Singular and the Specific* (Manchester: Manchester University Press, 2001); Martin Hägglund, *This Life: Secular Faith and Spiritual Freedom* (New York: Pantheon, 2019). This of course not to say that there is no engaged literary criticism here. For some examples, see: Marcus Boon, Eric Cazdyn, and Timothy Morton, *Nothing: Three Inquiries in Buddhism* (Chicago: University of Chicago Press, 2015); J. Jeffrey Franklin, *The Lotus and the Lion: Buddhism and the British Empire* (Ithaca, NY: Cornell University Press, 2008); Jane Iwamura, *Virtual Orientalism: Asian Religions and American Popular Culture* (Oxford: Oxford University Press, 2010); Josephine Park, *Apparitions of Asia: Modernist Form and Asian American Poetics* (New York: Oxford University Press, 2008); Linda Selzer, "Black American Buddhism: History and Representation," in *Writing as Enlightenment: Buddhist American Literature Into the Twenty-First Century*, ed. Gary Storhoff and John Whalen-Bridge (Albany: State University of New York Press, 2011), 37–69; John Whalen-Bridge and Gary Storhoff, eds., *The Emergence of Buddhist American Literature* (Albany: State University of New York Press, 2010); R. John Williams, *The Buddha in the Machine: Art, Technology, and the Meeting of East and West* (New Haven, CT: Yale University Press, 2014). I will return later to some minor disagreements I have with these authors. For some insights into literature and the arts more broadly from Buddhist studies scholars, see Lopez, "Introduction," *A Modern Buddhist Bible*; McMahan, *The Making of Buddhist Modernism*, chapter 8; Stanley Abe, "Inside the Wonder House: Buddhist Art and the West," in *Curators of the Buddha: The Study of Buddhism Under Colonialism*, ed. Donald S. Lopez Jr. (Chicago: University of Chicago Press, 1995), 63–106; Arnika Fuhrmann,

Ghostly Desires: Queer Sexuality and Vernacular Buddhism in Contempo-rary Thai Cinema (Durham, NC: Duke University Press, 2016); Justin Thomas McDaniel, "Strolling Through Temporary Temples: Bud-dhism and Installation Art in Modern Thailand," *Contemporary Bud-dhism* 18, no. 1 (January 2, 2017): 165–98; Gregory P. A. Levine, *Long Strange Journey: On Modern Zen, Zen Art, and Other Predicaments* (Honolulu: University of Hawaii Press, 2017). For a bibliography of scholarship on Buddhism and literature, see Kimberly Beek, "Bud-dhism and Modern Literature," in *Buddhism*, Oxford Bibliographies, 2016, https://www.oxfordbibliographies.com/view/document/obo-9780 195393521/obo-9780195393521-0230.xml?q=buddhism+and+modern+li terature.

10. My greatest debt here is to Justin McDaniel, Gauri Viswanathan, and Rebecca Walkowitz, whose probing questions during a book work-shop helped me understand so much better what I was trying to say with this book.

11. I take the concept of being embedded from Karl Polanyi, who showed that even the supposedly most free market remained embedded in social relations. While he was critical of how liberal economics sought to make society dependent on the economy, rather than the economy dependent on society, he showed clearly that such an overturning would destroy the very society that the market attempted to domi-nate: "Such an institution could not exist for any length of time with-out annihilating the human and natural substance of society; it would have physically destroyed man and transformed his surroundings into a wilderness." In thinking of art as linked to the processes of everyday life, I also follow John Dewey's aesthetic theory. Karl Polanyi, *The Great Transformation: The Political and Economic Origins of Our Time* (Boston: Beacon, 2001), 3; See also: Fred Block, "Introduction," in *The Great Transformation: The Political and Economic Origins of Our Time*, by Karl Polanyi (Boston: Beacon, 2001), xxiii–xxix; John Dewey, *Art as Experience* (New York: Perigee, 2005).

12. This makes a slight but not insignificant difference from how other philosophical models of literary criticism explore the relation between ideas and their effects in the world. Pheng Cheah, for example, has argued that while philosophy seeks to incarnate its ideals in the world, literature discloses our universal condition in which the very thing

that would make incarnation possible—the time of transformation—is also what makes it impossible, since time necessarily undoes what it has allowed in the next instant. I understand this point, but I am suggesting that the incarnation model is not as apparent from the start. Philosophical ideals are not put into the world; they are embedded. They do not come from elsewhere. They are always within the social. I owe this insight into the material conditions of abstraction to conversations about contemporary art with Anthea Behm. Pheng Cheah, *What Is a World?: On Postcolonial Literature as World Literature* (Durham, NC: Duke University Press, 2016).

13. There is some ongoing debate about this success. Enthusiasts like Robert Wright have suggested that Buddhism can truly help us overcome some of the more pernicious cycles of our thought. Critics like Evan Thompson say the science is still out. One mediating position is offered by David McMahan, who suggests that meditation "works" differently in different contexts, and should be understood within the cultural horizon of the practitioner. Thus we should at least appreciate the anecdotal evidence that it releases tension and anxiety. Robert Wright, *Why Buddhism Is True: The Science and Philosophy of Meditation and Enlightenment* (New York: Simon and Schuster, 2017); Thompson, *Why I Am Not a Buddhist*, 118–40; David McMahan, "How Meditation Works: Theorizing the Role of Cultural Context in Buddhist Contemplative Practices," in *Meditation, Buddhism, and Science*, ed. David McMahan and Erik Braun (New York: Oxford University Press, 2017), 21–46.

14. Thich Nhat Hanh, "History of Engaged Buddhism: A Dharma Talk by Thich Nhat Hanh—Hanoi, Vietnam, May 6–7, 2008," *Human Architecture* 6, no. 3 (Summer 2008): 3–4.

15. B. R. Ambedkar, *The Buddha and His Dhamma: A Critical Edition*, ed. Aakash Singh Rathore and Ajay Verma (New Delhi; Oxford; New York: Oxford University Press, 2011), xxxi.

16. Christopher S. Queen, "Dr. Ambedkar and the Hermeneutics of Buddhist Liberation," in *Engaged Buddhism: Buddhist Liberation Movements in Asia*, ed. Christopher S. Queen and Sallie B. King (Albany: State University of New York Press, 1996), 62.

17. Philip C. Almond, *The British Discovery of Buddhism* (Cambridge; New York: Cambridge University Press, 1988), 2.

18. Dan Arnold and Alicia Turner, "Opinion | Why Are We Surprised When Buddhists Are Violent?," *The New York Times*, March 5, 2018, sec. Opinion, https://www.nytimes.com/2018/03/05/opinion/buddhists-violence-tolerance.html.

19. Beth Blum, *The Self-Help Compulsion: Searching for Advice in Modern Literature* (New York: Columbia University Press, 2020).

20. Georges Dreyfus, *The Sound of Two Hands Clapping: The Education of a Tibetan Buddhist Monk* (Berkeley: University of California Press, 2003); Ann Gleig, *American Dharma: Buddhism Beyond Modernity* (New Haven, CT: Yale University Press, 2019); Thompson, *Why I Am Not a Buddhist*.

21. Thompson, *Why I Am Not a Buddhist*, 6–7.

22. Thompson, 8–19.

23. A study by Charles Prebish cited in Gleig, *American Dharma*, 15.

24. It was largely anthropologists of religion who originally helped move scholarship beyond a focus on texts and histories and into a study of how Buddhism was embedded in diverse cultural systems. See the overview in Ivette Vargas-O'Bryan, "Anthropology," in *Buddhism*, Oxford Bibliographies, 2013, https://www.oxfordbibliographies.com/view/document/obo-9780195393521/obo-9780195393521-0001.xml.

25. Gleig, *American Dharma*, 14–15.

26. Implicit here is Marx's critique of idealism, and the idea that we project real conditions of structural alienation onto a figure of religious alienation. I do not think—and I'm not quite convinced that Marx thought—that this alienation is because of religion *as such*. Rather, the concern here is when religious thinking displaces rather than reinvigorates our sense of commitment to transforming the world.

27. A longer version of this story would discuss the relationship between my interest in Buddhism and my youthful experimentation with hallucinogens, in which I am also not atypical. The feelings produced by drugs seem to at least approximate certain mystical states, as has recently been detailed extensively for a popular audience by Michael Pollan, and which has long been explored in diverse religious ceremonies and cultural practices. The specific connection with Buddhism is strong in Anglophone culture. It was written about by Richard Alpert

(to whom I am not related), Aldous Huxley, the Beat poets, and others. For an overview of this history, see Douglas Osto, *Altered States: Buddhism and Psychedelic Spirituality in America* (New York: Columbia University Press, 2016). For a classic Buddhist modernist account of the relation between drugs and Buddhism prompted by Huxley's writings, see Daisetz Teitaro Suzuki, "Religion and Drugs," in *Selected Works of D. T. Suzuki*, ed. Tomoe Moriya and Jeff Wilson (Berkeley: University of California Press, 2016), 233–38. Michael Pollan, *How to Change Your Mind: What the New Science of Psychedelics Teaches Us About Consciousness, Dying, Addiction, Depression, and Transcendence* (New York: Penguin, 2018).

28. For a full history of American Jewish-Buddhist relations, see Emily Sigalow, *American JewBu: Jews, Buddhists, and Religious Change* (Princeton, NJ: Princeton University Press, 2019).

29. Alan W. Watts, *The Way of Zen* (New York: Vintage, 1999), 66.

30. As I spent time with the monks, I was also surprised to see how many of them, unlike me, ate meat. But in fact this too has a long history in Tibetan Buddhism. See Geoffrey Barstow, *Food of Sinful Demons: Meat, Vegetarianism, and the Limits of Buddhism in Tibet* (New York: Columbia University Press, 2017). On violence, see, for example: Michael K. Jerryson and Mark Juergensmeyer, eds., *Buddhist Warfare* (New York: Oxford University Press, 2010). For a short overview of some misconceptions about Buddhism, see Bernard Faure, *Unmasking Buddhism* (West Sussex: Wiley, 2009).

31. On the Burmese side, see Braun, *The Birth of Insight*. For Thailand, see Cook, *Meditation in Modern Buddhism*.

32. Daisetz Teitaro Suzuki, "The Philosophy of Zen," *Philosophy East and West* 1, no. 2 (1951): 8.

33. The promise was not that after the experience of satori one is automatically "Zen." The insight must be worked through, according to Suzuki. See his autobiographical account of his first "enlightenment experience": Richard M. Jaffe, ed., "Early Memories," in *Selected Works of D. T. Suzuki, Volume I*, Zen (University of California Press, 2015), 202–10.

34. Sharf, "Buddhist Modernism and the Rhetoric of Meditative Experience," 244–45.

35. Michel Foucault, *The Hermeneutics of the Subject: Lectures at the Collège de France, 1981–1982*, trans. Graham Burchell (New York: Palgrave-Macmillan, 2005).

36. Foucault, *The Hermeneutics of the Subject*, 227n58. I do not agree with Foucault's seemingly Orientalist idea that Buddhism automatically instills a more direct route to realization than other philosophies. While meditative practice can help, it cannot replace the related concerns of institution building. This assumption is one of the concerns I have about the literary criticism around Buddhism. See, for example, the thoughts on Buddhism and actualization in Eve Kosofsky Sedgwick, *Touching Feeling: Affect, Pedagogy, Performativity* (Durham, NC: Duke University Press, 2003); Eve Kosofsky Sedgwick, *The Weather in Proust*, ed. Jonathan Goldberg (Durham, NC: Duke University Press, 2011).

37. Marshall Sahlins, "Two or Three Things That I Know About Culture," *The Journal of the Royal Anthropological Institute* 5, no. 3 (1999): 399–421.

38. There is of course now a vast literature on this point. The essays of Sanjay Subrahmanyam have been especially influential on my thinking. Sanjay Subrahmanyam, "La 'Religion,' Une Catégorie Déroutante: Perspectives Depuis l'Asie Du Sud," *Asdiwal: Revue Genevoise d'anthropologie et d'histoire Des Religions* 9 (2014): 79–90; Sanjay Subrahmanyam, "Global Intellectual History Beyond Hegel and Marx," *History and Theory* 54, no. 1 (February 2015): 126–37.

39. Almond's account, noted above, begins with this discrepancy between praise for Edwin Arnold's *Light of Asia* and critical responses from missionaries. Lopez, "Introduction," 1995.

40. Donald S. Lopez Jr., *The Story of Buddhism: A Concise Guide to Its History and Teachings* (San Francisco: HarperOne, 2001), 18. While the Lopez quote gives me a clear reference, the idea was actually brought home for me by Justin McDaniel, who, in a workshop of this book, showed me that what I was really doing was using stories to talk about global Buddhism. It was an invaluable insight for which I am deeply grateful.

41. Sam van Schaik, *Tibet: A History* (New Haven: Yale University Press, 2013).

42. See Toni Huber, *The Holy Land Reborn: Pilgrimage and the Tibetan Reinvention of Buddhist India* (Chicago: University of Chicago Press, 2008), 268–70.

43. As in most studies originating in scholarly research, I tend to position my understanding of Buddhism as more up to date and more accurate than that of predecessors in my field (literary studies). While this may be true for some, it is not the case for everyone, and my knowledge certainly pales in comparison to the work of those who have dedicated their lives to the study of Buddhism in its local and global forms. While I occasionally criticize other scholars for what appears as their insouciance toward engaging with Buddhism, I do not do so out of a sense that I am an expert, so much as someone who has tried to reach a little further into the field of study. I am hoping to advance a conversation, not declare my perfected knowledge on the topic. Indeed, as I rewrote this book, I was embarrassed by some of the mistakes I made in telling the history of diverse Buddhisms. I have done my best to check and cross-check sources, and to consult the most recent scholarship I can find (with the additional limitations of focusing on trends in the U.S.-American academy). But I am sure that some mistakes remain, and I would greatly appreciate future readers who take the time to point them out.

44. See for examples: Selzer, "Black American Buddhism: History and Representation"; Gleig, *American Dharma*; Ann Gleig, "Dharma Diversity and Deep Inclusivity at the East Bay Meditation Center: From Buddhist Modernism to Buddhist Postmodernism?," *Contemporary Buddhism* 15, no. 2 (July 3, 2014): 312–31.

45. I agree with Jeffrey Stout when he writes, "Theorists of interpretation have been highly successful exposing each other's weaknesses. My proposal [to argue not about meaning of texts but our different interests in texts] offers a way to recognize and inherit each other's strengths." Jeffrey Stout, "What Is the Meaning of a Text?," *New Literary History* 14, no. 1 (1982): 10.

I. ENLIGHTENMENT

1. Dogen, *Sounds of Valley Streams: Enlightenment in Dogen's Zen Translation of Nine Essays From Shobogenzo*, trans. Francis H. Cook (Albany: State University of New York Press, 1988), 89.

2. John Powers, *Introduction to Tibetan Buddhism* (Ithaca, NY: Snow Lion, 2007), 149–52.

3. There is some doubt, mentioned in Powers, as to whether the debate actually ever happened. Sam van Schaik has also provided an interesting account of how Zen survived in Tibetan Buddhist thought. Sam van Schaik, *Tibetan Zen: Discovering a Lost Tradition* (Boston: Shambhala, 2015).

4. Sam van Schaik, *Tibet: A History* (New Haven, CT: Yale University Press, 2013), chapter 6.

5. Sarat Chandra Das, *Journey to Lhasa and Central Tibet* (London: J. Murray, 1902), 180–81.

6. His monastery is called Tashi Lhunpo, so he is, in a sense, the Lama of Tashi. The Geluks are the most powerful of what are generally considered the four sects of Tibetan Buddhism. Das's claim of "universality" merely affirms Geluk claims to representing all Tibetans. The Dalai Lama and Panchen Lama were also historically political rivals at times, and, when he could secure a stronger patron, the Panchen became the most powerful. On sectarianism in Tibetan Buddhism and some of its violent repercussions, see Matthew T. Kapstein, *Tibetan Buddhism: A Very Short Introduction* (Oxford: Oxford University Press, 2013), 29–44.

7. Peter Hopkirk, *Quest for Kim: In Search of Kipling's Great Game* (Oxford: Oxford University Press, 2001), 224–26.

8. Karl E. Meyer and Shareen Blair Brysac, *Tournament of Shadows: The Great Game and the Race for Empire in Central Asia* (New York: Basic Books, 2009), 221.

9. Paul G. Hackett, *Theos Bernard, the White Lama: Tibet, Yoga, and American Religious Life* (New York: Columbia University Press, 2012), 133.

10. It is part of the erasure of Buddhism in this text that Harish Trivedi, in his 2011 introduction to the Penguin edition, confidently claims that "no such printed reference [in the Buddhist canon] has so far been traced." In fact, Buddhist studies scholar Stanley Abe had traced the textual history already in 1995. Trivedi, "Introduction," in Rudyard Kipling, *Kim*, ed. Harish Trivedi (New York: Penguin, 2011), xxvii. Abe, "Inside the Wonder House: Buddhist Art and the West," in *Curators of the Buddha: The Study of Buddhism Under Colonialism*, ed. Donald S. Lopez Jr. (Chicago: University of Chicago Press, 1995), 95n14.

11. The Wheel shows how ignorance produces rebirth in one of the six realms of existence. The diagram presents in condensed form a description of both why life is suffering and what the means of ending that suffering are. It demonstrates how our suffering is conditioned by our actions, and how by changing our actions we can become unconditioned and exit the cycle of reincarnation. For a helpful overview, see Rupert Gethin, *The Foundations of Buddhism* (Oxford: Oxford University Press, 1998), 149–59.

12. Edward W. Said, *Culture and Imperialism* (New York: Random House, 1993), 142, 140.

13. Srinivas Aravamudan, *Guru English: South Asian Religion in a Cosmopolitan Language* (Princeton, NJ: Princeton University Press, 2005), 83.

14. William Dillingham, *Rudyard Kipling: Hell and Heroism* (New York: Palgrave Macmillan, 2005), 248.

15. J. Jeffrey Franklin, *The Lotus and the Lion: Buddhism and the British Empire* (Ithaca, NY: Cornell University Press, 2008), 158.

16. Schaik, *Tibet*, chapter 6.

17. An early reader suggested that this was not the case in Dillingham's criticism (and I thank that reader for bringing his work to my attention). But while Dillingham is clear that the lama is not naïve as such, he does not go so far as to suggest that the lama is on a mission to find a new patron.

18. Kipling, *Kim*, ed. Trivedi, 240. Unfairly, since Russian Oriental studies on Tibet were arguably more advanced than the British. See John Snelling, *Buddhism in Russia: The Story of Agvan Dorzhiev, Lhasa's Emissary to the Tsar* (Rockport, MA: Element Books, 1993).

19. When the lama asks if the spies speak Hindi, Hurree replies, "A little, maybe." Kipling, *Kim*, 241. As more evidence of how an ideology of Buddhism overwrites critics' ability to read the text, Kinkeade-Weeks remarks, "When the Lama speaks, in Hindi so that all can understand, nobody listens." The whole point, as I take it, is that the lama is testing their knowledge, not their souls, which he knows, like Kim's, will still require transformation. Mark Kinkeade-Weekes, "Vision in Kipling's Novels," in *Kipling's Mind and Art: Selected Critical Essays*, ed. Andrew Rutherford (Palo Alto, CA: Stanford University Press, 1964), 228.

20. This is not intended as a comment on whether the current Dalai Lama should reincarnate, as he has hinted he may not in order to forestall Chinese claims that he has been reborn in mainland China. The point is that this leader of modern Buddhism is also making a political decision about what to do with this moment of enlightenment.

21. Toni Huber, *The Holy Land Reborn: Pilgrimage and the Tibetan Reinvention of Buddhist India* (Chicago: University of Chicago Press, 2008), 269.

22. Kipling, *Kim*, 235.

23. Kipling, 370n10.

24. Donald E. Garrett, *Borates: Handbook of Deposits, Processing, Properties, and Use* (San Diego, CA: Academic Press, 1998), 58–65.

25. Kipling, *Kim*, 183.

26. Kipling, 184.

27. Kipling, 235.

28. Alex McKay, "The Drowning of Lama Sengchen Kyabying: A Preliminary Enquiry from British Sources," *Tibet Journal* 36, no. 2 (2011): 5.

29. This is a very quick description of a very complex philosophy. There are many sources that explain this in greater depth. See, for example, Gethin, *The Foundations of Buddhism*, 149–59; Jan Westerhoff, *Nagarjuna's Madhyamaka: A Philosophical Introduction* (New York: Oxford University Press, 2009).

30. Dreyfus's work was very helpful to me in understanding this point. Georges Dreyfus, *The Sound of Two Hands Clapping: The Education of a Tibetan Buddhist Monk* (Berkeley: University of California Press, 2003), 186–88.

31. Steven Collins, *Nirvana: Concept, Imagery, Narrative* (New York: Cambridge University Press, 2010), 38. While Collins is describing what he calls the "Pali imaginaire," and thus not the Buddhism of Tibet directly, it is clear that enlightenment as a kind of extinguishing is what is at stake here. Of course, these distinctions within traditions do not always hold fast, and recent scholarship has questioned the strict boundaries within Buddhism. Further still, the association of Buddhism with annihilation in Victorian English would have been present for Kipling and his readers. On this, see Franklin, *The Lotus*

and the Lion. On questioning the boundaries between Buddhist communities, see Frank E. Reynolds and Charles Hallisey, "Buddhism: An Overview," in *Encyclopedia of Religion*, ed. Lindsay Jones (Detroit: Macmillan Reference, 2005).

32. Martin Hägglund has recently engaged Collins's book in an argument against "the religious life." For Hägglund, the religious life devalues our current, finite existence in the name of a future one that is infinite: "All world religions (Hinduism, Buddhism, Judaism, Islam, and Christianity) hold that the highest form of existence or the most desirable form of life is eternal rather than finite" (*This Life: Secular Faith and Spiritual Freedom* [New York: Pantheon, 2019], 8). Hägglund seems not to care about anything outside colonialism's purview of demarcating "world religions," but it is especially strange to find Buddhism in this list. Like so many other critics, Hägglund writes with authority about Buddhism based on very little knowledge: Collins is his only cited source in a critique that repeats throughout his book. But the presumption about what Buddhism is seems to overwrite even his understanding of Collins's argument. Nirvana, Collins makes clear, is most often *not* about eternity but about the escape from it. Before criticizing this conception of the universe, it is important to fully understand the position being articulated. Furthermore, while Collins is an important source, there are others as well. As in all fields of thought, nirvana is a contested concept.

33. Kipling, *Kim*, 262.

34. That Kim will prove to have this role is foretold in the text's earlier reference to a *Jātaka* tale about the necessity of a *chela* for achieving liberation. Kipling, 167.

35. Kipling, 289.

36. Kipling, 290.

37. For some context on how the Dalai Lama has sculpted his image in relation to visions of Tibet, see the competing claims in Donald S. Lopez Jr., *Prisoners of Shangri-La: Tibetan Buddhism and the West* (Chicago: University of Chicago Press, 1999), and Georges Dreyfus, "Are We Prisoners of Shangrila? Orientalism, Nationalism, and the Study of Tibet," *Journal of the International Association of Tibetan Studies* 1, no. 1 (2005): 1–21.

38. Robert Barnett, "Symbols and Protest: The Iconography of Demonstrations in Tibet, 1987–89," in *Resistance and Reform in Tibet: 40 Years On, Tibet 1950–90*, ed. Robert Barnett (Bloomington: University of Indiana Press, 1994), 238–58.

39. This is not to disparage "self-care," which began in response to the failure of systems to provide care for marginalized peoples. One can see this in the art practice of Simone Leigh, which included meditation and other self-care workshops during Black Lives Matter protests in New York. Aisha Harris, "A History of Self-Care," *Slate*, April 5, 2017, http://www.slate.com/articles/arts/culturebox/2017/04/the_history_of_self_care.html; Simone Leigh, *The Waiting Room*, The New Museum, September 2016, https://www.newmuseum.org/exhibitions/view/simone-leigh-the-waiting-room.

40. This was happening whether or not Enlightenment thinkers themselves subscribed to it, which remains an ongoing debate. Enlightenment *philosophes* like Voltaire and Leibniz believed in the light coming from Asia, as when Leibniz wrote of exchange between Europe and China as "A commerce, I say, of doctrine and mutual light." Cited in Franklin Perkins, *Leibniz and China: A Commerce of Light* (Cambridge; New York: Cambridge University Press, 2004), 121. But Enlightenment as a colonial mission is far from this hopeful belief. See Sankar Muthu, *Enlightenment Against Empire* (Princeton, NJ: Princeton University Press, 2003); John M. Hobson, *The Eurocentric Conception of World Politics: Western International Theory, 1760–2010* (Cambridge: Cambridge University Press, 2012). For a brief but poignant discussion of the complexity of this imagery in Conrad, see Benita Parry, "The Moment and After-Life of Heart of Darkness," in *Conrad in the Twenty-First Century: Contemporary Approaches and Perspectives*, ed. Carola Kaplan, Peter Mallios, and Andrea White, 1 edition (New York: Routledge, 2004), 41–42. For an extended treatment of the use of "enlightenment" in the colonies in a context not too far from Conrad's own, see Alice L. Conklin, *A Mission to Civilize: The Republican Idea of Empire in France and West Africa, 1895–1930* (Palo Alto, CA: Stanford University Press, 1997).

41. While critical attention has been drawn to the place of Buddhism in Conrad's work, it has yet to ask what connection there may be between Buddhism and politics in *Heart of Darkness*. For representative

examples, see H. C. Brashers, "Conrad, Marlow, and Gautama Buddha," *Conradiana* 1 (1969): 63–71; Peter Caracciolo, "Buddhist Typologies in *Heart of Darkness* and *Victory* and Their Contribution to the Modernism of Jacob Epstein, Wyndham Lewis, and T. S. Eliot," *The Conradian* 11, no. 1 (1986): 24–34; Bruce Johnson, "'Heart of Darkness' and the Problem of Emptiness," *Studies in Short Fiction* 9, no. 4 (1972): 387–400; William Byshe Stein, "The Lotus Posture and Heart of Darkness," *Modern Fiction Studies* 2 (1956): 235–37; Franklin, *The Lotus and the Lion*, 193–95. Johnson is unique in his argument, which I echo below, that Conrad was largely critical of Buddhism. Franklin represents a recent attempt to situate Conrad in a longer history of Victorian and modernist interest in Buddhism.

42. This is perhaps not surprising given "that Conrad seems quite incapable of 'believing in' any kind of thought-form, and his contempt is directed acidly toward a 'humanity [that] doesn't know what it wants. But it will swallow everything . . . It has swallowed Christianity, Buddhism, Mahomedanism, and the Gospel of Mrs. Eddy.'" William Wesley Bonney, *Thorns and Arabesques: Contexts for Conrad's Fiction* (Baltimore, MD: Johns Hopkins University Press, 1980), 8.

43. This is perhaps related to other forms found in "postsecular" narratives. John McClure has argued that the "weakening" of religion and its transformation into "partial faiths" is the hallmark of "postsecular fiction," which is marked by "plots of partial conversion, [a] project of ontological disruption . . . efforts at once to reassert and to weaken religious conceptions of reality, and . . . attempts to imagine a new, religiously inflected, form of progressive politics." This description speaks very well to some of the transformations of Buddhism in modernity at large. John A. McClure, *Partial Faiths: Postsecular Fiction in the Age of Pynchon and Morrison* (Athens: University of Georgia Press, 2007), 6.

44. For two important positions in this debate, see Chinua Achebe, "An Image of Africa," *The Massachusetts Review* 18, no. 4 (1977): 782–94; Wilson Harris, "The Frontier on Which 'Heart of Darkness' Stands," *Research in African Literatures* 12, no. 1 (1981): 86–93; Said, *Culture and Imperialism*.

45. Joseph Conrad, *Heart of Darkness: An Authoritative Text, Backgrounds and Sources, Criticism*, 3rd ed. (New York: Norton, 2005), 69.

46. Conrad, 7.

47. Conrad, 10.

48. Lester suggests that this Europeanization demonstrates Marlow's East-West "universality." But even without the broader context I am offering, the language here clearly separates Marlow *from* universality. John Lester, *Conrad and Religion* (New York: St. Martin's Press, 1988), 62.

49. On Schopenhauer and Conrad, see the overview in Owen Knowles and Gene Moore, eds., *Oxford Reader's Companion to Conrad* (Oxford: Oxford University Press, 2000), 323–25. The links among Schopenhauer, savagery, and Buddhism have gone undeveloped in recent accounts. Wollaeger, for example, does not even mention Buddhism, and Knowles only notes that Marlow's Buddha pose secures his comparative relation to Schopenhauer. It is this triangulation of concerns that I am working to explore here. Mark Wollaeger, *Joseph Conrad and the Fictions of Skepticism* (Stanford, CA: Stanford University Press, 1990).

50. Arthur Schopenhauer, *The World as Will and Representation*, trans. E.F.J. Payne, vol. 1 (New York: Dover, 1966), 333.

51. On the blurred relation to Hinduism and Buddhism, see Roger-Pol Droit, *The Cult of Nothingness: The Philosophers and the Buddha*, trans. Pamela Vohnson (Chapel Hill: University of North Carolina Press, 2003), 91–103.

52. This critique is noted by Georg Simmel in his overview of the relation between Schopenhauer and Nietzsche. "Contrary to Schopenhauer's claim that freedom means the irrevocable quality of will, the ultimate within us . . . is so by dwelling in the changes and vicissitudes of innermost life." Georg Simmel, *Schopenhauer and Nietzsche*, trans. Helmut Loiskandl, Deena Weinstein, and Michael Weinstein (Urbana: University of Illinois Press, 1991), 130.

53. Schopenhauer, *The World as Will and Representation*, 2:578.

54. For a more detailed and critical account that echoes the basic outline here, see Christopher Janaway, *Self and World in Schopenhauer's Philosophy* (Oxford: Oxford University Press, 1999), 5–12; 248–88.

55. Schopenhauer, *The World as Will and Representation*, 2:628; my emphasis.

56. On Schopenhauer's views on death and suicide and his curious exception for "accidental" self-starvation by ascetics, see Dale Jacquette, "Schopenhauer on Death," in *The Cambridge Companion to Schopenhauer*, ed. Christopher Janaway (New York: Cambridge University Press, 1999), 300–14.

57. John Bramble, *Modernism and the Occult* (New York: Palgrave Macmillan, 2015), 57.

58. David McMahan, *The Making of Buddhist Modernism* (Oxford; New York: Oxford University Press, 2008), 76.

59. Conrad, *Heart of Darkness*, 5.

60. While I appreciate LaCapra's concern that we bear in mind the parodic elements of Conrad's narrative, I think a close reading of the passage dispels his claim that "the metaphor is so convoluted that it seems to dissipate by the time one reaches its final terms." Dominick LaCapra, *History, Literature, Critical Theory* (Ithaca: Cornell University Press, 2013), 39.

61. Conrad, *Heart of Darkness*, 6.

62. On the ambiguity of the title, with its opposing imagery of a heart and darkness, see Ian Watt, *Conrad in the Nineteenth Century* (Berkeley: University of California Press, 1981), 199–200.

63. This is what strikes me as ironic about Miller's claim that this moment alerts us to "the presence *within* the novella of this inaccessible secret," since that would seem to imply that our goal is not the outside, but only to reach an even deeper internal truth. J. Hillis Miller, "Should We Read *Heart of Darkness*?," in *Joseph Conrad's Heart of Darkness*, ed. Harold Bloom (New York: Chelsea House, 2008), 124; my emphasis.

64. Conrad, *Heart of Darkness*, 39.

65. Conrad, 39.

66. Conrad, 39.

67. Conrad, 41, 42.

68. Conrad, 41–42.

69. Conrad, 42.

70. Conrad, 42.

71. My thoughts on the relation between an indeterminate universe and the making of human order have been formed to a large extent by the work of Cornelius Castoriadis, although I take strong exception to his

Eurocentrism. Cornelius Castoriadis, *Philosophy, Politics, Autonomy* (New York: Oxford University Press, 1991).

72. Conrad, *Heart of Darkness*, 57.

73. Conrad, 58.

74. Conrad, 49.

75. Conrad, 69.

76. In a philosophical mode, we might read this as the refusal of "the negation of the negation." We famously get this in the colonial context in Marx's early writing on India, where there is a desire for the negative destructive force of colonialism to break up the supposed negative stalemate of premodern life. What Kurtz sees, what he affirms that Marx early on did not (recent research has shown that he later broke with this stance), is that colonialism simply can have no positive effects. For Kurtz, in this reading, the horror is in both Africa and Belgium, India and England, in all human life, and these horrors can only compound each other. "The horror! The horror!" is thus resounding repetition rather than negation. This is not the space to explore the connections between Conrad's novella and Jean-Luc Godard's *Week end*, which I take to be a rewriting of *Heart of Darkness*, from the long tracking shot of car pileups, as if down a river, to the cannibalism at the end. But we could say that Godard rewrites "The horror! The horror!" to bring back the possibility of the negation of the negation. This occurs when his revolutionary leader proclaims, "The horror of the bourgeoisie can only be overcome by more horror [On ne peut dépassser l'horreur de la bourgeoisie que par plus d'horreur encore]." But Conrad may still have the last word, since even if we accept Godard's claim, we must see that it leads to endless cycles of horror and violence. Jean-Luc Godard, *Week end* (New York: New Yorker Video, 2005). On Marx's reconsideration of his writings on India, see Kevin Anderson, *Marx at the Margins: On Nationalism, Ethnicity, and Non-Western Societies* (Chicago: University of Chicago Press, 2010).

77. Conrad, *Heart of Darkness*, 51.

78. Conrad, 74.

79. Conrad, 75.

80. Conrad, 77.

81. Conrad, 29.

82. Conrad, 77.

83. Conrad, 11.

84. Conrad, 76; my emphasis.

85. This reading runs counter to Ian Watt's claim that Marlow has convinced the narrator, whose vision "is now coloured by the expansive power of Marlow's primary symbol." Other critics might also disagree with my interpretation. J. Hillis Miller, for example, holds that "the heart of darkness is the truth, but it is a truth that makes ordinary human life impossible." But this reading is dependent on the assumption that follows: "To know the darkness is to know the falsity of life, and to understand the leap into emptiness man made when he separated himself from the wild clamor of primitive life." Again, this need for separation, this vision of primitive darkness, is precisely what I am claiming the narrative as a whole denies. Watt, *Conrad in the Nineteenth Century*, 253. J. Hillis Miller, *Poets of Reality: Six Twentieth-Century Writers* (Cambridge, MA: Harvard University Press, 1965), 33–34.

86. Conrad, *Heart of Darkness*, 33.

87. Joseph Conrad, *Typhoon and Other Tales*, ed. Cedric Watts (Oxford; New York: Oxford University Press, 2009), 82.

88. Conrad, 17.

89. So far as I know, this meditative posture in the book has not been remarked on by any of the critics who discuss Buddhism. This is precisely the kind of textual detail that gets obscured by our narratives about Buddhism.

90. Cited in Adam Hochschild, *King Leopold's Ghost: A Story of Greed, Terror, and Heroism in Colonial Africa* (Boston: Houghton Mifflin, 1998), 114.

91. Joseph Conrad, *The Collected Letters of Joseph Conrad*, ed. Laurence Davies and J. H. Stape, vol. 7 (Cambridge; New York: Cambridge University Press, 2005), 13.

92. Conrad, *Typhoon and Other Tales*, 91.

93. Somboon Suksamran, *Buddhism and Politics in Thailand: A Study of Socio-Political Change and Political Activism of the Thai Sangha* (Singapore: Institute of Southeast Asian Studies, 1982), 14.

94. Suksamran, 15. For a broad-ranging analysis of this situation and a defense of those who decided to evade the state, see James C. Scott, *The Art of Not Being Governed: An Anarchist History of Upland Southeast Asia* (New Haven, CT: Yale University Press, 2009).

95. See especially Erik Braun, *The Birth of Insight: Meditation, Modern Buddhism, and the Burmese Monk Ledi Sayadaw* (Chicago: University of Chicago Press, 2013). Given this rise of embodied religious practice *because of* colonialism, it is interesting that there has been very little comparative analysis with respect to Buddhism in studies of secularism and corporeal practices. Even a scholar like David McMahan, who writes extensively about Buddhism and meditation, does not bring this up in his writing on Buddhism and secularism. On the importance of embodiment to studies of secularism, see, for example, Charles Hirschkind, "Is There a Secular Body?," *Cultural Anthropology* 26, no. 4 (November 2, 2012): 633–47; David McMahan, "Buddhism and Global Secularisms," *Journal of Global Buddhism* 18 (2017): 112–28.

96. Henry Alabaster and Thiphākǫnwongmahākōsāthibǫdī, *The wheel of the law: Buddhism, illustrated from Siamese sources by the Modern Buddhist, a Life of Buddha, and an account of the Phrabat* (London: Trübner, 1871), xv.

97. Charles F. Keyes, "Buddhist Politics and Their Revolutionary Origins in Thailand," *International Political Science Review/Revue Internationale de Science Politique* 10, no. 2 (1989): 121–42. For a critique of how this centralization of religion diminished the plurality of Buddhist practices, see Tiyavanich Kamala, *Forest Recollections: Wandering Monks in Twentieth-Century Thailand* (Honolulu: University of Hawaii Press, 1997), 1–10. As scholars like Thongchai Winichakul have further argued, this modernization occurred in the face of colonial threats, and its legacies have been complex, especially with regard to the linking of Thai identity to Buddhism. Thongchai Winichakul, "Buddhist Apologetics and a Genealogy of Comparative Religion in Siam," *Numen* 62, no. 1 (December 12, 2015): 76–99.

98. James C. Scott, *Weapons of the Weak: Everyday Forms of Peasant Resistance* (New Haven, CT: Yale University Press, 1985), 247, 250.

99. James C. Scott, *Domination and the Arts of Resistance: Hidden Transcripts* (New Haven, CT: Yale University Press, 1992), xiii.

100. Scott, *Domination and the Arts of Resistance*, 184; my emphasis.

2. REINCARNATION

1. Bernard Faure, *Unmasking Buddhism* (West Sussex: Wiley, 2009), 53. This is not to say that the act is without precedent, as in Siddhartha Gautama's own birth story.

2. For some examples, see Stephen Batchelor, *After Buddhism: Rethinking the Dharma for a Secular Age* (New Haven, CT: Yale University Press, 2015); Owen Flanagan, *The Bodhisattva's Brain: Buddhism Naturalized* (Cambridge, MA: MIT Press, 2013); Robert Wright, *Why Buddhism Is True: The Science and Philosophy of Meditation and Enlightenment* (New York: Simon and Schuster, 2017). For an exception to this trend, see the brief but poignant reflections in Eve Kosofsky Sedgwick, *Touching Feeling: Affect, Pedagogy, Performativity* (Durham: Duke University Press, 2003), 177–80.

3. Schopenhauer had noted this: "Thus we find the doctrine of metempsychosis, springing from the very earliest and noblest ages of the human race, always world-wide, as the belief of the great majority of mankind, in fact really as the doctrine of all religions, with the exception of Judaism and the two religions that have arisen from it." Arthur Schopenhauer, *The World as Will and Representation*, trans. E.F.J. Payne (New York: Dover, 1966), 2:504. He notes some exceptions in the Abrahamic faiths too (506).

4. Gananath Obeyesekere, *Imagining Karma: Ethical Transformation in Amerindian, Buddhist, and Greek Thought* (Berkeley: University of California Press, 2002), 75.

5. Steven Collins has written several excellent studies about selflessness and the concept of nirvana in early Buddhism. Steven Collins, *Selfless Persons: Imagery and Thought in Theravada Buddhism* (Cambridge: Cambridge University Press, 1990); Steven Collins, *Nirvana and Other Buddhist Felicities: Utopias of the Pali Imaginaire* (Cambridge: Cambridge University Press, 1998).

6. On this see Roger-Pol Droit, *The Cult of Nothingness: The Philosophers and the Buddha*, trans. Pamela Vohnson (Chapel Hill: University of North Carolina Press, 2003).

7. Ralph Waldo Emerson, *The Collected Works of Ralph Waldo Emerson*, ed. Alfred Riggs Ferguson, Joseph Slater, and Jean Ferguson Carr, vol. 2 (Cambridge, MA: Harvard University Press, 1971), 18. For more on

Emerson and the theme of "metempsychosis" in American literature, see John Michael Corrigan, *American Metempsychosis: Emerson, Whitman, and the New Poetry* (New York: Fordham University Press, 2012).

8. Emerson, *The Collected Works of Ralph Waldo Emerson*, 2:18.

9. Robert Chambers, *Vestiges of the Natural History of Creation and Other Evolutionary Writings* (Chicago: University of Chicago Press, 1994).

10. David McMahan, "Buddhism and Global Secularisms," *Journal of Global Buddhism* 18 (2017): 115.

11. Thomas Henry Huxley, *Evolution and Ethics*, ed. Michael Ruse (Princeton, NJ: Princeton University Press, 2009); T. W. Rhys Davids, *Lectures on the Origin and Growth of Religion as Illustrated by Some Points in the History of Indian Buddhism*, The Hibbert Lectures, 1881 (Edinburgh: Williams and Norgate, 1881), 93. For more context on Victorian ideas about reincarnation, see J. Jeffrey Franklin, *The Lotus and the Lion: Buddhism and the British Empire* (Ithaca, NY: Cornell University Press, 2008), chapter 3. See also Vijitha Rajapakse, "Buddhism in Huxley's 'Evolution and Ethics': A Note on a Victorian Evaluation and Its 'Comparativist Dimension,'" *Philosophy East and West* 35, no. 3 (1985): 295–304.

12. For a helpful overview of the scholarship, see: Greg Bailey, "Buddhism and Caste," in *Oxford Bibliographies* (Oxford: Oxford University Press, 2014), DOI: 10.1093/OBO/9780195393521-0191.

13. Some standard biographies held in U.S. libraries include: Jerry S. Piven, *The Madness and Perversion of Yukio Mishima* (Westport, CT: Praeger, 2004); John Nathan, *Mishima: A Biography* (Cambridge, MA: Da Capo Press, 2000); Henry Scott Stokes, *The Life and Death of Yukio Mishima* (New York: Cooper Square Press, 2000); Marguerite Yourcenar, *Mishima: A Vision of the Void*, trans. Alberto Manguel (Chicago: University of Chicago Press, 2001); Damian Flanagan, *Yukio Mishima* (London: Reaktion Books, 2014).

14. Yukio Mishima, *Runaway Horses: The Sea of Fertility*, 2, trans. Michael Gallagher (New York: Vintage, 2013), 337.

15. "Only now did he see it for what it was, the most fundamental emotion he had felt toward Kiyoaki and Isao, the source of all lyricism in intellectual man, envy." Yukio Mishima, *The Decay of the Angel: The Sea of Fertility*, 4, trans. Edward G. Seidensticker (New York: Vintage, 2013), 137–38.

16. Mishima, *Runaway Horses*, 219. See Sigmund Freud, "Mourning and Melancholia," in *The Standard Edition of the Complete Psychological Works of Sigmund Freud*, trans. Anna Freud and James Strachey, vol. 14 (London: Hogarth Press, 1953), 237–58.

17. Roy Starrs, *Deadly Dialectics: Sex, Violence, and Nihilism in the World of Yukio Mishima* (Honolulu: University of Hawaii Press, 1994), 59; Susan Jolliffe Napier, *Escape from the Wasteland: Romanticism and Realism in the Fiction of Mishima Yukio and Oe Kenzaburo* (Cambridge, MA: Council on East Asian Studies, Harvard University, 1995), 206.

18. Yukio Mishima, *The Temple of Dawn*, trans. E. Dale Saunders and Cecilia Segawa Seigle (New York: Vintage, 1990), 89.

19. Starrs, *Deadly Dialectics*, 59.

20. Sara Janet Shaw, ed., *The Jatakas: Birth Stories of the Bodhisatta* (New York: Penguin, 2007), 1.

21. Michele Marra, "The Development of Mappo Thought in Japan (I)," *Japanese Journal of Religious Studies* 15, no. 1 (1988): 25–54.

22. For an overview see Donald S. Lopez Jr., *The Story of Buddhism: A Concise Guide to Its History and Teachings* (San Francisco: HarperOne, 2001, 19–36.

23. Mishima, *The Temple of Dawn*, 108–10.

24. Giambattista Vico, *New Science*, trans. Dave Marsh (New York: Penguin Classics, 2000), 2.

25. Giuseppe Mazzotta, *The New Map of the World: The Poetic Philosophy of Giambattista Vico* (Princeton, NJ: Princeton University Press, 1999), 5.

26. Mazzotta, 211.

27. Mazzotta, 228.

28. Vico, *New Science*, 478.

29. Mishima, *Runaway Horses*, 397.

30. Vico, *New Science*, 490.

31. For a helpful overview, see Leon Pompa, *Vico: A Study of the "New Science"* (New York: Cambridge University Press, 1990), 15–50. The essential relation for Vico is between the individual mind and "common sense": "Since human judgment is by nature uncertain, it gains certainty from our common sense about what is necessary and useful to humankind. . . . Common sense is judgment without reflection, shared by an entire class, an entire people, an entire nation, or the entire human race." Vico, *New Science*, 79–80.

32. Mishima, *The Decay of the Angel*, 221.

33. Mishima, *The Decay of the Angel*, 235.

34. Mishima, *The Decay of the Angel*, 236.

35. Mishima, *The Temple of Dawn*, 316.

36. Kojin Karatani has suggested that this is the case with Mishima's own life, which he calls "ironic," in the philosophical sense of being an evasion of dealing with reality. Karatani calls instead for an engagement with the "institutional and popular forms of Buddhism." I can't speak to Mishima's life, but I do think his fiction takes up precisely these questions. We can see this very well also in his novel *The Temple of the Golden Pavilion*. Kojin Karatani, *History and Repetition*, ed. Seiji Lippit (New York: Columbia University Press, 2011), 81, 186.

37. Quoted in a story by Richard Bernstein, "How One Fantasy Land Holds Onto the Heart of Another," *New York Times*, March 19, 1997, sec. C.

38. Jamyang Norbu, "Trapped by Buddha," *The New Humanist*, May 31, 2007, https://newhumanist.org.uk/articles/904/trapped-by-buddha.

39. See, for example, Jamyang Norbu, "The Great Middle Way Referendum Swindle," *Shadow Tibet* (blog), September 3, 2014, http://www.jamyangnorbu.com/blog/2014/09/03/the-great-middleway-referendum-swindle/.

40. Jamyang Norbu, *The Mandala of Sherlock Holmes* (New Delhi: Harper-Collins India, 2001), 267.

41. Steven Venturino, noting that Moriarty and Holmes struggle over a *material* stone in their epic battle, writes: "In the novel Tibetan Buddhism may help rescue the Dalai Lama and 'save the day,' but other, explicitly material forces will be required if Tibet and its contemporary population are to be saved." And David Damrosch notes that Holmes, in Norbu's hands, becomes a "strikingly otherworldly figure, even as Norbu uses crime fiction for very worldly political ends." Steven Venturino, "Placing Tibetan Fiction in a World of Literary Studies: Jamyang Norbu's *The Mandala of Sherlock Holmes*," in *Modern Tibetan Literature and Social Change*, ed. Lauran R. Hartley and Patricia Schiaffini-Vedani (Durham, NC: Duke University Press, 2008), 318. David Damrosch, "A Sinister Chuckle: Sherlock in Tibet," in

Crime Fiction as World Literature, ed. Louise Nilsson, David Damrosch, and Theo D'haen (New York: Bloomsbury, 2017), 257.

42. Kristin Guest, "Norbu's *The Mandala of Sherlock Holmes*: Neo-Victorian Occupations of the Past," *Neo-Victorian Studies* 3, no. 2 (2010): 85–86.

43. See, for example, the work on vision and light symbolism in Mahayana Buddhism in David McMahan, *Empty Vision: Metaphor and Visionary Imagery in Mahayana Buddhism* (New York: Routledge, 2013). Guest, "Norbu's *The Mandala of Sherlock Holmes*," 85–86.

44. Damrosch, "A Sinister Chuckle: Sherlock in Tibet," 267.

45. See Norbu, "Trapped by Buddha."

46. Chris Buckley, "China's Tensions With Dalai Lama Spill Into the Afterlife," *The New York Times*, March 11, 2015, http://www.nytimes.com/2015/03/12/world/asia/chinas-tensions-with-dalai-lama-spill-into-the-afterlife.html.

47. Jamyang Norbu, "The Real Threat to the Dalai Lama," *Shadow Tibet* (blog), February 5, 2016, http://www.jamyangnorbu.com/blog/2016/02/05/the-real-threat-to-the-dalai-lama/.

48. I understand Norbu to be undertaking the kind of anthropology described by David Scott, albeit from an "insider's" perspective: "On this view, the business of anthropology is not to seek to discover the authentic meaning of symbolic practice, but to grasp its *position* in that discursive tradition, and the social projects within which it is employed." Scott says this leads to the question, "Through what kinds of social practices authorized through what kinds of social discourses is a distinctive tradition established among the people being studied, and how within it do they learn to recognize themselves as distinctive subjects?" Norbu, I take it, is trying to shift the discursive tradition and the place Tibetans find themselves within it. This is different than Scott's concern for how an outside anthropologist understands *their own* conceptual baggage, but I find the general frame he (among others) enunciates for thinking about ritual as a kind of contested social power of use in understanding what Norbu is attempting. David Scott, *Formations of Ritual: Colonial and Anthropological Discourses on the Sinhala Yaktovil* (Minneapolis: University of Minnesota Press, 1994), xxii, xxiii.

49. Quoted in Norbu, *The Mandala of Sherlock Holmes*, epigraph.

50. Venturino writes incisively about this erasure of Tibet in "Placing Tibetan Fiction in a World of Literary Studies," 319–20.

51. Norbu, *The Mandala of Sherlock Holmes*, 6.

52. Norbu, 80.

53. Norbu, 36.

54. Dante Alighieri, *Inferno*, trans. Allen Mandelbaum (New York: Bantam Classics, 1982), I.1–3.

55. Joan M. Ferrante, *The Political Vision of the "Divine Comedy"* (Princeton, NJ: Princeton University Press, 1984), 3.

56. Norbu, *The Mandala of Sherlock Holmes*, 260; Dante Alighieri, *Paradiso*, trans. Allen Mandelbaum (New York: Bantam Classics, 1986), XXXIII.145.

57. See, for example, Kelsang Gyaltsen, "'Umaylam'—The Middle Way Approach," Central Tibetan Administration, September 29, 2014, http://tibet.net/2014/09/umaylam-the-middle-way-approach/.

58. See, for examples: Jamyang Norbu, "Not the Buddha's Middle Way," *Shadow Tibet* (blog), January 30, 2011, http://www.jamyangnorbu.com/blog/2011/01/30/not-the-buddhas-middle-way/; Norbu, "The Great Middle Way Referendum Swindle."

59. Norbu, "Not the Buddha's Middle Way."

60. Norbu, *The Mandala of Sherlock Holmes*, 145.

61. Norbu, "Trapped by Buddha."

62. Norbu, "Trapped by Buddha."

63. For scholarship on this point, see Alex Owen, *The Place of Enchantment: British Occultism and the Culture of the Modern* (Chicago: University of Chicago Press, 2007); Gauri Viswanathan, "In Search of Madame Blavatsky: Reading the Exoteric, Retrieving the Esoteric," *Representations* 141, no. 1 (February 2018): 67–94.

64. Guest, "Norbu's *The Mandala of Sherlock Holmes*," 81; Norbu, *The Mandala of Sherlock Holmes*, xxiv, 72, 76, 149.

65. Janet Gyatso, *Being Human in a Buddhist World: An Intellectual History of Medicine in Early Modern Tibet* (New York: Columbia University Press, 2015), 106.

66. Gyatso, 6–10, 108–25.

67. Robert A. F. Thurman, *Essential Tibetan Buddhism* (San Francisco: HarperOne, 1996), 6.

68. Thurman, 7.
69. Thurman, 8. The language of "quantum leap" is not incidental—there is a long tradition of suggesting that Buddhism anticipates modern science. See Donald S. Lopez Jr., *Buddhism and Science: A Guide for the Perplexed* (Chicago: University of Chicago Press, 2009).
70. Thurman, *Essential Tibetan Buddhism*, 8.
71. Thurman, 9; Donald S. Lopez Jr., *Prisoners of Shangri-La: Tibetan Buddhism and the West* (Chicago: University of Chicago Press, 1999), 207.
72. Lopez, *Prisoners of Shangri-La*, 207.
73. Norbu, *The Mandala of Sherlock Holmes*, 176–77.
74. Viswanathan expressed this idea to me in a workshop on this manuscript. October 4, 2019.
75. Norbu, *The Mandala of Sherlock Holmes*, 268; C. G. Jung, *Civilization in Transition*, ed. Gerhard Adler, trans. R.F.C. Hull, vol. 10 (Princeton, NJ: Princeton University Press, 1970), 388.
76. Norbu, *The Mandala of Sherlock Holmes*, 270; Jung, *Civilization in Transition*, 10:328.
77. Norbu, *The Mandala of Sherlock Holmes*, 270–71; Jung, *Civilization in Transition*, 10:328.
78. Jung, *Civilization in Transition*, 10:165.
79. Norbu, *The Mandala of Sherlock Holmes*, 120–36.
80. Jamyang Norbu, "Cult of Victimhood: Two Studies," *Shadow Tibet* (blog), March 31, 2010, http://www.jamyangnorbu.com/blog/2010/03/31/cult-of-victimhood-two-studies/.
81. Avram Alpert, *Global Origins of the Modern Self, from Montaigne to Suzuki* (Albany: State University of New York Press, 2019).
82. Guest, "Norbu's *The Mandala of Sherlock Holmes*," 91.
83. Norbu, *The Mandala of Sherlock Holmes*, xvi.
84. See, for examples, Derek Attridge, "A Writer's Life: J. M. Coetzee's *Elizabeth Costello*," *Virginia Quarterly Review* 80, no. 4 (Fall 2004); David Atwell, "The Life and Times of Elizabeth Costello: J. M. Coetzee and the Public Sphere," in *J. M. Coetzee and the Idea of the Public Intellectual*, ed. Jane Poyner (Athens: Ohio University Press, 2006), 25–41.
85. J. M. Coetzee, *Elizabeth Costello* (New York: Penguin, 2003), 77.
86. James Wood, "A Frog's Life," *London Review of Books*, October 23, 2003, https://www.lrb.co.uk/v25/n20/james-wood/a-frogs-life.

204 ℂ 2. REINCARNATION

87. Leo Tolstoi, *The Death of Ivan Ilyich*, trans. Richard Pevear and Larissa Volokhonsky (New York: Vintage, 2012), 32.

88. Sextus Empiricus, *Sextus Empiricus: Outlines of Scepticism*, ed. Julia Annas and Jonathan Barnes (Cambridge: Cambridge University Press, 2000), 120.

89. Richard Northover finds some common ground between Coetzee and Schopenhauer, while Jonathan Lamb links Coetzee's thoughts on animal life to a tradition of thinking the transmigration of souls between humans and animals. Richard Allen Northover, "Schopenhauer and Secular Salvation in the Work of J. M. Coetzee," *English in Africa* 41, no. 1 (September 22, 2015): 35–54. Jonathan Lamb, "Modern Metamorphoses and Disgraceful Tales," *Critical Inquiry* 28, no. 1 (2001): 133–66.

90. Coetzee, *Elizabeth Costello*.

91. Stephen Mulhall, *The Wounded Animal: J. M. Coetzee and the Difficulty of Reality in Literature and Philosophy* (Princeton, NJ: Princeton University Press, 2009), 176.

92. Eduardo Viveiros de Castro, "Zeno and the Art of Anthropology: Of Lies, Beliefs, Paradoxes, and Other Truths," trans. Antonia Walford, *Common Knowledge* 17, no. 1 (February 25, 2011): 132.

93. James Joyce, *Ulysses* (New York: Vintage, 1986), 52–53.

94. On Gaelic see Maria Tymoczko, *The Irish Ulysses* (Berkeley: University of California Press, 1997), 43–49. On Buddhism see the classic notes in Stuart Gilbert, *James Joyce's Ulysses: A Study*, 2nd rev. ed. (New York: Vintage, 1952), 33–37.

95. Joyce, *Ulysses*, 156, 137.

96. Coetzee, *Elizabeth Costello*, 20.

97. Coetzee, 22.

98. Coetzee, 31.

99. Coetzee, 80.

100. Coetzee, 133.

101. Coetzee, 177.

102. Coetzee, 220.

103. Coetzee, 1, 224.

104. Coetzee, 230.

105. J. M. Coetzee, *Inner Workings: Literary Essays 2000–2005* (London: Penguin, 2008), 10.

106. J. M. Coetzee, *Doubling the Point: Essays and Interviews*, ed. David Atwell (Cambridge: Harvard University Press, 1992), 248.

107. J. M. Coetzee, "Awakening," *The New York Review of Books*, October 23, 2003, https://www.nybooks.com/articles/2003/10/23/awakening/.

108. Coetzee, *Elizabeth Costello*, 127.

109. Collins, *Nirvana and Other Buddhist Felicities*, 250.

110. Collins, *Selfless Persons*, 193.

111. This is especially the case in popular accounts, such as those by Nhat Hanh, which are nevertheless very sophisticated. See Thich Nhat Hanh, *Interbeing: Fourteen Guidelines for Engaged Buddhism* (Berkeley: Parallax Press, 1987). For a critique of the interconnectedness approach, see Mark Siderits, "Is Everything Connected to Everything Else? What the Gopis Know," in *Moonshadows: Conventional Truth in Buddhist Philosophy*, by Cowherds (Oxford; New York: Oxford University Press, 2011), 167–80.

112. In her reading of *Elizabeth Costello*, Elizabeth Anker utilizes a concept of "interbeing" from the work of Maurice Merleau-Ponty. This concept is different to the extent that it lacks the agnostic moment and is not meant to have a connection to calm. While engaged by the possibilities this phenomenological conception of being-in-the-world with others offers, Anker still appreciates, as I do, that it does not resolve questions of ethics and embodiment. Rather, it simply allows us a new angle on the problem. Elizabeth Susan Anker, "*Elizabeth Costello*, Embodiment, and the Limits of Rights," *New Literary History* 42, no. 1 (2011): 169–92.

113. Coetzee, *Elizabeth Costello*, 115.

114. Coetzee, *Elizabeth Costello*, 31.

115. Franz Kafka, *The Metamorphosis: And Other Stories*, trans. Edwin Muir and Willa Muir (New York: Schocken, 1995), 173–84.

116. Coetzee, *Elizabeth Costello*, 221.

117. Coetzee, *Elizabeth Costello*, 203.

118. Coetzee, *Elizabeth Costello*, 20.

119. Karl Marx and Friedrich Engels, *The Marx-Engels Reader*, ed. Robert C. Tucker (New York: Norton, 1978), 595.

120. Coetzee, *Elizabeth Costello*, 225.

3. LIBERATION

1. For some recent examples, see: Thea N. Riofrancos and Daniel Denvir, "The 'Identity Politics' Debate Is Splintering the Left. Here's How We Can Move Past It," *In These Times*, February 14, 2017, http://inthesetimes .com/article/19902/heres-how-we-can-move-pastthe-identity-politics -debate-splintering-the-left; Suzanna Danuta Walters, "In Defense of Identity Politics," *Signs: Journal of Women in Culture and Society* 43, no. 2 (November 15, 2017): 473–88; Asad Haider, *Mistaken Identity: Race and Class in the Age of Trump* (New York: Verso, 2018).

2. bell hooks, "Waking Up to Racism," *Tricycle*, Fall 1994, https://tricycle .org/magazine/waking-racism/; bell hooks, "Agent of Change: An Interview with Bell Hooks," *Tricycle*, accessed August 3, 2013, http:// www.tricycle.com/special-section/agent-change-an-interview-with -bell-hooks.

3. Ann Gleig, "Queering Buddhism or Buddhist De-Queering?: Reflecting on Differences Amongst Western LGBTQI Buddhists and the Limits of Liberal Convert Buddhism," *Theology and Sexuality* 18, no. 3 (January 2012): 198–99.

4. Gleig, "Queering Buddhism or Buddhist De-Queering?," 199.

5. Ann Gleig, "Dharma Diversity and Deep Inclusivity at the East Bay Meditation Center: From Buddhist Modernism to Buddhist Post-modernism?" *Contemporary Buddhism* 15, no. 2 (July 3, 2014): 312–31.

6. Severo Sarduy, *Cobra and Maitreya*, trans. Susan Jill Levine (Normal, IL: Dalkey Archive Press, 1995), 36.

7. For this summary, I am indebted to previous critical work, especially Roberto González Echevarría, *La ruta de Severo Sarduy* (Hanover: Ediciones del Norte, 1987); Vilashini Cooppan, *Worlds Within: National Narratives and Global Connections in Postcolonial Writing* (Palo Alto, CA: Stanford University Press, 2009).

8. Rubén Gallo, "Sarduy avec Lacan: The Portrayal of French Psycho-analysis in *Cobra* and *La simulación*," *Revista Hispánica Moderna* 60, no. 1 (2007): 41.

9. Sarduy, *Cobra*, 149; translation emended. For more on the odd history of this phrase in its Western reception, see chapter 4 of Donald S. Lopez Jr., *Prisoners of Shangri-La: Tibetan Buddhism and the West* (Chicago: University of Chicago Press, 1999).

10. Jorge Aguilar Mora, *Severo Sarduy* (Madrid: Editorial Fundamentos, 1976), 30–31; Julia Alexis Kushigian, *Orientalism in the Hispanic Literary Tradition: In Dialogue with Borges, Paz, and Sarduy* (Albuquerque: University of New Mexico Press, 1991), 93; Echevarría, *La ruta de Severo Sarduy*, 161; Peter Hallward, *Absolutely Postcolonial: Writing Between the Singular and the Specific* (Manchester: Manchester University Press, 2001), 294–98; Cooppan, *Worlds Within*, 253–59; Cooppan, 253–59. Perhaps the most disappointing reading here is Hallward's; he spends a fair amount of time discussing Buddhism in his book, only to conclude that it is a regressive philosophical system that vitiates our political capacities. In spite of his calls for a "specific" criticism that takes context and relation seriously, Hallward fails to view Buddhism through such a critical lens. He registers *none* of the critical Buddhist studies that had been written throughout the 1980s and '90s. And even given all the Shambhala and Wisdom publications he cites, Hallward's claims about Buddhism are almost entirely wrong, or, at the very least, far outside of what is generally accepted. Unlike Sedgwick's writings from the same era, which recognize Buddhist diversity, Hallward seeks out the "essential" teaching of Buddhism. *Absolutely Postcolonial*, 10–11.

11. Sarduy, *Cobra*, 102.

12. Daisetz Teitaro Suzuki, *An Introduction to Zen Buddhism* (New York: Grove Press, 1964), 33.

13. Sarduy, *Cobra*, 102.

14. Sarduy, 103.

15. Hallward, *Absolutely Postcolonial*, 10.

16. See Lopez, *Prisoners of Shangri-La*, chapter 2, for the strange history of this book and title.

17. Sarduy, *Cobra*, 130.

18. Sarduy, 86.

19. Sarduy, 146.

20. Sarduy, 134.

21. Sarduy, 149. Given Sarduy's interest in contemporary American art, it is worth asking if the "Zen-inspired" Fluxus might have been on his mind, especially the neon-light tubes of Dan Flavin. This would add the possibility of signaling a possible small redemption through the circulation of ideas and the movements of history.

22. Sarduy, 149.

23. Cited in Lopez, *Prisoners of Shangri-La*, 120.

24. Sarduy, *Cobra*, 149; translation emended.

25. Lopez, *Prisoners of Shangri-La*, 132; Robert E. Buswell and Donald S. Lopez Jr., *The Princeton Dictionary of Buddhism* (Princeton, NJ: Princeton University Press, 2013), 82.

26. Although saying it is correct masks the fact that, as Lopez has argued, there are competing ideas within the history of Tibetan Buddhism as well. Many Tibetans are more concerned with the ritual practice that surrounds the phrase than the meaning, anyway. Lopez, *Prisoners of Shangri-La*, 132–34.

27. Lopez, 122–23.

28. Lopez, 133. That Buddhism itself was once a conqueror in Tibet shows the limitations of pointing to a pure Tibet prior to Chinese rule. On thinking through overlapping colonialisms more generally, see the provocative essay: Bruce Robbins, "Prolegomena to a Cosmopolitanism in Deep Time," *Interventions* 18, no. 2 (March 3, 2016): 172–86.

29. Sarduy, *Cobra*, 59.

30. Severo Sarduy, "Escrito sobre un cuerpo," in *Ensayos generales sobre el Barroco* (Mexico-Buenos Aires: Fondo de Cultura Económica, 1987), 258–63.

31. Sarduy, "Escrito sobre un cuerpo," 263.

32. In thinking about Sarduy's writings on "travestismo," I profited from the work of Ben Sifuentes-Jáuregui and Kzyrzstof Kuwalik. I follow Sifuentes-Jáuregui over Kuwalik in looking at Sarduy more as a thinker about the perpetual inversion rather than overcoming of categories. Ben Sifuentes-Jáuregui, *Transvestism, Masculinity, and Latin American Literature* (New York: Palgrave Macmillan, 2002), chapter 4; Krzysztof Kulawik, "Las Múltiples Faces Del Travesti: La Dispersión Del Sujeto En Los Espacios Transculturales de La Narrativa Neobarroca de Severo Sarduy," *Literatura: Teoría, Historia, Crítica* 17, no. 1 (2015): 207–44.

33. Janet Gyatso, "One Plus One Makes Three: Buddhist Gender, Monasticism, and the Law of the Non-Excluded Middle," *History of Religions* 43, no. 2 (2003): 94.

34. Gyatso, 99.

35. Gyatso, 100–101.
36. Gyatso, 104.
37. Gyatso, 104.
38. Avram Alpert, "Buddhism and the Postmodern Novel: Severo Sarduy's *Cobra*," *Twentieth Century Literature* 62, no. 1 (2016): 32–55.
39. In a provocative reading of the novel, Clare Counihan suggests that the seeming utopic end—almost taken for granted in most criticism—is in fact a continued vision of a failed postcolonial landscape: "Escaping a hell created by the delimiting and impossible narratives of racial and gendered identity, Elizabeth enters into a hell unrecognized by herself or her companions, one defined by the absence of difference and the death of desire." While I will disagree with Counihan in what follows, I found her reading helpfully troubled certain assumptions about Head's novel and forced me to read more closely the twists and turns of Elizabeth's mind and social life. Clare Counihan, "The Hell of Desire: Narrative, Identity and Utopia in *A Question of Power*," *Research in African Literatures* 42, no. 1 (2011): 80.
40. Bessie Head, *A Question of Power* (Oxford: Heinemann, 1974), 35.
41. Head, 199; in italics in original.
42. It would be interesting to read the many references to and apparent solidarity with Jewish people in the novel as part of this project, especially the explicit link between Buddha and David and Buddha's wife and Bathsheba. Those who praise "harmony with the earth" as part of a new ecological politics often overlook the fact that such an argument has potentially dangerous (though not inherent) connections with fascistic "blood and soil" arguments. The Jews, as forced nomads (or, in Daniel Boyarin's reading, as a people constituted by the meaningfulness of diaspora in relation to textual traditions), are often seen in dark times as being opposed to such an ethics. Bringing Jews and Buddhists together, Head shows the complexity of thinking a relation between exile (her own, the Buddha's own) and belonging, and how each is a dialectical concept with no necessary positive ethical force. On references in the novel, see Head, 18, 43, 46–47, 65, 86, 199. For Boyarin's provocative and learned argument, see Daniel Boyarin, *A Traveling Homeland: The Babylonian Talmud as Diaspora* (Philadelphia: University of Pennsylvania Press, 2015).

43. This point is, I think, missed by some of Head's critics, who tend to view her as either abandoning Buddhism or fully embracing some generic version of its philosophy. For contrasting examples see Paul H. Lorenz, "Colonization and the Feminine in Bessie Head's *A Question of Power*," *MFS Modern Fiction Studies* 37, no. 3 (1991): 591–605; June Campbell, "Beyond Duality: A Buddhist Reading of Bessie Head's *A Question of Power*," *The Journal of Commonwealth Literature* 28 (1993): 64–81.

44. My thanks to an anonymous reader for reminding me of the need to see the whole myth. Rewriting it is also fundamental to Ambedkar's vision of the Buddha's life. B. R. Ambedkar, *The Buddha and His Dhamma: A Critical Edition*, ed. Aakash Singh Rathore and Ajay Verma (New Delhi; Oxford; New York: Oxford University Press, 2011).

45. There are numerous studies here. For an interesting overview of early doctrinal matters, see Alice Collett, ed., *Women in Early Indian Buddhism: Comparative Textual Studies* (New York: Oxford University Press, 2014). For some recent ethnographic works that give very different conclusions based on region and topic, and also provide helpful comparative background, see Tessa J. Bartholomeusz, *Women Under the Bo Tree: Buddhist Nuns in Sri Lanka* (Cambridge: Cambridge University Press, 1994); Steven Collins and Justin McDaniel, "Buddhist 'Nuns' (Mae Chi) and the Teaching of Pali in Contemporary Thailand," *Modern Asian Studies* 44, no. 06 (November 2010): 1373–1408; Kim Gutschow, *Being a Buddhist Nun: The Struggle for Enlightenment in the Himalayas* (Cambridge, MA: Harvard University Press, 2004); Nirmala Salgado, *Buddhist Nuns and Gendered Practice: In Search of the Female Renunciant* (Oxford: Oxford University Press, 2013).

46. Head, *A Question of Power*, 18.

47. Miranda Shaw, *Passionate Enlightenment: Women in Tantric Buddhism* (Princeton, NJ: Princeton University Press, 1995), 145.

48. Shaw, 143.

49. Liz Wilson, "Introduction: Family and the Construction of Religious Communities," in *Family in Buddhism*, ed. Liz Wilson (Albany: State University of New York Press, 2013), 2.

50. John S. Strong, "A Family Quest: The Buddha, Yaśodharā, and Rāhula in the Mūlasarvāstivāda Vinaya," in *Sacred Biography in the*

Buddhist Traditions of South and Southeast Asia, ed. Juliane Schober (Honolulu: University of Hawai'i Press, 1997), 116.

51. Head, *A Question of Power*, 11, 12.

52. Head, 191.

53. Head, 11.

54. Head, 190.

55. Head, 32.

56. Head, 33.

57. Head, 43.

58. Head, 201–2.

59. Head, 202.

60. Head, 206.

61. Jacqueline Rose has written an intriguing essay on how madness—as something that embodies many voices in one individual—is part of the universal logic of the novel. Jacqueline Rose, "On the 'Universality' of Madness: Bessie Head's 'A Question of Power,'" *Critical Inquiry* 20, no. 3 (April 1, 1994): 401–18.

62. Head, *A Question of Power*, 47.

63. Head, 161.

64. For a prehistory and general overview of this series, see Henrik H. Sørensen, "A Study of the 'Ox-Herding Theme' as Sculptures at Mt. Baoding in Dazu County, Sichuan," *Artibus Asiae* 51, no. 3/4 (1991): 210–14.

65. Steven Heine, "When There Are No More Cats to Argue About: Chan Buddhist Views of Animals in Relation to Universal Buddha-Nature," *Journal of Chinese Philosophy* 43, no. 3/4 (September 2016): 242; Sørensen, "A Study of the 'Ox-Herding Theme,'" 210.

66. Charles Johnson, *Oxherding Tale* (New York: Plume, 1995), xiii.

67. These include Rudolph P. Byrd, *Charles Johnson's Novels: Writing the American Palimpsest* (Bloomington: Indiana University Press, 2005); Jonathan Little, *Charles Johnson's Spiritual Imagination* (Columbia: University of Missouri Press, 1997); William R. Nash, *Charles Johnson's Fiction* (Urbana: University of Illinois Press, 2003); Linda Selzer, *Charles Johnson in Context* (Amherst: University of Massachusetts Press, 2009); Gary Storhoff, *Understanding Charles Johnson* (Columbia: University of South Carolina Press, 2004).

68. Charles Johnson, *Turning the Wheel: Essays on Buddhism and Writing* (New York: Scribner, 2003).

69. Charles Taylor, *Sources of the Self: The Making of the Modern Identity* (Cambridge: Cambridge University Press, 1989), 129, 131.

70. Taylor, 131–32.

71. Taylor, 132.

72. Johnson, *Oxherding Tale*, 119.

73. Edmund Husserl, *Cartesian Meditations: An Introduction to Phenomenology* (The Hague: M. Nijhoff, 1966), 157. On Husserl's own somewhat spare interest in other cultures, see Robert Bernasconi, "Lévy-Bruhl Among the Phenomenologists: Exoticisation and the Logic of 'the Primitive,'" *Social Identities* 11, no. 3 (May 1, 2005): 229–45.

74. Maurice Merleau-Ponty, *Phenomenology of Perception* (London; New York: Routledge, 2002), xii.

75. Johnson, *Oxherding Tale*, 153.

76. Johnson, xvii.

77. Frantz Fanon, *Black Skin, White Masks*, trans. Richard Philcox (New York: Grove Press, 2008), xvii.

78. Fanon, 91.

79. Johnson, *Oxherding Tale*, 52.

80. Johnson, 76–77, 147. Hence I agree with Rudolph Byrd that Johnson's narrative is deeply indebted to another literary model of moving through different "ways," namely, Hesse's *Siddhartha*. There is also something of Hegel's *Phenomenology* here, which itself borrows from *Wilhelm Meister* and the *Odyssey*. And yet again, this is also available to us in the *Rig Veda* and the "Ten Oxherding Pictures." The point in Johnson is always to comprehend the multiplicity of origins on the way to whole sight. This is also why I don't follow Gleason's mapping of the narrative onto the ten pictures—the narrative just has too many other interlocutors and too many other paths on its way. Rudolph P. Byrd, "*Oxherding Tale* and *Siddhartha*: Philosophy, Fiction, and the Emergence of a Hidden Tradition," *African American Review* 30, no. 4 (1996): 549–58; William Gleason, "The Liberation of Perception: Charles Johnson's *Oxherding Tale*," *Black American Literature Forum* 25, no. 4 (1991): 705–28.

81. hooks, "Agent of Change: An Interview with Bell Hooks."

82. Johnson, *Oxherding Tale*, 120.
83. Johnson, 140.
84. See the discussions of *satori* in Daisetz Teitaro Suzuki, *Zen Buddhism: Selected Writings*, ed. William Barrett (Garden City, NY: Doubleday, 1956).
85. This is even the case in Suzuki. Daisetz Teitaro Suzuki, "An Autobiographical Account," in *A Zen Life: D. T. Suzuki Remembered*, ed. Masao Abe (New York: Weatherhill, 1986), 13–26.
86. Johnson, *Oxherding Tale*, 147.
87. Johnson here appears to deconstruct the famous distinction between the householder and the money-maker in the first chapter Aristotle's *Politics*. Again, if we refuse the separation and home and world, then we insist that there must be an ethical way to engage in business—one that is beyond profit motives.
88. Johnson, *Oxherding Tale*, 173.
89. Johnson, 174.
90. Johnson, 176. Johnson here is likely responding to the classic kōan: "What was your original face like before your parents were born?" For Johnson, it seems, it was many faces. This kōan also makes an appearance in Natsume Soseki's much more Zen-skeptical novel, *The Gate* (1910).
91. The idea that touch opens us to others and to broader visions of life is of course a theme from many places, but, as Rudolph Byrd notes, it most locally echoes the scenes of enlightenment by touch in Hesse's *Siddhartha*. Byrd, "*Oxherding Tale* and *Siddhartha*."
92. Johnson, *Oxherding Tale*, 176.
93. Matthew J. Moore, "Political Theory in Canonical Buddhism," *Philosophy East and West* 65, no. 1 (February 2, 2015): 43. Moore's point is that the canonical texts suggest an enlightened monarchy is best suited to these ends, but the goal does not of course preclude other modes of governance.
94. I do think that Hallward is closer to his target with Johnson than with Sarduy, although his ultimate claim here may again go too far: "Johnson works toward the immediate equation of an . . . African-American place with placelessness itself." It is clear that there is something like this at work in the novel's conclusion, but it ignores the very real and

embodied work of reconstruction that Johnson's characters continue to undertake. In other words, the two truths are missing in Hallward's analysis, but not necessarily in Johnson's story. Hallward, *Absolutely Postcolonial*, 137.

4. AUTHENTICITY

1. Gabriel García Márquez, *Los funerales de la Mamá Grande* (New York: Vintage Espanol, 2010), 31.

2. Karl Marx and Friedrich Engels, *The Marx-Engels Reader*, ed. Robert C. Tucker (New York: Norton, 1978), 595.

3. Jean-Paul Sartre, *Anti-Semite and Jew* (New York: Schocken, 1965), 42. Sartre, curiously enough, has an important if accidental place in the history of authenticity in modern Buddhism, since it was the translation of his term *engagé* by Vietnamese Buddhists that led to the naming of "Engaged Buddhism." Elise A. DeVido, "The Influence of Chinese Master Taixu on Buddhism in Vietnam," *Journal of Global Buddhism* 10 (2009): 436–37.

4. Charles Taylor, *The Ethics of Authenticity* (Cambridge, MA: Harvard University Press, 1992), 2–10.

5. Michael D. Coogan, Marc Z. Brettler, and Carol Newsom, eds., *The Holy Bible: New Revised Standard Version* (New York: Oxford University Press, 1989), Isaiah 29:13.

6. Robert Sharf, *Coming to Terms with Chinese Buddhism: A Reading of the Treasure Store Treatise* (Honolulu: University of Hawaii Press, 2005), 14.

7. Martin Heidegger, *Being and Time: A Translation of* Sein Und Zeit, trans. Joan Stambaugh (Albany: State University of New York Press, 1996), 47.

8. Heidegger, *Being and Time*.

9. W. E. B. Du Bois, *The Souls of Black Folk*, ed. Henry Louis Gates Jr. and Terri Hume Oliver, Norton Critical Editions (New York: Norton, 1999), 11.

10. Lewis R. Gordon, "Rockin' It in Blue: A Black Existential Essay on Jimi Hendrix," *Discourse* 39, no. 2 (September 14, 2017): 218.

11. Lewis R. Gordon, "Rarely Kosher: Studying Jews of Color in North America," *American Jewish History* 100, no. 1 (January 7, 2016): 115.

12. Lewis R. Gordon, *Bad Faith and Antiblack Racism* (Amherst, NY: Humanity Books, 1995), 59–64, 149–55.

13. Gordon, *Bad Faith and Antiblack Racism*, 182; Taylor, *The Ethics of Authenticity*, 91; Lionel Trilling, *Sincerity and Authenticity* (Cambridge, MA: Harvard University Press, 1973), 11; Sartre, *Anti-Semite and Jew*, chapter 3. This is not the canonical account in Sartre, but it is one of his clearest expositions. Gordon's claim overlaps with Stanley Cavell's ideas about "acknowledgment," which I discuss at the end of this chapter.

14. Alan W. Watts, "Beat Zen, Square Zen, and Zen," *Chicago Review* 12, no. 2 (1958): 6.

15. Cited in Kemmyō Taira Sato, "D. T. Suzuki and the Question of War," trans. Thomas Kirchner, *Eastern Buddhist* 39, no. 1 (2008): 117.

16. There is a long-standing debate about this. See, for examples: Brian Daizen Victoria, *Zen at War* (Lanham, MD: Rowman & Littlefield, 2006); Sato, "D. T. Suzuki and the Question of War"; Christopher Ives, *Imperial-Way Zen: Ichikawa Hakugen's Critique and Lingering Questions for Buddhist Ethics* (Honolulu: University of Hawai'i Press, 2009).

17. For critical replies that also give overviews of Žižek's positions, see: William D. Hart, "Slavoj Žižek and the Imperial/Colonial Model of Religion," *Nepantla: Views from South* 3, no. 3 (December 19, 2002): 553–78; Eske Møllgaard, "Slavoj Žižek's Critique of Western Buddhism," *Contemporary Buddhism* 9, no. 2 (November 1, 2008): 167–80; Marcus Boon, Eric Cazdyn, and Timothy Morton, *Nothing: Three Inquiries in Buddhism* (Chicago: University of Chicago Press, 2015); Toni J. Koivulahti, "Compassionate Apocalypse: Slavoj Žižek and Buddhism," *Critical Research on Religion* 5, no. 1 (April 1, 2017): 34–47.

18. Slavoj Žižek, *Less Than Nothing: Hegel and the Shadow of Dialectical Materialism*, reprint edition (London: Verso, 2013), 135.

19. Jamie Hubbard and Paul Swanson, eds., *Pruning the Bodhi Tree: The Storm Over Critical Buddhism* (Honolulu: University of Hawai'i Press, 1997); James Mark Shields, "Liberation as Revolutionary Praxis: Rethinking Buddhist Materialism," *Journal of Buddhist Ethics* 20 (2013): 461–99.

20. Žižek, *Less Than Nothing*, 135.

21. J. D. Salinger, *The Catcher in the Rye* (Boston: Little, Brown, 1991), 224.

22. Arthur Danto, "Upper West Side Buddhism," in *Buddha Mind in Contemporary Art*, ed. Jacquelynn Baas and Mary Jane Jacob (Berkeley: University of California Press, 2004), 54.

23. J. D. Salinger, *Raise High the Roof Beam, Carpenters and Seymour: An Introduction* (Boston: Little, Brown, 1963), 242.

24. For a bibliography of earlier discussions of Salinger and Zen, see Dennis McCort, "Hyakujo's Geese, Amban's Doughnuts and Rilke's Carrousel: Sources East and West for Salinger's 'Catcher,'" *Comparative Literature Studies* 34, no. 3 (1997): 276n2. McCort's own essay makes the standard general claims about Zen. The one piece of critical Zen scholarship he cites, by Bernard Faure, criticizes how "the complex reality of Chan was gradually replaced by a simplistic image of its mythic past." While McCort is appreciative of Faure, this problematic does not fully enter into his analysis. Bernard Faure, *The Rhetoric of Immediacy: A Cultural Critique of Chan/Zen Buddhism* (Princeton, NJ: Princeton University Press, 1991), 19.

25. J. D. Salinger, *Franny and Zooey* (Boston: Little, Brown, 1961), 36, 37.

26. Salinger, 40.

27. Salinger, 65.

28. Salinger, 66.

29. The lectures, which were recently published in Japan by Matsugaoka Bunko, Suzuki's archive, will be widely available soon from Columbia University Press, edited by Richard Jaffe.

30. For an overview, see Jaffe, "Introduction," in *Selected Works of D. T. Suzuki, Volume I: Zen*, by Daisetsu Teitaro Suzuki (Berkeley: University of California Press, 2014(, xi–lvi.

31. Daisetz Teitaro Suzuki, "An Autobiographical Account," in *A Zen Life: D. T. Suzuki Remembered*, ed. Masao Abe (New York: Weatherhill, 1986), 27.

32. Daisetz Teitaro Suzuki, *An Introduction to Zen Buddhism* (New York: Grove Press, 1964), 21.

33. On the former point, see Jane Iwamura, *Virtual Orientalism: Asian Religions and American Popular Culture* (Oxford: Oxford University Press, 2010). And on the latter see Suzuki himself: *Zen and Japanese Culture* (Princeton, NJ: Princeton University Press, 2010).

34. Watts, *The Way of Zen* (New York: Vintage, 1999), 20; John Cage, *A Year from Monday: New Lectures and Writings* (Middletown, CT: Wesleyan University Press, 1967), 96.

35. Ichikawa Hakugen, "A Preliminary Conception of Zen Social Ethics," *Journal of Indian and Buddhist Studies* 11, no. 1 (1963): 356–55.

36. Hakamaya Noriaki, "Critical Philosophy Versus Topical Philosophy," in *Pruning the Bodhi Tree: The Storm Over Critical Buddhism*, ed. Jamie Hubbard and Paul Swanson (Honolulu: University of Hawai`i Press, 1997), 74.

37. Robert Sharf, "The Zen of Japanese Nationalism," *History of Religions* 33, no. 1 (1993): 1–43.

38. Victor Hori, "Kōan and Kenshō in the Rinzai Zen Curriculum," in *The Koan: Texts and Contexts in Zen Buddhism*, ed. Steven Heine and Dale Wright (New York: Oxford University Press, 2000), 309.

39. Avram Alpert, *Global Origins of the Modern Self, from Montaigne to Suzuki* (Albany: State University of New York Press, 2019), chapter 7. Some of the discussion of Suzuki here is adapted from this earlier work.

40. Ross Posnock, *Renunciation: Acts of Abandonment by Writers, Philosophers, and Artists* (Cambridge, MA: Harvard University Press, 2016), 161.

41. Posnock, 162.

42. Posnock, 43.

43. Robert Sharf, "Buddhist Modernism and the Rhetoric of Meditative Experience," *Numen* 42, no. 3 (1995): 244.

44. Amy Hungerford, *Postmodern Belief: American Literature and Religion Since 1960* (Princeton, NJ: Princeton University Press, 2010), 9.

45. Hungerford, 11.

46. Hungerford, 10.

47. Hungerford, 11.

48. Salinger, *Franny and Zooey*, 103–4.

49. Salinger, 139.

50. Cited in Manfred Frank, *The Philosophical Foundations of Early German Romanticism*, trans. Elizabeth Millan-Zaibert (Albany: State University of New York Press, 2004), 50.

51. Salinger, *Franny and Zooey*, 119.

52. Salinger, 76.

53. Salinger, 149.

54. See, for example, Gregory Schopen, *Buddhist Monks and Business Matters: Still More Papers on Monastic Buddhism in India* (Honolulu: University of Hawaii Press, 2004).

55. Trilling, *Sincerity and Authenticity*, 124.

56. Salinger, *Franny and Zooey*, 198–99.

57. This is in part why I do not find Hungerford's "no doctrine" reading sufficient. There are real differences in doctrine here.

58. According to Taylor, this is the grounding idea (traceable to Herder) of much of the modern discourse on authenticity. Taylor, *The Ethics of Authenticity*, 28–29.

59. Daisetz Teitaro Suzuki, *Zen Buddhism: Selected Writings*, ed. William Barrett (Garden City, NY: Doubleday, 1956), 325. The quote appears in the "Zooey" story, originally published in 1957. Suzuki's name appears in the original version. J. D. Salinger, "Zooey," *The New Yorker*, May 4, 1957, 38.

60. William Barrett, "Zen for the West," in Suzuki, *Zen Buddhism*, xii.

61. For example: Suzuki writes, "By acquiring the intellectual freedom the soul is in full possession of itself; birth and death no longer torment it; for there are no such dualities anywhere; we live even through death." While Heidegger maintains, "Only being free *for* death gives Da-sein its absolute goal and knocks existence into its finitude. The finitude of existence thus seized upon tears one back out of endless multiplicity of possibilities offering themselves . . . [and] brings Da-sein to the simplicity of its *fate*." Suzuki, *An Introduction*, 60. Heidegger, *Being and Time*, 351; emphases in original.

62. I put "existentialism" in scare quotes because Heidegger famously rejected the label in his "Letter on Humanism."

63. William Barrett, *Irrational Man: A Study in Existential Philosophy* (New York: Anchor, 1958), 225–26; my emphasis. For the 1947 discussion, see William Barrett, *What Is Existentialism?* (New York: Partisan Review, 1947), 32–36.

64. Salinger, *Franny and Zooey*, 202; emphases mine.

65. It is perhaps not surprising that every so often there is a call to reevaluate Suzuki, which I have joined here and elsewhere. See also:

Luis O. Gomez, "D. T. Suzuki's Contribution to Modern Buddhist Scholarship," in *A Zen Life: D. T. Suzuki Remembered*, ed. Francis Haar and Masao Abe (New York: Weatherhill, 1986); Thomas Kasulis, "Reading D. T. Suzuki Today," *Eastern Buddhist* 38, no. 1/2 (2007): 41–57; Jaffe, "Introduction."

66. "The Official Homepage for Lama Zopa Rinpoche—FPMT," accessed July 13, 2018, https://fpmt.org/teachers/zopa/.

67. Thubten Zopa and Lama Zopa Rinpoche, *Ultimate Healing: The Power of Compassion* (New York: Simon and Schuster, 2001), 174.

68. Zadie Smith, *The Autograph Man* (New York: Vintage, 2002), 40.

69. Smith, 279.

70. Jonathan Sell, for example, finds it a subterfuge for the novel's thoroughly materialist logic. He concludes: "The reader who attempts to find Kabbalistic or Zen significances in the events of each chapter in the two books is engaged on a hermeneutic wild goose-chase." At the opposite end of the critical spectrum is Songyun Zheng, who argues that there is "substantial influence of the original Ten bulls on Smith's writing." Tracing this through the narrative, Zheng sees Alex becoming selfless and enlightened. Jonathan P.A. Sell, "Chance and Gesture in Zadie Smith's *White Teeth* and *The Autograph Man*: A Model for Multicultural Identity?," *The Journal of Commonwealth Literature* 41, no. 3 (September 1, 2006): 34. Songyun Zheng, "Postsecular Return of Religion: Jewish and Zen Elements in Zadie Smith's *The Autograph Man*," *Neohelicon*, June 25, 2018, 1–15, https://doi.org/10.1007/s11059-018-0439-8.

71. Smith, *The Autograph Man*, 54, 119.

72. Smith, 97, 198.

73. Smith, 341.

74. Smith, 342.

75. Virginia Woolf, *Moments of Being* (San Diego: Mariner Books, 1985), 142; my emphasis.

76. Wallace as cited in Zadie Smith, *Changing My Mind: Occasional Essays* (New York: Penguin, 2009), 281; Smith's emphasis.

77. Ludwig Wittgenstein, *Philosophical Investigations*, trans. G. E. M. Anscombe (Oxford: Basil Blackwell, 1968), section 19.

78. Stanley Cavell, *Must We Mean What We Say?: A Book of Essays* (New York: Cambridge University Press, 2002), 324.

79. Stanley Cavell, *The Claim of Reason: Wittgenstein, Skepticism, Morality, and Tragedy* (New York: Oxford University Press, 1979), xxi.

BIBLIOGRAPHY

Abe, Stanley. "Inside the Wonder House: Buddhist Art and the West." In *Curators of the Buddha: The Study of Buddhism Under Colonialism*, ed. Donald S. Lopez Jr., 63–106. Chicago: University of Chicago Press, 1995.

Achebe, Chinua. "An Image of Africa." *The Massachusetts Review* 18, no. 4 (1977): 782–94.

Aguilar Mora, Jorge. *Severo Sarduy*. Madrid: Editorial Fundamentos, 1976.

Alabaster, Henry, and Thiphākōnwongmahākōsāthibōdī. *The wheel of the law: Buddhism, illustrated from Siamese sources by the Modern Buddhist, a Life of Buddha, and an account of the Phrabat*. London: Trübner, 1871.

Alighieri, Dante. *Inferno*. Trans. Allen Mandelbaum. New York: Bantam Classics, 1982.

——. *Paradiso*. Trans. Allen Mandelbaum. New York: Bantam Classics, 1986.

Almond, Philip C. *The British Discovery of Buddhism*. Cambridge; New York: Cambridge University Press, 1988.

Alpert, Avram. "Buddhism and the Postmodern Novel: Severo Sarduy's Cobra." *Twentieth Century Literature* 62, no. 1 (2016): 32–55.

——. *Global Origins of the Modern Self, from Montaigne to Suzuki*. Albany: State University of New York Press, 2019.

Ambedkar, B. R. *The Buddha and His Dhamma: A Critical Edition*. Ed. Aakash Singh Rathore and Ajay Verma. New Delhi; Oxford; New York: Oxford University Press, 2011.

Anderson, Kevin. *Marx at the Margins: On Nationalism, Ethnicity, and Non-Western Societies.* Chicago: University of Chicago Press, 2010.

Anker, Elizabeth Susan. *"Elizabeth Costello,* Embodiment, and the Limits of Rights." *New Literary History* 42, no. 1 (2011): 169–92.

Aravamudan, Srinivas. *Guru English: South Asian Religion in a Cosmopolitan Language.* Princeton, NJ: Princeton University Press, 2005.

Arnold, Dan, and Alicia Turner. "Opinion | Why Are We Surprised When Buddhists Are Violent?" *The New York Times,* March 5, 2018, sec. Opinion. https://www.nytimes.com/2018/03/05/opinion/buddhists-violence -tolerance.html.

Attridge, Derek. "A Writer's Life: J. M. Coetzee's *Elizabeth Costello." Virginia Quarterly Review* 80, no. 4 (Fall 2004).

Atwell, David. "The Life and Times of Elizabeth Costello: J. M. Coetzee and the Public Sphere." In *J. M. Coetzee and the Idea of the Public Intellectual,* ed. Jane Poyner, 25–41. Athens: Ohio University Press, 2006.

Bailey, Greg. "Buddhism and Caste." In *Oxford Bibliographies.* Oxford: Oxford University Press, 2014. DOI: 10.1093/OBO/9780195393521-0191.

Barnett, Robert. "Symbols and Protest: The Iconography of Demonstrations in Tibet, 1987–89." In *Resistance and Reform in Tibet: 40 Years On, Tibet 1950–90,* ed. Robert Barnett, 238–58. Bloomington: Indiana University Press, 1994.

Barrett, William. *Irrational Man: A Study in Existential Philosophy.* New York: Anchor, 1958.

——. *What Is Existentialism?* New York: Partisan Review, 1947.

——. "Zen for the West." In *Zen Buddhism: Selected Writings,* by Daisetz Teitaro Suzuki. Garden City, NY: Doubleday, 1956.

Barstow, Geoffrey. *Food of Sinful Demons: Meat, Vegetarianism, and the Limits of Buddhism in Tibet.* New York: Columbia University Press, 2017.

Bartholomeusz, Tessa J. *Women Under the Bō Tree: Buddhist Nuns in Sri Lanka.* Cambridge: Cambridge University Press, 1994.

Batchelor, Stephen. *After Buddhism: Rethinking the Dharma for a Secular Age.* New Haven, CT: Yale University Press, 2015.

Beckett, Samuel. *Endgame and Act Without Words.* New York: Grove, 2009.

——. *Nohow On: Company, Ill Seen Ill Said, and Worstward Ho.* New York: Grove, 2014.

Beek, Kimberly. "Buddhism and Modern Literature." In *Buddhism*. Oxford Bibliographies, 2016. https://www.oxfordbibliographies.com/view/docu ment/obo-9780195393521/obo-9780195393521-0230.xml?q=buddhism+ and+modern+literature.

Bernasconi, Robert. "Lévy-Bruhl Among the Phenomenologists: Exoticisation and the Logic of 'the Primitive.'" *Social Identities* 11, no. 3 (May 1, 2005): 229–45.

Bernstein, Richard. "How One Fantasy Land Holds Onto the Heart of Another." *New York Times,* March 19, 1997, sec. C.

Block, Fred. "Introduction." In *The Great Transformation: The Political and Economic Origins of Our Time*, by Karl Polanyi. Boston: Beacon Press, 2001.

Blum, Beth. *The Self-Help Compulsion: Searching for Advice in Modern Literature.* New York: Columbia University Press, 2020.

Bonney, William Wesley. *Thorns and Arabesques: Contexts for Conrad's Fiction.* Baltimore, MD: Johns Hopkins University Press, 1980.

Boon, Marcus, Eric Cazdyn, and Timothy Morton. *Nothing: Three Inquiries in Buddhism.* Chicago: University of Chicago Press, 2015.

Borchert, Thomas. "Worry for the Dai Nation: Sipsongpannā, Chinese Modernity, and the Problems of Buddhist Modernism." *The Journal of Asian Studies* 67, no. 1 (February 2008): 107–42.

Boyarin, Daniel. *A Traveling Homeland: The Babylonian Talmud as Diaspora.* Philadelphia: University of Pennsylvania Press, 2015.

Bramble, John. *Modernism and the Occult.* New York: Palgrave Macmillan, 2015.

Brashers, H. C. "Conrad, Marlow, and Gautama Buddha." *Conradiana* 1 (1969): 63–71.

Braun, Erik. *The Birth of Insight: Meditation, Modern Buddhism, and the Burmese Monk Ledi Sayadaw.* Chicago: University of Chicago Press, 2013.

Buckley, Chris. "China's Tensions With Dalai Lama Spill Into the Afterlife." *The New York Times*, March 11, 2015. http://www.nytimes.com/2015 /03/12/world/asia/chinas-tensions-with-dalai-lama-spill-into-the -afterlife.html.

Buswell, Robert E., and Donald S. Lopez Jr. *The Princeton Dictionary of Buddhism.* Princeton, NJ: Princeton University Press, 2013.

Byrd, Rudolph P. *Charles Johnson's Novels: Writing the American Palimpsest.* Bloomington: Indiana University Press, 2005.

Byrd, Rudolph P. "Oxherding Tale and Siddhartha: Philosophy, Fiction, and the Emergence of a Hidden Tradition." *African American Review* 30, no. 4 (1996): 549–58.

Cage, John. *A Year from Monday: New Lectures and Writings*. Middletown: Wesleyan University Press, 1967.

Campbell, June. "Beyond Duality: A Buddhist Reading of Bessie Head's *A Question of Power*." *The Journal of Commonwealth Literature* 28 (1993): 64–81.

Caracciolo, Peter. "Buddhist Typologies in *Heart of Darkness* and *Victory* and Their Contribution to the Modernism of Jacob Epstein, Wyndham Lewis, and T. S. Eliot." *The Conradian* 11, no. 1 (1986): 24–34.

Castoriadis, Cornelius. *Philosophy, Politics, Autonomy*. New York: Oxford University Press, 1991.

de Castro, Eduardo Viveiros. "Zeno and the Art of Anthropology: Of Lies, Beliefs, Paradoxes, and Other Truths." Trans. Antonia Walford. *Common Knowledge* 17, no. 1 (February 25, 2011): 128–45.

Cavell, Stanley. *The Claim of Reason: Wittgenstein, Skepticism, Morality, and Tragedy*. New York: Oxford University Press, 1979.

——. *Must We Mean What We Say?: A Book of Essays*. New York: Cambridge University Press, 2002.

Chambers, Robert. *Vestiges of the Natural History of Creation and Other Evolutionary Writings*. Chicago: University of Chicago Press, 1994.

Cheah, Pheng. *What Is a World?: On Postcolonial Literature as World Literature*. Durham, NC: Duke University Press, 2016.

Coetzee, J. M. *Doubling the Point: Essays and Interviews*. Ed. David Atwell. Cambridge, MA: Harvard University Press, 1992.

——. *Elizabeth Costello*. New York: Penguin, 2003.

——. *Inner Workings: Literary Essays 2000–2005*. London: Penguin, 2008.

Collett, Alice, ed. *Women in Early Indian Buddhism: Comparative Textual Studies*. New York: Oxford University Press, 2014.

Collins, Steven. *Nirvana: Concept, Imagery, Narrative*. New York: Cambridge University Press, 2010.

——. *Nirvana and Other Buddhist Felicities: Utopias of the Pali Imaginaire*. Cambridge: Cambridge University Press, 1998.

——. *Selfless Persons: Imagery and Thought in Theravada Buddhism*. Cambridge: Cambridge University Press, 1990.

Collins, Steven, and Justin McDaniel. "Buddhist 'Nuns' (Mae Chi) and the Teaching of Pali in Contemporary Thailand." *Modern Asian Studies* 44, no. 06 (November 2010): 1373–1408.

Conklin, Alice L. *A Mission to Civilize: The Republican Idea of Empire in France and West Africa, 1895–1930.* Palo Alto, CA: Stanford University Press, 1997.

Conrad, Joseph. *The Collected Letters of Joseph Conrad.* Ed. Laurence Davies and J. H. Stape. Vol. 7. Cambridge; New York: Cambridge University Press, 2005.

——. *Heart of Darkness: An Authoritative Text, Backgrounds and Sources, Criticism.* 3rd ed. New York: Norton, 2005.

——. *Typhoon and Other Tales.* Ed. Cedric Watts. Oxford; New York: Oxford University Press, 2009.

Coogan, Michael D., Marc Z. Brettler, and Carol Newsom, eds. *The Holy Bible: New Revised Standard Version.* New York: Oxford University Press, 1989.

Cook, Joanna. *Meditation in Modern Buddhism: Renunciation and Change in Thai Monastic Life.* Cambridge; New York: Cambridge University Press, 2010.

Cooppan, Vilashini. *Worlds Within: National Narratives and Global Connections in Postcolonial Writing.* Palo Alto, CA: Stanford University Press, 2009.

Corrigan, John Michael. *American Metempsychosis: Emerson, Whitman, and the New Poetry.* New York: Fordham University Press, 2012.

Counihan, Clare. "The Hell of Desire: Narrative, Identity and Utopia in *A Question of Power*." *Research in African Literatures* 42, no. 1 (2011): 68–86.

Damrosch, David. "A Sinister Chuckle: Sherlock in Tibet." In *Crime Fiction as World Literature*, ed. Louise Nilsson, David Damrosch, and Theo D'haen, 257–70. New York: Bloomsbury, 2017.

Danto, Arthur. "Upper West Side Buddhism." In *Buddha Mind in Contemporary Art*, ed. Jacquelynn Baas and Mary Jane Jacob, 49–60. Berkeley: University of California Press, 2004.

Das, Sarat Chandra. *Journey to Lhasa and Central Tibet.* London: J. Murray, 1902.

Davids, T. W. Rhys. *Lectures on the Origin and Growth of Religion as Illustrated by Some Points in the History of Indian Buddhism.* The Hibbert Lectures, 1881. Edinburgh: Williams and Norgate, 1881.

DeVido, Elise A. "The Influence of Chinese Master Taixu on Buddhism in Vietnam." *Journal of Global Buddhism* 10 (2009): 413–58.

Dewey, John. *Art as Experience*. New York: Perigee, 2005.

Dillingham, William. *Rudyard Kipling: Hell and Heroism*. New York: Palgrave Macmillan, 2005.

Dogen. *Sounds of Valley Streams: Enlightenment in Dogen's Zen Translation of Nine Essays from Shobogenzo*. Trans. Francis H. Cook. Albany: State University of New York Press, 1988.

Dreyfus, Georges. "Are We Prisoners of Shangrila? Orientalism, Nationalism, and the Study of Tibet." *Journal of the International Association of Tibetan Studies* 1, no. 1 (2005): 1–21.

——. *The Sound of Two Hands Clapping: The Education of a Tibetan Buddhist Monk*. Berkeley: University of California Press, 2003.

Droit, Roger-Pol. *The Cult of Nothingness: The Philosophers and the Buddha*. Trans. Pamela Vohnson. Chapel Hill: University of North Carolina Press, 2003.

Du Bois, W. E. B. *The Souls of Black Folk*. Ed. Henry Louis Gates Jr. and Terri Hume Oliver. Norton Critical Editions. New York: Norton, 1999.

Echevarría, Roberto González. *La ruta de Severo Sarduy*. Hanover: Ediciones del Norte, 1987.

Emerson, Ralph Waldo. *The Collected Works of Ralph Waldo Emerson*. Ed. Alfred Riggs Ferguson, Joseph Slater, and Jean Ferguson Carr. Vol. 2. Cambridge, MA: Harvard University Press, 1971.

Empiricus, Sextus. *Sextus Empiricus: Outlines of Scepticism*. Ed. Julia Annas and Jonathan Barnes. Cambridge: Cambridge University Press, 2000.

Fanon, Frantz. *Black Skin, White Masks*. Trans. Richard Philcox. New York: Grove Press, 2008.

Faure, Bernard. *The Rhetoric of Immediacy: A Cultural Critique of Chan/Zen Buddhism*. Princeton, NJ: Princeton University Press, 1991.

——. *Unmasking Buddhism*. West Sussex: Wiley, 2009.

Ferrante, Joan M. *The Political Vision of the "Divine Comedy."* Princeton, NJ: Princeton University Press, 1984.

Flanagan, Damian. *Yukio Mishima*. London: Reaktion Books, 2014.

Flanagan, Owen. *The Bodhisattva's Brain: Buddhism Naturalized*. Cambridge, MA: MIT Press, 2013.

Foucault, Michel. *The Hermeneutics of the Subject: Lectures at the Collège de France, 1981–1982*. Trans. Graham Burchell. New York: Palgrave-Macmillan, 2005.

Frank, Manfred. *The Philosophical Foundations of Early German Romanticism*. Trans. Elizabeth Millan-Zaibert. Albany: State University of New York Press, 2004.

Franklin, J. Jeffrey. *The Lotus and the Lion: Buddhism and the British Empire*. Ithaca, NY: Cornell University Press, 2008.

Freud, Sigmund. "Mourning and Melancholia." In *The Standard Edition of the Complete Psychological Works of Sigmund Freud*, trans. Anna Freud and James Strachey, 14:237–58. London: Hogarth Press, 1953.

Fuhrmann, Arnika. *Ghostly Desires: Queer Sexuality and Vernacular Buddhism in Contemporary Thai Cinema*. Durham, NC: Duke University Press, 2016.

Gallo, Rubén. "Sarduy avec Lacan: The Portrayal of French Psychoanalysis in *Cobra* and *La simulación*." *Revista Hispánica Moderna* 60, no. 1 (2007): 34–60.

García Márquez, Gabriel. *Los funerales de la Mamá Grande*. New York: Vintage Espanol, 2010.

Garrett, Donald E. *Borates: Handbook of Deposits, Processing, Properties, and Use*. San Diego: Academic Press, 1998.

Gethin, Rupert. *The Foundations of Buddhism*. Oxford: Oxford University Press, 1998.

Gilbert, Stuart. *James Joyce's* Ulysses*: A Study*. 2nd rev. ed. New York: Vintage, 1952.

Gleason, William. "The Liberation of Perception: Charles Johnson's Oxherding Tale." *Black American Literature Forum* 25, no. 4 (1991): 705–28.

Gleig, Ann. *American Dharma: Buddhism Beyond Modernity*. New Haven, CT: Yale University Press, 2019.

——. "Dharma Diversity and Deep Inclusivity at the East Bay Meditation Center: From Buddhist Modernism to Buddhist Postmodernism?" *Contemporary Buddhism* 15, no. 2 (July 3, 2014): 312–31.

——. "Queering Buddhism or Buddhist De-Queering?: Reflecting on Differences Amongst Western LGBTQI Buddhists and the Limits of Liberal Convert Buddhism." *Theology and Sexuality* 18, no. 3 (January 2012): 198–214.

Godard, Jean-Luc. *Week end*. New York: New Yorker Video, 2005.

Gomez, Luis O. "D. T. Suzuki's Contribution to Modern Buddhist Scholarship." In *A Zen Life: D. T. Suzuki Remembered*, ed. Francis Haar and Masao Abe. New York: Weatherhill, 1986.

Gordon, Lewis R. *Bad Faith and Antiblack Racism*. Amherst, NY: Humanity Books, 1995.

——. "Rarely Kosher: Studying Jews of Color in North America." *American Jewish History* 100, no. 1 (January 7, 2016): 105–16.

——. "Rockin' It in Blue: A Black Existential Essay on Jimi Hendrix." *Discourse* 39, no. 2 (September 14, 2017): 216–29.

Guest, Kristin. "Norbu's *The Mandala of Sherlock Holmes*: Neo-Victorian Occupations of the Past." *Neo-Victorian Studies* 3, no. 2 (2010): 73–95.

Gutschow, Kim. *Being a Buddhist Nun: The Struggle for Enlightenment in the Himalayas*. Cambridge, MA: Harvard University Press, 2004.

Gyaltsen, Kelsang. "'Umaylam'—The Middle Way Approach." Central Tibetan Administration, September 29, 2014. http://tibet.net/2014/09/umaylam-the-middle-way-approach/.

Gyatso, Janet. *Being Human in a Buddhist World: An Intellectual History of Medicine in Early Modern Tibet*. New York: Columbia University Press, 2015.

——. "One Plus One Makes Three: Buddhist Gender, Monasticism, and the Law of the Non-Excluded Middle." *History of Religions* 43, no. 2 (2003): 89–115.

Hackett, Paul G. *Theos Bernard, the White Lama: Tibet, Yoga, and American Religious Life*. New York: Columbia University Press, 2012.

Hägglund, Martin. *This Life: Secular Faith and Spiritual Freedom*. New York: Pantheon, 2019.

Haider, Asad. *Mistaken Identity: Race and Class in the Age of Trump*. New York: Verso, 2018.

Hakugen, Ichikawa. "A Preliminary Conception of Zen Social Ethics." *Journal of Indian and Buddhist Studies* 11, no. 1 (1963): 359–48.

Hallward, Peter. *Absolutely Postcolonial: Writing Between the Singular and the Specific*. Manchester: Manchester University Press, 2001.

Hanh, Thich Nhat. "History of Engaged Buddhism: A Dharma Talk by Thich Nhat Hanh—Hanoi, Vietnam, May 6–7, 2008." *Human Architecture* 6, no. 3 (Summer 2008): 29–36.

———. *Interbeing: Fourteen Guidelines for Engaged Buddhism*. Berkeley, CA: Parallax Press, 1987.

Harris, Aisha. "A History of Self-Care." *Slate*, April 5, 2017. http://www .slate.com/articles/arts/culturebox/2017/04/the_history_of_self_care .html.

Harris, Wilson. "The Frontier on Which 'Heart of Darkness' Stands." *Research in African Literatures* 12, no. 1 (1981): 86–93.

Hart, William D. "Slavoj Zizek and the Imperial/Colonial Model of Religion." *Nepantla: Views from South* 3, no. 3 (December 19, 2002): 553–78.

Head, Bessie. *A Question of Power*. Oxford: Heinemann, 1974.

Heidegger, Martin. *Being and Time: A Translation of Sein Und Zeit*. Trans. Joan Stambaugh. Albany: State University of New York Press, 1996.

Heine, Steven. "When There Are No More Cats to Argue About: Chan Buddhist Views of Animals in Relation to Universal Buddha-Nature." *Journal of Chinese Philosophy* 43, no. 3/4 (September 2016): 239–58.

Hirschkind, Charles. "Is There a Secular Body?" *Cultural Anthropology* 26, no. 4 (November 2, 2012): 633–47.

Hobson, John M. *The Eurocentric Conception of World Politics: Western International Theory, 1760–2010*. Cambridge: Cambridge University Press, 2012.

Hochschild, Adam. *King Leopold's Ghost: A Story of Greed, Terror, and Heroism in Colonial Africa*. Boston: Houghton Mifflin, 1998.

hooks, bell. "Agent of Change: An Interview with Bell Hooks." Tricycle. Accessed August 3, 2013. http://www.tricycle.com/special-section/agent -change-an-interview-with-bell-hooks.

———. "Waking Up to Racism." *Tricycle*, Fall 1994. http://www.tricycle.com /special-section/waking—racism.

Hopkirk, Peter. *Quest for Kim: In Search of Kipling's Great Game*. Oxford: Oxford University Press, 2001.

Hori, Victor. "Kōan and Kenshō in the Rinzai Zen Curriculum." In *The Koan: Texts and Contexts in Zen Buddhism*, ed. Steven Heine and Dale Wright. New York: Oxford University Press, 2000.

Hubbard, Jamie, and Paul Swanson, eds. *Pruning the Bodhi Tree: The Storm Over Critical Buddhism*. Honolulu: University of Hawai'i Press, 1997.

Huber, Toni. *The Holy Land Reborn: Pilgrimage and the Tibetan Reinvention of Buddhist India*. Chicago: University of Chicago Press, 2008.

Hungerford, Amy. *Postmodern Belief: American Literature and Religion Since 1960*. Princeton, NJ: Princeton University Press, 2010.

Husserl, Edmund. *Cartesian Meditations: An Introduction to Phenomenology*. The Hague: M. Nijhoff, 1966.

Huxley, Thomas Henry. *Evolution and Ethics*. Ed. Michael Ruse. Princeton, NJ: Princeton University Press, 2009.

Ives, Christopher. *Imperial-Way Zen: Ichikawa Hakugen's Critique and Lingering Questions for Buddhist Ethics*. Honolulu: University of Hawai'i Press, 2009.

Iwamura, Jane. *Virtual Orientalism: Asian Religions and American Popular Culture*. Oxford: Oxford University Press, 2010.

Jacquette, Dale. "Schopenhauer on Death." In *The Cambridge Companion to Schopenhauer*, ed. Christopher Janaway, 293–317. New York: Cambridge University Press, 1999.

Jaffe, Richard M., ed. "Early Memories." In *Selected Works of D. T. Suzuki, Volume I*, 202–10. Berkeley: University of California Press, 2015.

——. "Introduction." In *Selected Works of D. T. Suzuki, Volume I: Zen*, by Daisetsu Teitaro Suzuki, xi–lvi. Berkeley: University of California Press, 2014.

——. "Seeking Sakyamuni: Travel and the Reconstruction of Japanese Buddhism." *The Journal of Japanese Studies* 30, no. 1 (2004): 65–96.

Janaway, Christopher. *Self and World in Schopenhauer's Philosophy*. Oxford: Oxford University Press, 1999.

Jerryson, Michael K., and Mark Juergensmeyer, eds. *Buddhist Warfare*. New York: Oxford University Press, 2010.

Johnson, Bruce. "'Heart of Darkness' and the Problem of Emptiness." *Studies in Short Fiction* 9, no. 4 (1972): 387–400.

Johnson, Charles. *Oxherding Tale*. New York: Plume, 1995.

——. *Turning the Wheel: Essays on Buddhism and Writing*. New York: Scribner, 2003.

Josephson, Jason Ananda. *The Invention of Religion in Japan*. Chicago: University of Chicago Press, 2012.

Joyce, James. *Ulysses*. New York: Vintage, 1986.

Jung, C. G. *Civilization in Transition*. Ed. Gerhard Adler. Trans. R. F. C. Hull. Vol. 10. Princeton, NJ: Princeton University Press, 1970.

Kafka, Franz. *The Metamorphosis: And Other Stories*. Trans. Edwin Muir and Willa Muir. New York: Schocken, 1995.

Kamala, Tiyavanich. *Forest Recollections: Wandering Monks in Twentieth-Century Thailand.* Honolulu: University of Hawaii Press, 1997.

Kapstein, Matthew T. *Tibetan Buddhism: A Very Short Introduction.* Oxford: Oxford University Press, 2013.

Karatani, Kojin. *History and Repetition.* Ed. Seiji Lippit. New York: Columbia University Press, 2011.

Kasulis, Thomas. "Reading D. T. Suzuki Today." *Eastern Buddhist* 38, no. 1/2 (2007): 41–57.

Kemper, Steven. *Rescued from the Nation: Anagarika Dharmapala and the Buddhist World.* Chicago: University of Chicago Press, 2015.

Keyes, Charles F. "Buddhist Politics and Their Revolutionary Origins in Thailand." *International Political Science Review/Revue Internationale de Science Politique* 10, no. 2 (1989): 121–42.

Kinkeade-Weekes, Mark. "Vision in Kipling's Novels." In *Kipling's Mind and Art: Selected Critical Essays,* ed. Andrew Rutherford, 197–234. Palo Alto, CA: Stanford University Press, 1964.

Kipling, Rudyard. *Kim.* Ed. Harish Trivedi. New York: Penguin, 2011.

Knowles, Owen, and Gene Moore, eds. *Oxford Reader's Companion to Conrad.* Oxford: Oxford University Press, 2000.

Koivulahti, Toni J. "Compassionate Apocalypse: Slavoj Žižek and Buddhism." *Critical Research on Religion* 5, no. 1 (April 1, 2017): 34–47.

Kulawik, Krzysztof. "Las Múltiples Faces Del Travesti: La Dispersión Del Sujeto En Los Espacios Transculturales de La Narrativa Neobarroca de Severo Sarduy." *Literatura: Teoría, Historia, Crítica* 17, no. 1 (2015): 207–44.

Kushigian, Julia Alexis. *Orientalism in the Hispanic Literary Tradition: In Dialogue with Borges, Paz, and Sarduy.* Albuquerque: University of New Mexico Press, 1991.

LaCapra, Dominick. *History, Literature, Critical Theory.* Ithaca, NY: Cornell University Press, 2013.

Lamb, Jonathan. "Modern Metamorphoses and Disgraceful Tales." *Critical Inquiry* 28, no. 1 (2001): 133–66.

Leigh, Simone. *The Waiting Room.* September 2016. Installation. The New Museum. https://www.newmuseum.org/exhibitions/view/simone-leigh-the-waiting-room.

Lester, John. *Conrad and Religion.* New York: St. Martin's Press, 1988.

Levine, Gregory P. A. *Long Strange Journey: On Modern Zen, Zen Art, and Other Predicaments.* Honolulu: University of Hawaii Press, 2017.

Little, Jonathan. *Charles Johnson's Spiritual Imagination*. Columbia: University of Missouri Press, 1997.

Lopez, Donald S., Jr. *Buddhism and Science: A Guide for the Perplexed*. Chicago: University of Chicago Press, 2009.

——. "Buddhism in Practice." In *Asian Religions in Practice: An Introduction*, ed. Donald S. Lopez Jr., 56–87. Princeton, NJ: Princeton University Press, 1999.

——. "Introduction." In *Curators of the Buddha: The Study of Buddhism Under Colonialism*, ed. Donald S. Lopez Jr., 1–30. Chicago: University of Chicago Press, 1995.

——. "Introduction." In *A Modern Buddhist Bible: Essential Readings from East and West*, ed. Donald S. Lopez Jr., vii–xli. Boston: Beacon Press, 2004.

——. *Prisoners of Shangri-La: Tibetan Buddhism and the West*. Chicago: University of Chicago Press, 1999.

——. *The Story of Buddhism: A Concise Guide to Its History and Teachings*. San Francisco: HarperOne, 2001.

Lorenz, Paul H. "Colonization and the Feminine in Bessie Head's *A Question of Power*." *MFS Modern Fiction Studies* 37, no. 3 (1991): 591–605.

Marra, Michele. "The Development of Mappo Thought in Japan (I)." *Japanese Journal of Religious Studies* 15, no. 1 (1988): 25–54.

Marx, Karl, and Friedrich Engels. *The Marx-Engels Reader*. Ed. Robert C. Tucker. New York: Norton, 1978.

Mazzotta, Giuseppe. *The New Map of the World: The Poetic Philosophy of Giambattista Vico*. Princeton, NJ: Princeton University Press, 1999.

McClure, John A. *Partial Faiths: Postsecular Fiction in the Age of Pynchon and Morrison*. Athens: University of Georgia Press, 2007.

McCort, Dennis. "Hyakujo's Geese, Amban's Doughnuts and Rilke's Carrousel: Sources East and West for Salinger's 'Catcher.'" *Comparative Literature Studies* 34, no. 3 (1997): 260–78.

McDaniel, Justin Thomas. "Strolling Through Temporary Temples: Buddhism and Installation Art in Modern Thailand." *Contemporary Buddhism* 18, no. 1 (January 2, 2017): 165–98.

McKay, Alex. "The Drowning of Lama Sengchen Kyabying: A Preliminary Enquiry from British Sources." *Tibet Journal* 36, no. 2 (2011): 3–18.

McMahan, David. "Buddhism and Global Secularisms." *Journal of Global Buddhism* 18 (2017): 112–28.

——. *Empty Vision: Metaphor and Visionary Imagery in Mahayana Buddhism*. New York: Routledge, 2013.

——. "How Meditation Works: Theorizing the Role of Cultural Context in Buddhist Contemplative Practices." In *Meditation, Buddhism, and Science*, ed. David McMahan and Erik Braun, 21–46. New York: Oxford University Press, 2017.

——. *The Making of Buddhist Modernism*. Oxford; New York: Oxford University Press, 2008.

Merleau-Ponty, Maurice. *Phenomenology of Perception*. London; New York: Routledge, 2002.

Meyer, Karl E., and Shareen Blair Brysac. *Tournament of Shadows: The Great Game and the Race for Empire in Central Asia*. New York: Basic Books, 2009.

Miller, J. Hillis. *Poets of Reality: Six Twentieth-Century Writers*. Cambridge, MA: Harvard University Press, 1965.

——. "Should We Read *Heart of Darkness*?" In *Joseph Conrad's Heart of Darkness*, ed. Harold Bloom. New York: Chelsea House, 2008.

Mishima, Yukio. *Runaway Horses: The Sea of Fertility, 2*. Trans. Michael Gallagher. New York: Vintage, 2013.

——. *The Decay of the Angel: The Sea of Fertility, 4*. Trans. Edward G. Seidensticker. New York: Vintage, 2013.

——. *The Temple of Dawn*. Trans. E. Dale Saunders and Cecilia Segawa Seigle. New York: Vintage, 1990.

Møllgaard, Eske. "Slavoj Žižek's Critique of Western Buddhism." *Contemporary Buddhism* 9, no. 2 (November 1, 2008): 167–80.

Moore, Matthew J. "Political Theory in Canonical Buddhism." *Philosophy East and West* 65, no. 1 (February 2, 2015): 36–64.

Mulhall, Stephen. *The Wounded Animal: J. M. Coetzee and the Difficulty of Reality in Literature and Philosophy*. Princeton, NJ: Princeton University Press, 2009.

Muthu, Sankar. *Enlightenment Against Empire*. Princeton, NJ: Princeton University Press, 2003.

Napier, Susan Jolliffe. *Escape from the Wasteland: Romanticism and Realism in the Fiction of Mishima Yukio and Oe Kenzaburo*. Cambridge, MA:

Council on East Asian Studies, Harvard University: Distributed by Harvard University Press, 1995.

Nash, William R. *Charles Johnson's Fiction*. Urbana: University of Illinois Press, 2003.

Nathan, John. *Mishima: A Biography*. Cambridge, MA: Da Capo Press, 2000.

Norbu, Jamyang. "Cult of Victimhood: Two Studies." *Shadow Tibet* (blog), March 31, 2010. http://www.jamyangnorbu.com/blog/2010/03/31/cult-of -victimhood-two-studies/.

——. "The Great Middle Way Referendum Swindle." *Shadow Tibet* (blog), September 3, 2014. http://www.jamyangnorbu.com/blog/2014/09/03/the -great-middleway-referendum-swindle/.

——. *The Mandala of Sherlock Holmes*. New Delhi: HarperCollins India, 2001.

——. "Not the Buddha's Middle Way." *Shadow Tibet* (blog), January 30, 2011. http://www.jamyangnorbu.com/blog/2011/01/30/not-the-buddhas -middle-way/.

——. "The Real Threat to the Dalai Lama." *Shadow Tibet* (blog), February 5, 2016. http://www.jamyangnorbu.com/blog/2016/02/05/the-real -threat-to-the-dalai-lama/.

——. "Trapped by Buddha." *The New Humanist*, May 31, 2007. https:// newhumanist.org.uk/articles/904/trapped-by-buddha.

Noriaki, Hakamaya. "Critical Philosophy Versus Topical Philosophy." In *Pruning the Bodhi Tree: The Storm Over Critical Buddhism*, ed. Jamie Hubbard and Paul Swanson, 56–80. Honolulu: University of Hawai'i Press, 1997.

Northover, Richard Allen. "Schopenhauer and Secular Salvation in the Work of J. M. Coetzee." *English in Africa* 41, no. 1 (September 22, 2015): 35–54.

Obeyesekere, Gananath. "Buddhism and Conscience: An Exploratory Essay." *Daedelus* 120, no. 3 (1991): 219–39.

——. *Imagining Karma: Ethical Transformation in Amerindian, Buddhist, and Greek Thought*. Berkeley: University of California Press, 2002.

"The Official Homepage for Lama Zopa Rinpoche—FPMT." Accessed July 13, 2018. https://fpmt.org/teachers/zopa/.

Osto, Douglas. *Altered States: Buddhism and Psychedelic Spirituality in America*. New York: Columbia University Press, 2016.

Owen, Alex. *The Place of Enchantment: British Occultism and the Culture of the Modern*. Chicago: University of Chicago Press, 2007.

Park, Josephine. *Apparitions of Asia: Modernist Form and Asian American Poetics*. New York: Oxford University Press, 2008.

Parry, Benita. "The Moment and After-Life of *Heart of Darkness*." In *Conrad in the Twenty-First Century: Contemporary Approaches and Perspectives*, ed. Carola Kaplan, Peter Mallios, and Andrea White, 39–54. New York: Routledge, 2004.

Perkins, Franklin. *Leibniz and China: A Commerce of Light*. Cambridge; New York: Cambridge University Press, 2004.

Piven, Jerry S. *The Madness and Perversion of Yukio Mishima*. Westport, CT: Praeger, 2004.

Polanyi, Karl. *The Great Transformation: The Political and Economic Origins of Our Time*. Boston: Beacon Press, 2001.

Pollan, Michael. *How to Change Your Mind: What the New Science of Psychedelics Teaches Us About Consciousness, Dying, Addiction, Depression, and Transcendence*. New York: Penguin, 2018.

Pompa, Leon. *Vico: A Study of the "New Science."* New York: Cambridge University Press, 1990.

Posnock, Ross. *Renunciation: Acts of Abandonment by Writers, Philosophers, and Artists*. Cambridge, MA: Harvard University Press, 2016.

Powers, John. *Introduction to Tibetan Buddhism*. Ithaca, NY: Snow Lion, 2007.

Queen, Christopher S. "Dr. Ambedkar and the Hermeneutics of Buddhist Liberation." In *Engaged Buddhism: Buddhist Liberation Movements in Asia*, ed. Christopher S. Queen and Sallie B. King, 45–71. Albany: State University of New York Press, 1996.

Queen, Christopher S., and Sallie B. King, eds. *Engaged Buddhism: Buddhist Liberation Movements in Asia*. Albany: State University of New York Press, 1996.

Rajapakse, Vijitha. "Buddhism in Huxley's 'Evolution and Ethics': A Note on a Victorian Evaluation and Its 'Comparativist Dimension.'" *Philosophy East and West* 35, no. 3 (1985): 295–304.

Reynolds, Frank E., and Charles Hallisey. "Buddhism: An Overview." In *Encylopedia of Religion*, ed. Lindsay Jones, 2:1087–1101. Detroit: Macmillan Reference, 2005.

Riofrancos, Thea N., and Daniel Denvir. "The 'Identity Politics' Debate Is Splintering the Left. Here's How We Can Move Past It." *In These Times*, February 14, 2017. http://inthesetimes.com/article/19902/heres-how-we-can-move-pastthe-identity-politics-debate-splintering-the-left.

Robbins, Bruce. "Prolegomena to a Cosmopolitanism in Deep Time." *Interventions* 18, no. 2 (March 3, 2016): 172–86.

Rose, Jacqueline. "On the 'Universality' of Madness: Bessie Head's 'A Question of Power.'" *Critical Inquiry* 20, no. 3 (April 1, 1994): 401–18.

Sahlins, Marshall. "Two or Three Things That I Know About Culture." *The Journal of the Royal Anthropological Institute* 5, no. 3 (1999): 399–421.

Said, Edward W. *Culture and Imperialism.* New York: Random House, 1993.

Salgado, Nirmala. *Buddhist Nuns and Gendered Practice: In Search of the Female Renunciant.* Oxford: Oxford University Press, 2013.

Salinger, J. D. *The Catcher in the Rye.* Boston: Little, Brown, 1991.

——. *Franny and Zooey.* Boston: Little, Brown, 1961.

——. *Raise High the Roof Beam, Carpenters and Seymour: An Introduction.* Boston: Little, Brown, 1963.

——. "Zooey." *The New Yorker*, May 4, 1957, 32–139.

Sarduy, Severo. *Cobra and Maitreya.* Trans. Susan Jill Levine. Normal, IL: Dalkey Archive Press, 1995.

——. "Escrito sobre un cuerpo." In *Ensayos generales sobre el Barroco*, 229–317. Mexico-Buenos Aires: Fondo de Cultura Económica, 1987.

Sartre, Jean-Paul. *Anti-Semite and Jew.* New York: Schocken, 1965.

Sato, Kemmyō Taira. "D. T. Suzuki and the Question of War." Trans. Thomas Kirchner. *Eastern Buddhist* 39, no. 1 (2008): 61–120.

Schaik, Sam van. *Tibet: A History.* New Haven, CT: Yale University Press, 2013.

——. *Tibetan Zen: Discovering a Lost Tradition.* Boston: Shambhala, 2015.

Schopen, Gregory. *Buddhist Monks and Business Matters: Still More Papers on Monastic Buddhism in India.* Honolulu: University of Hawaii Press, 2004.

Schopenhauer, Arthur. *The World as Will and Representation*. Trans. E.F.J. Payne. 2 vols. New York: Dover, 1966.

Scott, David. *Formations of Ritual: Colonial and Anthropological Discourses on the Sinhala Yaktovil*. Minneapolis: University of Minnesota Press, 1994.

Scott, James C. *The Art of Not Being Governed: An Anarchist History of Upland Southeast Asia*. New Haven, CT: Yale University Press, 2009.

——. *Domination and the Arts of Resistance: Hidden Transcripts*. New Haven, CT: Yale University Press, 1992.

——. *Weapons of the Weak: Everyday Forms of Peasant Resistance*. New Haven, CT: Yale University Press, 1985.

Sedgwick, Eve Kosofsky. *Touching Feeling: Affect, Pedagogy, Performativity*. Durham, NC: Duke University Press, 2003.

——. *The Weather in Proust*. Ed. Jonathan Goldberg. Durham, NC: Duke University Press, 2011.

Sell, Jonathan P.A. "Chance and Gesture in Zadie Smith's *White Teeth* and *The Autograph Man*: A Model for Multicultural Identity?" *The Journal of Commonwealth Literature* 41, no. 3 (September 1, 2006): 27–44.

Selzer, Linda. "Black American Buddhism: History and Representation." In *Writing as Enlightenment: Buddhist American Literature Into the Twenty-First Century*, ed. Gary Storhoff and John Whalen-Bridge, 37–69. Albany: State University of New York Press, 2011.

——. *Charles Johnson in Context*. Amherst: University of Massachusetts Press, 2009.

Sharf, Robert. "Buddhist Modernism and the Rhetoric of Meditative Experience." *Numen* 42, no. 3 (1995): 228–83.

——. *Coming to Terms with Chinese Buddhism: A Reading of the Treasure Store Treatise*. Honolulu: University of Hawaii Press, 2005.

——. "The Zen of Japanese Nationalism." *History of Religions* 33, no. 1 (1993): 1–43.

Shaw, Miranda. *Passionate Enlightenment: Women in Tantric Buddhism*. Princeton, NJ: Princeton University Press, 1995.

Shaw, Sara Janet, ed. *The Jatakas: Birth Stories of the Bodhisatta*. New York: Penguin, 2007.

Shields, James Mark. "Liberation as Revolutionary Praxis: Rethinking Buddhist Materialism." *Journal of Buddhist Ethics* 20 (2013): 461–99.

Siderits, Mark. "Is Everything Connected to Everything Else? What the Gopis Know." In *Moonshadows: Conventional Truth in Buddhist Philosophy*, by Cowherds, 167–80. Oxford; New York: Oxford University Press, 2011.

Sifuentes-Jáuregui, Ben. *Transvestism, Masculinity, and Latin American Literature*. New York: Palgrave Macmillan, 2002.

Sigalow, Emily. *American JewBu: Jews, Buddhists, and Religious Change*. Princeton, NJ: Princeton University Press, 2019.

Simmel, Georg. *Schopenhauer and Nietzsche*. Trans. Helmut Loiskandl, Deena Weinstein, and Michael Weinstein. Urbana: University of Illinois Press, 1991.

Smith, Zadie. *The Autograph Man*. New York: Vintage, 2002.

——. *Changing My Mind: Occasional Essays*. New York: Penguin, 2009.

Snelling, John. *Buddhism in Russia: The Story of Agvan Dorzhiev, Lhasa's Emissary to the Tsar*. Rockport, MA: Element Books, 1993.

Sørensen, Henrik H. "A Study of the 'Ox-Herding Theme' as Sculptures at Mt. Baoding in Dazu County, Sichuan." *Artibus Asiae* 51, no. 3/4 (1991): 207–33.

Starrs, Roy. *Deadly Dialectics: Sex, Violence, and Nihilism in the World of Yukio Mishima*. Honolulu: University of Hawaii Press, 1994.

Stein, William Byshe. "The Lotus Posture and *Heart of Darkness*." *Modern Fiction Studies* 2 (1956): 235–37.

Stokes, Henry Scott. *The Life and Death of Yukio Mishima*. New York: Cooper Square Press, 2000.

Storhoff, Gary. *Understanding Charles Johnson*. Columbia: University of South Carolina Press, 2004.

Stout, Jeffrey. "What Is the Meaning of a Text?" *New Literary History* 14, no. 1 (1982): 1–12.

Strong, John S. "A Family Quest: The Buddha, Yaśodharā, and Rāhula in the Mūlasarvāstivāda Vinaya." In *Sacred Biography in the Buddhist Traditions of South and Southeast Asia*, ed. Juliane Schober, 113–28. Honolulu: University of Hawai'i Press, 1997.

Subrahmanyam, Sanjay. "Global Intellectual History Beyond Hegel and Marx." *History and Theory* 54, no. 1 (February 2015): 126–37.

——. "La 'Religion,' Une Catégorie Déroutante: Perspectives Depuis l'Asie Du Sud." *Asdiwal: Revue Genevoise d'anthropologie et d'histoire Des Religions* 9 (2014): 79–90.

Suksamran, Somboon. *Buddhism and Politics in Thailand: A Study of Socio-Political Change and Political Activism of the Thai Sangha.* Singapore: Institute of Southeast Asian Studies, 1982.

Suzuki, Daisetz Teitaro. "An Autobiographical Account." In *A Zen Life: D. T. Suzuki Remembered,* ed. Masao Abe, 13–26. New York: Weatherhill, 1986.

——. *An Introduction to Zen Buddhism.* New York: Grove Press, 1964.

——. "The Philosophy of Zen." *Philosophy East and West* 1, no. 2 (1951): 3–15.

——. "Religion and Drugs." In *Selected Works of D.T. Suzuki,* ed. Tomoe Moriya and Jeff Wilson, 233–38. Berkeley: University of California Press, 2016.

——. *Zen and Japanese Culture.* Princeton, NJ: Princeton University Press, 2010.

——. *Zen Buddhism: Selected Writings.* Ed. William Barrett. Garden City, NY: Doubleday, 1956.

Taylor, Charles. *The Ethics of Authenticity.* Cambridge, MA: Harvard University Press, 1992.

——. *Sources of the Self: The Making of the Modern Identity.* Cambridge: Cambridge University Press, 1989.

Thompson, Evan. *Why I Am Not a Buddhist.* New Haven, CT: Yale University Press, 2020.

Thurman, Robert A. F. *Essential Tibetan Buddhism.* San Francisco: HarperOne, 1996.

Tolstoy, Leo. *The Death of Ivan Ilyich.* Trans. Richard Pevear and Larissa Volokhonsky. New York: Vintage, 2012.

Trilling, Lionel. *Sincerity and Authenticity.* Cambridge, MA: Harvard University Press, 1973.

Tymoczko, Maria. *The Irish Ulysses.* Berkeley: University of California Press, 1997.

Vargas-O'Bryan, Ivette. "Anthropology." In *Buddhism.* Oxford Bibliographies, 2013. https://www.oxfordbibliographies.com/view/document/obo-9780195393521/obo-9780195393521-0001.xml.

Venturino, Steven. "Placing Tibetan Fiction in a World of Literary Studies: Jamyang Norbu's *The Mandala of Sherlock Holmes.*" In *Modern Tibetan Literature and Social Change,* ed. Lauran R. Hartley and Patricia Schiaffini-Vedani, 301–26. Durham, NC: Duke University Press, 2008.

Vico, Giambattista. *New Science.* Trans. Dave Marsh. New York: Penguin Classics, 2000.

Victoria, Brian Daizen. *Zen at War.* Lanham: Rowman & Littlefield, 2006.

Viswanathan, Gauri. "In Search of Madame Blavatsky: Reading the Exoteric, Retrieving the Esoteric." *Representations* 141, no. 1 (February 2018): 67–94.

Walters, Suzanna Danuta. "In Defense of Identity Politics." *Signs: Journal of Women in Culture and Society* 43, no. 2 (November 15, 2017): 473–88.

Watt, Ian. *Conrad in the Nineteenth Century.* Berkeley: University of California Press, 1981.

Watts, Alan W. "Beat Zen, Square Zen, and Zen." *Chicago Review* 12, no. 2 (1958): 3–11.

——. *The Way of Zen.* New York: Vintage, 1999.

Westerhoff, Jan. *Nagarjuna's Madhyamaka: A Philosophical Introduction.* New York: Oxford University Press, 2009.

Whalen-Bridge, John, and Gary Storhoff, eds. *The Emergence of Buddhist American Literature.* Albany: State University of New York Press, 2010.

Williams, R. John. *The Buddha in the Machine: Art, Technology, and the Meeting of East and West.* New Haven, CT: Yale University Press, 2014.

Wilson, Liz. "Introduction: Family and the Construction of Religious Communities." In *Family in Buddhism,* ed. Liz Wilson. Albany: State University of New York Press, 2013.

Winichakul, Thongchai. "Buddhist Apologetics and a Genealogy of Comparative Religion in Siam." *Numen* 62, no. 1 (December 12, 2015): 76–99.

Wittgenstein, Ludwig. *Philosophical Investigations.* Trans. G. E. M. Anscombe. Oxford: Basil Blackwell, 1968.

Wollaeger, Mark. *Joseph Conrad and the Fictions of Skepticism.* Stanford: Stanford University Press, 1990.

Wood, James. "A Frog's Life." *London Review of Books,* October 23, 2003. https://www.lrb.co.uk/v25/n20/james-wood/a-frogs-life.

Woolf, Virginia. *Moments of Being.* San Diego: Mariner Books, 1985.

Wright, Robert. *Why Buddhism Is True: The Science and Philosophy of Meditation and Enlightenment.* New York: Simon and Schuster, 2017.

Yourcenar, Marguerite. *Mishima: A Vision of the Void.* Trans. Alberto Manguel. Chicago: University of Chicago Press, 2001.

Žižek, Slavoj. *Less Than Nothing: Hegel and the Shadow of Dialectical Materialism*. Reprint edition. London: Verso, 2013.

Zopa, Thubten, and Lama Zopa Rinpoche. *Ultimate Healing: The Power of Compassion*. New York: Simon and Schuster, 2001.

INDEX

Abe, Stanley, 186n10

accidents, 173–74; authenticity and, 165, 169–71; in *Autograph Man*, 162–63, 169, 171

Alabaster, Henry, 59

Ambedkar, B. R., 6–7, 18–19; on enlightenment, 40; four new Noble Truths, 7

Animal Liberation Fund, 161–62

Anker, Elizabeth, 205n112

anthropology of religion, 10, 182n24

anticolonialism, 1, 2; meditation as, 14, 59–61

anti-Semitism, 104

anxiety: authenticity and, 16; in Buddhism, 12, 13–14; enlightenment and, 27–28, 40; existentialism and, 15–16; meditation and, 14

Aravamudan, Srinivas, 31–32

Aristotle, 213n87

Arnold, Edwin, 113–14

Augustine, 129–30, 130–31

authenticity, 5, 139–45; accidents and, 165, 169–71; anxiety and, 16; in *Autograph Man*, 145, 163, 166, 169; "Being Zen," 143, 145; Buddhism and, 96, 139, 141, 143–44; in *Catcher in the Rye*, 146–47; in *Cobra*, 161; double consciousness and, 142; embeddedness of, 23–24; enlightenment and, 16; existentialism and, 16; in *Franny and Zooey*, 145, 160–61; individualism and, 140; modern Buddhism and, 2, 15–16, 23–24, 171–72, 174–78; modernity and, 140–41; nationalism and, 142; in *Oxherding Tale*, 161; personal, 147; pluralism and, 170; Suzuki and, 143–44, 147, 150–51; textual, 147–48; Zen and, 16–18, 147, 150, 153–54, 164–65, 170

Autograph Man, The (Smith), 22, 162–70; accidents in, 162–63, 169, 171; authenticity in, 145,

Autograph Man (*continued*)
163, 166, 169; Kabbalah in,
163–64, 219n70; selflessness in,
168; Wittgenstein in, 164,
166–68; Zen in, 163–64, 219n70
awakening, 9, 150. *See also*
enlightenment; *satori*

Barrett, William, 157–59
Barthes, Roland, 107, 149, 152
Beckett, Samuel, 3–4, 46, 65
Benjamin, Walter, 164
Borges, Jorge Luis, 23, 46, 149
Boyarin, Daniel, 209n42
Buddhism: alienation and, 111;
anxiety in, 12, 13–14;
authenticity and, 96, 139, 141,
143–44; class and, 23, 67; desire
and, 124; embeddedness of, 6,
19, 36–37, 111, 114–15, 182n24;
enlightenment and, 17, 39, 41;
ethical theory of, 96; feminism
and, 108; gender and, 23, 104,
116–18; homophobia and, 106;
interconnectedness in, 96,
205nn111–112; liberation and,
14, 17, 65, 118, 138, 162;
modernity and, 4, 24–25;
nationalism and, 103–4; as
nihilistic, 65; Orientalism and,
13, 18–19, 171; patriarchy and,
119, 138; as philosophy, 1, 4, 9,
12, 19–20, 31–32, 64, 109–11;
politics and, 29–30, 32–33, 35,
37, 58–59, 190n41; race and, 23,
104, 108; science and, 77,

203n69; scriptural history of, 1;
selflessness and, 65, 70, 103;
sexuality and, 23, 117–18, 122;
the social in, 72; social
contract, 7; suffering and, 3–4,
7, 95–96, 124; as "superstition,"
64; third sex and, 117. *See also*
Buddhism, Tibetan;
Buddhism, Thai; Zen
Buddhism, modern, 1–2; as
antiracist, 1, 2; authenticity and,
2, 15–16, 23–24, 171–72, 174–78;
communal practices of, 10; as
democratic, 1; as egalitarian, 1;
embeddedness of, 4–5, 29, 43;
enlightenment in, 34, 120, 171;
as feminist, 1; founding myth
of, 121–22; global, 2, 4; identity,
critique of, 105; liberation and,
23–24; literary history of, 3,
20–21, 23; as meditation
practice, 4, 14, 59; as pacifist, 1,
2; as philosophic, 1, 4, 37–38;
politics and, 188n20;
reincarnation and, 64, 100–101;
Sharf critique of, 17–18, 152–53;
suffering and, 15; Western
philosophy and, 15. *See also*
Buddhism
Buddhism, Thai, 59
Buddhism, Tibetan, 27–28, 186n6;
in *Cobra*, 111–12; middle path of,
80–81; politics and, 77–78;
reincarnation in, 63; science
and, 77; sex and gender in,
117–18

Buddhist studies, 4; critical
  Buddhist studies, 24;
  practicing scholars, 9; Suzuki
  in, 152
Byrd, Rudolph, 212n80, 213n91

Cage, John, 149, 151
Campbell, June, 116
Castoriadis, Cornelius, 193n71
Catcher in the Rye, The (Salinger),
  146–47
Cavell, Stanley, 168–69, 215n13
Cheah, Pheng, 180n12
class: Buddhism and, 23, 67
Cobra (Sarduy), 22, 23, 107–19;
  authenticity in, 161; Buddhism
  in, 110–11; enlightenment in, 111;
  exile in, 112; gender in, 107;
  "Indian Journal" section, 112–13;
  liberation in, 109, 111, 118; *om
  mani padme hum* chant in, 109,
  113–16; plot summary, 108–9;
  reincarnation in, 116, 117;
  sexuality in, 115–17; Tibetan
  Buddhism in, 111–12; Zen and,
  109, 111
Coetzee, J. M., 65–66, 204n89;
  Costello lectures, 89; *Elizabeth
  Costello*, 22–23, 88–100; on
  Gordimer, 94; salvation in,
  94–95, 99; on Schopenhauer, 93;
  suffering in, 94. See also
  Elizabeth Costello (Coetzee)
Collins, Steven: on
  interdependence, 95–96; on
  nirvana, 37, 188n31, 189n32

colonialism, 194n76; anticolonialism,
  1, 2, 14, 59–61; genocide and, 113;
  in *Heart of Darkness*, 5, 43, 55;
  liberation and, 113; meditation
  and, 14; politics of, 107
Columbus, Christopher, 112–13
Conan Doyle, Arthur, 79, 80
Conrad, Joseph: "Falk: A
  Reminiscence," 54–55, 57–58;
  Heart of Darkness, 5, 22–23,
  41–44, 46–61; influence of
  Schopenhauer on, 45, 52–53,
  55–56; meditative stillness in,
  56–57; skepticism of, 57–58,
  191n42; spectral illumination in,
  3–4, 42–43. See also *Heart of
  Darkness* (Conrad)
Counihan, Clare, 209n39
Critical Buddhism, 144

Dalai Lama, 18, 28, 29, 76, 84; as
  embodiment of enlightenment,
  39; on enlightenment, 40; on
  nationalism, 103–4;
  reincarnation of, 32–33, 63, 78,
  188n20; relationship with
  Panchen Lama, 32, 186n6
Damrosch, David, 77, 200n41
Dante: in *Mandala of Sherlock
  Holmes*, 80–81, 82
Das, Sarat Chandra, 36, 186n6;
  prophecy of, 29–30, 33, 35
Davids, T. W. Rhys, 67
Death of Ivan Ilyich (Tolstoy),
  89, 96
de Castro, Eduardo Viveiros, 91

Dharmapala, Anagarika, 18
Dillingham, William, 32, 187n17
Dipankara, 71
Dōgen, 27–28
Dreyfus, Georges, 8, 188n30
Du Bois, W. E. B., 142

Elizabeth Costello (Coetzee), 22–23,
    88–100; beginning of, 90–91;
    ethics of, 88, 90, 96, 98–99, 100;
    gender in, 95, 209n39;
    reincarnation in, 90, 91–95,
    97–98
Emerson, Ralph Waldo: on
    transmigration, 66
Engaged Buddhism, 6–7, 214n3
enlightenment, 5, 25, 29, 134;
    anxiety and, 27–28, 40;
    authenticity and, 16; Buddhist,
    17, 39, 41; in *Cobra*, 111;
    embeddedness of, 23–24; empire
    and, 33, 34, 39; as extinguishing,
    188n31; in *Heart of Darkness*, 5,
    42, 51–52; in *Kim*, 29, 31, 33, 38;
    liberal ideal of, 41–42; light as
    metaphor for, 77; in modern
    Buddhism, 34, 120, 171;
    modernism and, 36; modernity
    and, 134; in *Oxherding Tale*,
    135–36, 137; partial, 6, 47, 61–62;
    politics and, 29, 35, 36–37, 40; in
    Question of Power, 123, 124;
    reincarnation and, 71; sexuality
    and, 122; spectral illumination
    and, 42, 61–62; sudden, 40, 75,
    162; suffering and, 40

exile, 13, 84; in *Cobra*, 111; hell as,
    80; *Question of Power* and,
    209n42
existentialism, 15–16, 103; anxiety
    and, 15–16; authenticity and, 16;
    Buddhism and, 15–16; in *Franny
    and Zooey*, 158–61; Suzuki on,
    15–18; Zen and, 157

Fanon, Frantz, 132
Faure, Bernard, 63, 216n24
Finnegan's Wake (Joyce), 92, 93
Foucault, Michel, 15, 20, 149;
    Orientalism of, 184n36; on
    practice, 17–18
Franklin, Jeffrey, 32, 33, 191n41
Franny and Zooey (Salinger), 145,
    147–49, 152–61; authenticity in,
    145, 160–61; detachment in,
    156–57; existentialism in,
    158–61; materialism in, 154–55;
    satori in, 154; spectral
    illumination in, 147–49; Suzuki
    in, 149, 153–54, 157–58; Zen in,
    152–54, 156–58

García Márquez, Gabriel, 139
Geluks, 21, 28, 29–30, 186n6
gender: Buddhism and, 23, 104, 116;
    in *Cobra*, 107; in *Elizabeth
    Costello*, 95, 209n39; in *Question
    of Power*, 119–20; in Tibetan
    Buddhism, 117–18
Gleason, William, 212n80
Gleig, Ann, 9, 10, 105–6, 120
Godard, Jean-Luc, 194n76

Goenka, S. N., 14
Goldstein, Joseph, 11
Gordimer, Nadine, 94
Gordon, Lewis, 142–43, 215n13
Guest, Kristin, 77, 82, 88
Gyatso, Janet, 82, 117–18

Hägglund, Martin, 179n9,
    189n32
Hallward, Peter, 179n9, 207n10,
    213n94
Hanh, Thich Nhat, 6–7, 12, 14,
    18–19, 205n111; on
    enlightenment, 40
Head, Bessie, 106. See also
    Question of Power, A (Head)
Heart of Darkness (Conrad), 5,
    22–23, 41–44, 46–61, 192n48,
    194n76; Buddha allusions in, 42,
    47, 54, 56–57; Buddhism in,
    55–56; colonialism in, 5, 43, 55;
    enlightenment in, 5, 42, 51–52;
    interpretation in, 46–48, 55;
    laborers, meditative posture of,
    56–61, 195n89; philosophy in,
    53–57; politics in, 190n41;
    sacrifice in, 53–54; savagery in,
    49–52, 55; spectral illumination
    in, 46–49, 51, 53, 62
Heidegger, Martin, 149,
    157–59, 218n61; on authenticity,
    141–42
homophobia: Buddhism and, 106;
    in *Question of Power*, 126
hooks, bell, 105, 106, 120, 133, 149
Huber, Toni, 34–35

Hungerford, Amy, 148, 153
Husserl, Edmund, 129–30

identity, 103–4; liberation and,
    103–7; Mahayana Buddhism
    and, 104; modern Buddhist
    critique of, 105; queer, 106
identity politics, 105
individuality, 44–45
Inferno, The (Dante), 80
Insight Meditation Society (IMS),
    11–12
interpretation, 185n45; in *Heart of
    Darkness*, 46–48, 55

JewBus, 11, 12
Johnson, Bruce, 191n41
Johnson, Charles, 128, 129, 151, 163;
    See also *Oxherding Tale*
    (Johnson)
Joyce, James, 91–92
Jung, Carl, 85–86, 149; on
    mandalas, 86; views on Jews,
    86–87

Kafka, Franz, 97, 98, 129
Kalachakra Tantra, 83–84, 88; Dalai
    Lama and, 84
Kamenetz, Roger, 11
Karatani, Kojin, 200n36
Kierkegaard, Søren, 12, 15
Kim (Kipling), 21–22, 30–41, 56,
    189n34; Buddhism, critical
    erasure of, 31–32, 186n10; Das
    prophecy in, 35; empire in,
    38–39, 41; enlightenment in, 29,

Kim (Kipling) (*continued*)
31, 33, 38; geopolitics of, 31–34,
36–37; Panchen Lama in, 33–34,
187n17; politics in, 34, 40;
reincarnation in, 38, 79; Wheel
of Life in, 31, 37–38
Kinkeade-Weeks, Mark, 187n19
Kipling, Rudyard, 30. See also *Kim*
(Kipling)
Kornfield, Jack, 11
Kuwalik, Kzryrzstof, 208n32

LaCapra, Dominick, 193n60
Leibniz, Gottfried Wilhelm,
190n40
Leigh, Simone, 190n39
Levine, Jill, 113, 114
liberal economics, 180n11
liberation, 5, 103; Buddhism and,
14, 17, 65, 118, 138, 162; in *Cobra*,
109, 111, 118; colonization and,
113; embeddedness of, 23–24;
identity and, 103–7; modern
Buddhism and, 23–24; in
Oxherding Tale, 130, 133–37;
patriarchy and, 119; personal,
103, 107; political, 103, 107, 136;
in *Question of Power*, 125–26;
reincarnation and, 114; sex and,
117; solitude and, 125–26; as
struggle, 118
Light of Asia (Arnold), 113–14
Lopez, Donald S., Jr., 19, 84, 116,
184n40; on *om mani padme hum*
chant, 208n26
Lost Horizon (Hilton), 23

Mahayana Buddhism: identity
and, 104
Mandala of Sherlock Holmes, The
(Norbu), 22, 76–88, 200n41;
appendix to, 85;
cosmopolitanism of, 82, 88;
Dante in, 80–81, 82; history in,
85; inversion in, 79–80, 83, 87;
Kalachakra Tantra in, 83–84;
mysticism in, 77, 78, 85–86;
reincarnation in, 76–79, 82–83,
94; religious symbolism in, 78;
Tibet in, 79
Mandell, Jacqueline (neé
Schwartz), 11
Marx, Karl, 99, 140, 182n26,
194n76
Mazzotta, Giuseppe, 72, 74
McClure, John, 191n43
McCort, Dennis, 216n24
McDaniel, Justin, 184n40
McMahan, David, 46, 66–67,
181n13, 196n95
meditation, 1; as anticolonial, 14,
59–61; anxiety and, 14; British
colonialism and, 14; cultural
context and, 5, 181n13; limits of,
9; mindfulness meditation, 6; as
modern Buddhist practice, 4,
14, 59; modernity and, 5; as
resistance, 61; suffering and,
174–75
Melville, Herman, 133
Merleau-Ponty, Maurice, 205n112;
critique of Augustine, 130; race
and, 132

Miller, J. Hillis, 193n63, 195n85

Mishima, Yukio, 65–66, 67–68, 160; failed coup of, 68, 71. See also *Sea of Fertility, The* (Mishima)

modernism: enlightenment and, 36; reincarnation and, 66; self-help and, 8

modernity: authenticity and, 140–41; Buddhism and, 4, 24–25; enlightenment and, 134; meditation and, 5

Moheyan, Heshang, 28

Moore, Matthew J., 136, 213n93

Mulhall, Stephen, 91

mysticism, 1; in *Mandala of Sherlock Holmes*, 77, 78, 85–86

nationalism: authenticity and, 142; Buddhism and, 103–4, 142; Tibetan, 104

Nietzsche, Friedrich, 45, 192n51

nirvana, 28, 37–38, 188n31, 189n32. *See also* enlightenment; *satori*

Norbu, Jamyang, 41, 65–66, 76, 174, 201n48; critique of Dalai Lama, 76; critique of empire, 67; critique of "Middle Way," 81, 85; *Mandala of Sherlock Holmes*, 22, 76–88; as radical pluralist, 87–88; skepticism of Tibetan Buddhism, 77; on tradition, 82; See also *Mandala of Sherlock Holmes, The* (Norbu)

Novalis, 155

Obeyesekere, Gananath, 64, 70

oneness, 103

Orientalism, 1; Buddhism and, 13, 18–19, 171; of Foucault, 184n36; Russian, 33, 187n18; of Schopenhauer, 44–45

Oxherding Tale (Johnson), 128–37, 213n87; authenticity in, 161; desire in, 137; differences from traditional tale, 132–33; enlightenment in, 135–36, 137; epigraphs in, 129; first-personal universal narration of, 131; influences on, 212n80; interdependence in, 136; intersubjectivity in, 130; liberation in, 130, 133–37; philosophy in, 128, 131; race in, 106, 131–37; slave narratives in, 129; utopic ending of, 137

Panchen Lama, 21, 29–30; in *Kim*, 33–34, 187n17; relationship with Dalai Lama, 32, 186n6

Pascal, 96

philosophy, 14–15; Buddhism as, 1, 4, 9, 12, 19–20, 31–32, 64, 109–11; as embedded, 181n12; in *Heart of Darkness*, 53–57; modern Buddhism as, 1, 4, 37–38; in *Oxherding Tale*, 128, 131; Western, 1, 15. *See also* existentialism; Schopenhauer, Arthur

Polanyi, Karl, 180n11

Posnock, Ross, 148, 152
Powers, John, 186n5

Queen, Christopher, 7
queer Buddhism, 105–6
Question of Power, A (Head), 23;
  Buddha in, 120–21, 123–25, 126;
  Buddhist tradition in, 123–25;
  enlightenment in, 123, 124; exile
  and, 209n42; gender in, 119–20;
  homophobia in, 126;
  interdependence in, 120–21;
  Jewish people in, 209n42;
  liberation in, 125–26; madness
  in, 211n61; race in, 119–20;
  sexuality in, 122, 126–27;
  universality of, 126–27; utopic
  ending of, 120, 209n39

race: Buddhism and, 23, 104, 108;
  embeddedness of, 132; Merleau-
  Ponty and, 132; in *Oxherding
  Tale*, 106, 131–37; in *Question of
  Power*, 119–20
Rama IV, 59
reincarnation, 5, 95–96, 187n11;
  atman, 65–66; in *Cobra*, 116, 117;
  of Dalai Lama, 32–33, 63, 78,
  188n20; in *Elizabeth Costello*, 90,
  91–95, 97–98; enlightenment
  and, 71; ethicization, 64–65; as
  evolution, 66–67; in *Kim*, 38, 79;
  liberation and, 88, 114; in
  Mandala of Sherlock Holmes,
  76–79, 82–83, 94; melancholia
  and, 69; modern Buddhism

and, 64, 100–101; modernism
  and, 66; salvation and, 99; in
  Sea of Fertility, 68–76, 94; the
  social and, 75; as "superstition,"
  75, 82; in Tibetan Buddhism, 63;
  transmigration and, 63;
  universality of, 64–65, 197n3
Rimbaud, Arthur, 92
Rohingya: genocidal campaign
  against, 8, 142
Rose, Jacqueline, 211n61

Sahlins, Marshall, 18
Said, Edward: on *Kim*, 22, 31
Salinger, J. D., 141, 149; *Catcher in
  the Rye, The*, 146–47; *Franny and
  Zooey*, 145, 147–49, 152–61;
  Seymour–An Introduction, 147,
  153; Zen in, 147–49, 164;
  "Zooey," 218n59. See also
  Franny and Zooey (Salinger)
Salzberg, Sharon, 11
Sarduy, Severo, 22, 23, 207n11;
  Buddhism in, 107; *Cobra*,
  107–19; *Maitreya*, 107; on
  "transvestismo," 116, 208n32.
  See also *Cobra* (Sarduy)
Sartre, Jean-Paul, 15–16, 140, 143,
  214n3, 215n13; authenticity in,
  165
satori, 134, 143, 148–51, 160; fascism
  and, 151; in *Franny and Zooey*,
  154
Schopenhauer, Arthur, 3, 44–46,
  47, 192n51, 204n89; asceticism
  of, 45; influence on Conrad, 45,

52–53, 55–56; interpretation of
Buddhism, 45–46, 192n49;
Orientalism of, 44–45; on
reincarnation, 197n3
Scott, David, 201n48
Scott, James C., 60
Sea of Fertility, The (Mishima),
68–76; envy in, 69, 198n15;
history in, 75; melancholia in,
69; reincarnation in, 68–76, 94;
the social in, 70–71, 75; suicide
in, 68; Vico in, 72, 73
Sedgwick, Eve Kosofsky, 207n10
self-care, 190n39
self-help, 8
selflessness, 65, 70; in *Autograph
Man*, 168; Buddhism and, 65,
70, 103; queer identity and, 106;
in Suzuki, 158; Zen, 157
Sengchen Lama, 36
sexuality: Buddhism and, 9, 23,
117–18, 122; in *Cobra*, 115–17;
enlightenment and, 122; in
Question of Power, 122, 126–27;
third sex, 117
Seymour–An Introduction (Salinger),
147, 153
Sharf, Robert, 17, 18, 141, 151;
critique of modern Buddhism,
17–18, 152–53
Shaw, Miranda, 121–22
Siddhartha (Hesse), 23, 212n80,
213n91
Siddhartha Gautama, 71, 83, 197n1
Sifuentes-Jarugui, Ben, 208n32
Simmel, Georg, 192n51

skepticism, 169; in Conrad, 57–58,
191n42; in Norbu, 77
Smith, Zadie, 162; on Wallace,
167–68, 169–70. See also
Autograph Man, The (Smith)
spectral illumination, 24–25; in
Conrad, 3–4, 42–43; in *Franny
and Zooey*, 147–49; in *Heart of
Darkness*, 46–49, 51, 53, 62; as
partial enlightenment, 47,
61–62; of resistance, 60
Starrs, Roy, 69–70, 71
Stevens, Wallace, 11
Stout, Jeffrey, 185n45
Strong, John, 122
suffering: Buddhism and, 3–4, 7, 15,
95–96, 124; in Coetzee, 94;
enlightenment and, 40;
meditation and, 174–75; modern
Buddhism and, 15
Suksamran, Somboon, 58
Suzuki, D. T., 12, 109–10, 132,
149–52, 183n33; authenticity and,
17, 143–44, 147, 150–51; in
Buddhist studies, 152; on
enlightenment, 134; on
existentialism, 15–18; in *Franny
and Zooey*, 149, 153–54, 157–58;
"Oxherding Tale," 127–28; *satori*,
148–51; selflessness in, 158; in
"Zooey," 218n59. See also Zen

Taixu, 18, 66–67
Tantric Buddhism, 121–22, 126
Taylor, Charles, 129, 218n58; on
authenticity, 140, 142

"Ten Cow-Herding Pictures, The" (Kakuan), 127–29

Thompson, Evan, 178n8, 181n13; critique of modern Buddhism, 9–10

Thurman, Robert, 76, 83–84

Tibet: British invasion of, 34–35; Chinese colonization of, 13, 28, 76, 78–79, 106, 208n28; geopolitics of, 39–40; human rights in, 40, 76; sovereignty of, 81. *See also* Buddhism, Tibetan

transmigration, 13–14, 28, 66; reincarnation and, 63. *See also* reincarnation

Trilling, Lionel, 143, 158

Trivedi, Harish, 186n10

Tsongkhapa, 28

UFOs, 85–86

Ulysses (Joyce), 91

Upanishads, 65

van Schaik, Sam, 186n5

Vedas, 129, 130

Venturino, Steven, 200n41

Vico, Giambattista, 91, 199n31; historical theory of, 72–74; *The New Science*, 73–74; in *Sea of Fertility*, 72, 73; theory of reincarnation, 68

Virgil, 80

Viswanathan, Gauri, 85

Wallace, David Foster, 167–68

Watts, Alan, 12, 15–18, 151, 195n85; authenticity and, 143; on enlightenment, 40

Week-end (Godard film), 194n76

West, Paul, 92–93

Wheel of Life, 187n11; in *Kim*, 31, 37–38

Wilson, Liz, 122

Winichakul, Thongchai, 196n97

Wittgenstein, Ludwig: in *Autograph Man*, 164, 166–68

Wollaeger, Mark, 192n49

Wood, James, 89

Woolf, Virginia, 45; in *Autograph Man*, 166–68

Wright, Robert, 181n13

Zen, 18, 28; authenticity and, 16–18, 147, 150, 153–54, 164–65, 170; in *Autograph Man*, 163–64, 219n70; *Cobra* and, 109, 111; in *Franny and Zooey*, 152–54, 156–58; in Salinger, 147–49, 152–54, 156–58, 164; selflessness and, 157. *See also* Suzuki, D. T.

Zen paradox, 109–10

Žižek, Slavoj, 144–45

Zopa Rinpoche, 161–62